ACCLAIM FOR
JUST HERE TRYING TO SAVE A FEW LIVES

"Spellbinding . . . gritty . . . after a few chapters, TV's so-called slices of emergency-room life begin to look like a tea party."
—*Biography* **magazine**

"Descriptive language and a vivid narrative style . . . fascinating reading. . . . Her colorful descriptions are worthwhile reading for all."
—**from a review by Linda A. Khym, M.A., in the**
New England Journal of Medicine

"While the medical know-how is impressive in these dramas . . . even more so is Grim's humanity. . . . An acute observer and a compassionate doctor [who] pulls no punches . . . brutally realistic. . . . Readers can only hope she doesn't stop writing."
—*Kirkus Reviews* **(starred review)**

"Reads like dispatches from the front. . . . Pamela Grim has peered into our contemporary heart of darkness and in so doing has illuminated us and herself as well."
—**Marc Flitter, M.D., author of** *Judith's Pavilion*

"Transcends reality TV . . . a fascinating tour. . . . Grim's pacing is sure, and her writing is deft and often lyrical . . . introduces us to characters and scenes we can see vividly."
—*Winston-Salem Journal*

more . . .

D0066718

JUST HERE
TRYING TO
SAVE A FEW LIVES

Tales of Life and Death from the ER

P AMELA G RIM , M.D.

WARNER BOOKS

An AOL Time Warner Company

The events described in this book happened, but some of the names and identifying details about persons and entities depicted in this book have been modified or presented in composite form.

WARNER BOOKS EDITION

Copyright © 2000 by Dr. Pamela Grim
All rights reserved.

Warner Books, Inc., 1271 Avenue of the Americas, New York, NY 10020

Visit our Web site at www.twbookmark.com.

For more information on Time Warner Trade Publishing's online publishing program, visit www.ipublish.com.

W An AOL Time Warner Company

Printed in the United States of America
Originally published in hardcover by Warner Books, Inc.
First Trade Printing: January 2002
10 9 8 7 6 5 4 3 2 1

ISBN: 0-446-52423-9 (hardcover)
LCCN: 00-103208

ISBN: 0-446-67757-4 (pbk.)

Cover design by Brigid Pearson
Cover photograph by Rick Neibel/Stock Connection/Picture Quest

To Al, Barb and the other Pam.

CONTENTS

JUST HERE
TRYING TO
SAVE A FEW LIVES

1

A TAXONOMY OF GRIEF

IT'S TEN AT NIGHT and I am making a run back to the hospital to check on a patient. Two new roadblocks have been set up since the night before. They don't even seem like roadblocks, really; it's just the lights shining in our eyes that make us stop. It could be anyone behind those flashlights—we can't tell even when we pull up. Only by straining can we see the soldiers. Our driver rolls his window down and waves our paperwork. There is a long exchange in Hausa, and finally a black face, washed out by the glare of the light, says, "*Médecins sans Frontières*. Oh, oh, well, okay." He waves us on.

I am in Nigeria with Doctors without Borders, an international humanitarian organization widely respected as a provider of medical care to various third- and fourth-world countries, often under hazardous circumstances. We are here doing crisis medicine, handling a meningitis outbreak in the heart of the sub-Sahara. The outbreak is killing thousands and thousands of people, and we have come because the Nigerian government is unable (read too inefficient, corrupt and useless) to muster anything near the resources needed to fight back. There are about thirty of us expatriates in Kano, five doctors, ten nurses and the rest "administrative." Unfortunately, there were not enough of us to begin with, even before the cholera cases started.

I am an emergency medicine physician; I have been for over

ten years, a long enough period of time, I have discovered, to forget why I went into the field to begin with. Over those ten years I have played trauma doctor, social worker, breaker of bad news, heart failure doctor, Band-Aid placer, substance abuse counselor, frontline medic, post-traumatic-stress victim and a thousand other roles. The result was not surprising: I needed a change. I needed a new perspective. Hence Africa.

To be honest, before I came here I had imagined an experience I thought to be very Albert Schweitzer–like. This image had me working in a jungle camp of friendly natives where I serenely administered vaccinations under a tented canopy of brilliant green leaves. The truth: it is a squalid disaster here. We are understaffed and underequipped. The hospital we use had been closed for fifty years. Our staff is made up largely of Nigerian nursing students, most of whom have never even seen an IV before, much less started one. There is no sanitation, no windows, dirt floors, a single hand pump for water, and flies everywhere. Overall we have at least two hundred patients at any one time, but that is just a fraction of the total number of victims. The mortality rate averages about 20 percent.

But it would have been 100 percent without us.

The meningitis outbreak is not a pandemic, not quite on the scale of the cholera outbreak for Rwandan refugees in Zaire, but even so, every morning I have to clear away the dead or the near dead from the front porch of the emergency clinic to make room for the dying. I am currently in charge of the meningitis "emergency room," formerly a one-room post office. I examine everyone on a bare wooden table, where I also diagnose, treat (chloramphenicol and/or ampicillin) and arrange for a "bed." (Usually a bed is a piece of swept earth. The few beds we have sport only bare wire springs, no mattresses.) When I first arrive in the morning, it is so busy that if someone dies inside the clinic we put him or her on the floor and just step over the body until the relatives come to take it away. The atmosphere is that of complete chaos, but we have saved lives here, in this small room and throughout the hospital. We will save more, if the government allows us to stay on.

There's a measles outbreak as well.

We see most of the desperately ill in the morning. They come in early, after curfew lifts, and they sit and wait for me. The first hour is always a disaster. I wade down the hallway doing triage. "This one's sick, get him in now." "This one's dead, forget it." "This one's almost dead, just leave him be." To the families, it must seem as though we are passing judgment from on high: this one lives, this one doesn't. I don't think they have any idea what it is I see in each patient when I pass my sentence. I don't know if they know it has nothing to do with me at all, that I have no special power. Still, they accept what I say. No one argues, or rarely do they; no one pleads with me to change my mind, to take one more look. No one reaches out to hold me back, to convince me. Everyone in this line accepts the judgment I pass on to them, even if it is a death sentence.

In the afternoon I round on my intensive care verandah and three intensive care tents. These are where most of the critical cases are, not that we can do a whole lot of intensive care. *Médecins sans Frontières* has shipped down over four tons of supplies, but it is pitiful to see how little four tons of supplies is for those of us who practice Western-style medicine. We have liter bags of normal saline, IVs, IV tubing, and a few drugs: ampicillin, phenobarbital, Valium and paracetamol—a form of injectable Tylenol. The backbone of our therapy is something called oily chloramphenicol, an oil-based slurry of a venerable antibiotic; it is long lasting and dirt cheap. Listing what we have makes it seem like a lot, but simple things go missing. For example, we have no tape to tape the IV catheters down. Fortunately, someone at the start of the mission figured out that you could take the labels off the saline bags and tear them into strips. With these strips you can tack the IVs in place. We also have no gloves—but this may be, partly, a cultural thing. The first day I worked, the first time I went to start an IV, I looked around automatically for the glove box—de rigueur in America. There was nothing like this, so I asked Pierre, our chief logistician and head of supplies, for gloves.

He gave me a funny look. "Gloves?" he asked. "You're just staiving an IV. What do you need gloves for?" He shook his head and raised his eyes heavenward. "Americans," he said, tapping his forehead and walking away.

I started after him. *"'No gloves' is not an American thing, it's a French thing. You guys are crazy."*

He didn't look back; he just raised his hand over his head and waved at me. "Okay, okay," he shouted back to me.

He found me a box of gloves.

The other French thing is the smoking. I had dinner before I left with another American who had spent six months in Burundi with a French crew. I don't know what his medical experiences were like because all he could talk about was how much the French smoked. "Meetings, dinner, lunch, at work, after work, in the wards, in the *shower* for Christ's sake."

The first thing the mission director asked me when I arrived was: "You don't have that American thing about smoking, do you?"

I raised my hands. "No, no," I said, "not at all."

This apparently was all the mission director wanted to know from me. Afterward I never saw or talked to him again.

Back in the car, we continue on past the roadblock, down a street lit by the shallow beam of our one working headlight. The shops and stores that line the main roadway are all shuttered. This is a street that is packed with hundreds and thousands of people during the day. It's dead quiet now.

Pierre, of the gloves argument, is sitting in the backseat trying to read some shipping labels by starlight. As the chief logistician, he has the unenviable job of trying to maintain some small degree of order in a whole sea of African chaos. He is returning tonight to bring in a fresh supply of oily chloramphenicol. I am going back to see a patient who, with luck, might still be alive. I admitted her just before I went home. A little girl. I had been starting an IV on an older woman, deathly ill from meningitis (she died about twenty minutes later), when I looked up and saw a young couple scurry across the open field in front of the ICU tents. I waved them over and they stopped breathlessly before me. The man handed me the bundle he held in his arms. It was a baby, maybe eight months old, and the baby was seizing. Great spasms, with arms extended, joints locked and legs twitching. She could have been seizing from anything, malaria, meningitis, cysticercosis, even a simple febrile seizure. What to do?

In the U.S. the workup would begin now: hundred of dollars of laboratory tests, x-rays, IVs. The poorest child in America would have a bed covered with a spotless sheet and a half dozen people crowded around it, trying to save someone's precious baby. But *this* baby, now, was examined on a mat on the ground with flies everywhere. The only diagnostic tool I had was my stethoscope. I couldn't look in the child's blood for signs of malaria. I couldn't tap the spinal fluid to make certain of a diagnosis of meningitis. (After the first week, when the epidemic was confirmed, we never tapped anyone. There wasn't time or equipment. If the patients were sick, you treated them for meningitis. If they didn't have meningitis, they would die.)

I squatted down by the child and pulled down on one arm while Simon, my nursing assistant, knelt down over the other. We had to use old IV tubing as tourniquets; there wasn't anything else. Simon and I squatted there, tap, tap, tapping the arm, up and down, looking for a vein to administer the IV. Babies this age are the hardest, even when they are not seizing. Their veins are thread-like and deep under the skin. This time I got one in before Simon. Usually he's a much better shot.

The father took my scribbled note and ran off to the pharmacy. We squatted there watching the baby seize, watching minutes tick by. Finally the father returned, triumphant, with the ampules. Simon broke them open and I drew up what we needed. I injected the baby slowly with phenobarbital, 5 mg, 10 mg and on. This should have stopped the seizure. Nothing. She kept twitching, seizing. I tried to get an idea from the family how long this had been going on. If it hadn't been long, the baby had a chance. A seizure lasting over an hour or more, though, meant there was not much use in even trying. I tried to ask, but either I couldn't make myself understood to Simon or Simon couldn't make himself understood to the parents, because I never did get any information.

We drew up more phenobarb and gave it slowly through the IV. Still, the baby seized. I had nothing more, no oxygen, no monitor. No other medication. If this didn't work, the baby was dead. After a few minutes I drew up another 20 mg and injected it slowly. Nothing else I could do. As I sat there brooding about this, the baby's spasms slowed a bit and became almost hiccuplike. Then, suddenly, the spasms were gone; the baby sighed deeply and was still.

We gave her ampicillin, oily chloramphenicol, and paracetamol for her fever. The nurses found a place for her between another young child with mild meningitis and a woman who had been desperately sick but now was doing much better, even walking a little today. "I'll be back later," I told the nursing students. "Don't anyone touch that IV."

So now I'm back. It's quiet at the hospital and dead black. The night-shift nurses are dozing at the two tables wedged between the tents and the verandah. A single candle lights up one table. I jostle Chuckie, Mark and Amos to wake them up. It's funny to think that I get on French nerves as much as they can get on mine. My first act in coming to the hospital was to award each nursing student an "American" name, a modification of whatever their name was in Hausa. My righthand man, Siminu, became Simon. Umar became Omar, Chafu became Chucky, et cetera. The French hate this. "That is so colonialist!" Pierre would tell me—but the nursing students love it. They laugh and clap each other on the back. "Now I shall go to America," one tells me dreamily, and I know that feeling—everyone has it when they are young—and sometimes I think I've never lost it: that feeling that somewhere in the world—not here but somewhere—there is a place one can find oneself . . . where someone could be who he or she really is. In Nigeria it is America. Oh, America.

I poke at the students. "The baby that was seizing," I whisper. "I've come back to check on her."

They all yawn and stretch, looking around. They seem as puzzled and astonished to find themselves here as I feel sometimes. Someone scrambles for another candle for us to round with. Silently, or as silently as we can, we creep through the verandah and on to the tent. I am holding the candle high, not sure where we deposited that family. There are no beds at all in the tents. Each patient has a mat—brought in by the family—that serves as a sickbed. At the foot of each mat a family member sits—or, as now, dozes. The family member serves as the patient's caretaker—making dinner, feeding, washing. The hospital merely supplies and administers the drugs. If a patient requires any drug beyond that which our meager pharmacy supplies, the patient's family must get it from an outside pharmacy and bring it for us to administer.

I walk cautiously through the tent, past the sleeping figures. Bags of saline are randomly tied to the tent cross beams; we have no IV poles. Tubing snakes down here and there to a patient, who stirs restlessly or lies still as death as my little entourage and I pass by.

The baby is there, sleeping comfortably. The sign I made is still in place. For some reason the night nurses regarded it as one of their duties to remove all the IVs sometime during the course of the night. No matter how much I begged, pleaded, bargained, requested, the IVs were always gone in the morning. Finally, I scrounged up a single roll of tape, which I used to tape a sign over the IVs. The sign reads:

I, Dr. Grim,
will kill you if
you touch this IV.

I also added a homemade skull and crossbones, a sign universal enough, apparently, so that even Nigerian nursing students understand what it means.

My seizing patient still has her IV in place. She is sleeping peacefully in her mother's arms. The mother is sitting there pretty much as I left her, bolt upright and wide awake. She looks transfixed by the saline bag and the loop of IV tubing that dangles from it, dripping precious Western medicine into her child's vein. I flick open the baby's eyes, and she shakes herself restlessly, sighs and sleeps on. Normal respiratory pattern, heart rate, pulse. I hold the candle up to her face. It is not the face of the dying child I left, but the face of a sleeping angel.

I turn to look up at the nursing students. "Well, we've saved another life here," I tell them. Someone translates this into Hausa and there is a nervous murmur of confirmation. They are all so proud of their work.

I hold the candle up and look around. Shadows dance everywhere in its light. I can see the baby's IV tubing more clearly now and see that it is covered with flies. There are flies almost everywhere you look. During the day the constant fanning of the relatives keeps the tent somewhat clear of them, but now, at night, they range free. The woman on the next mat over, unconscious and with no relatives, has a dozen of them feasting at the edges of her closed eyes.

Across the tent I see the policeman's child. His father is chief of the local police bureau. He makes, according to Simon, $20 a month when the government remembers to pay him. This is much too little to be able to take his son to one of the private clinics. I get up and go over there to say hello to his mother. I gaze down at the child for a moment, remembering. He came in sick, very sick. We gave him chloramphenicol and he only got sicker. One evening during rounds I found him, blue-black, scarcely breathing, sweating, as close to death as I had ever seen anything that was still alive. Again I had no way to tell if this was meningitis or malaria or anything else. He had "failed" chloramphenicol, for whatever reason. I could only give him what medicine we had left, ampicillin and chloroquine. But first we had to get an IV in, which turned out to be impossible in this dehydrated, almost prune-like little boy. Simon tried and I tried, over and over. The child lay there dying, and his only hope was for us to get a butterfly needle threaded into one of his hair-sized veins. But we couldn't get anything. Finally one of the senior nurses came by, looked down his nose through his rimless spectacles, cluck-clucked, and knelt down beside me to examine the arm. He got it in, first try.

We gave the child IV ampicillin, and within a few hours his fever broke. Still, when morning came, the child looked deathly ill. His mother spooned teaspoons of water into his mouth, but he didn't move, didn't swallow. The water spilled out along the edges of his lips. Why didn't you just let him die? I thought to myself. Now he's just going to suffer longer.

Suffer. To suffer. Suffering.

That afternoon I stopped by again to see him, and he was making little sipping movements with his lips and actually swallowing the water. His mother sat there, cross-legged, her scarf covering her hair. Her son's head rested in her lap. She was always there, always awake, always watching her boy. A day or two ago he actually opened his eyes and could lift his hand weakly to touch his mother's arm. Earlier today I had come in and found him sitting upright, very precariously, with his stick limbs girdered to give him some balance.

His father, the policeman, had pulled me aside yesterday evening as I was rounding. He held his hands out, cupped, as if he were offering me water.

"Thank you," he said to me. He was as formal as his freshly pressed uniform. "Thank you, thank you." That was all, but what else could he say or do?

Tonight the mother is wide awake, with the child sleeping beside her. She sits in dignified silence watching her son. She nods to me as I kneel beside her. I pull my stethoscope out of my bush jacket and press the bell against the child's bare rib cage.

"Breathing good," I tell her in Hausa. I know a total of four phrases in Hausa. The others are "Getting better, little by little," "It was Allah's will" and "He's dead."

Next to the child, though, is an empty space where there was a patient of mine when I left a few hours earlier. It was a young woman tended by her husband. We were treating her for both meningitis and malaria, but I'm not really sure she had either. The ampicillin and the chloramphenicol we poured into her seemed to do nothing. She wasn't very sick to begin with, but she got sicker as the days wore on. For the last two days it was clear she was dying. Her husband never left her. He nursed her with what he had, a little soup, a cool wet rag to her forehead. He would patiently wave away flies for hours at a time. He never asked us for anything; he never seemed to do more than to accept what fate doled out to him. When I tried to explain that I was going to try to treat his wife with IV chloroquine for malaria, he nodded and said nothing. What will be, will be.

I point to the empty space and look at Simon. He shrugs.

That woman was all that man had.

It's late. I check my watch again by candlelight but can't see more than a shadow. Outside, the night is as black as before. I look around for Pierre but he must still be at the measles ward, so I walk up to the pharmacy to try to find something to drink. There is no moon. The trees carry their giant canopy of leaves like great black clouds boiling overhead. The air is close; the wind has died down. There is a touch of dampness in the air. Perfect weather for an epidemic.

I fish out my key to unlock the pharmacy door. Everything here has to be locked up and guarded; the pilfering is unending. There are some Cokes hidden behind a stack of saline bags. I pull one out and root around, candle held high, for the bottle opener. How long has it been since I've used a bottle opener in America? I find it, go back out and sit on the front steps where it's cooler. The stars are all out, all brilliant. Out of habit I search for the Big Dipper, the Little Dipper, Cassiopeia, but nothing I see looks familiar.

Why am I in Nigeria? I wonder this for the hundredth time as I look up at the stars. There is the thin arc of a comet up above one of the trees. The answer is simple burnout. I am here so I won't be there. So I won't be back at home and in the ER. A crisis of faith brought me here to Nigeria. I had been thinking more and more that I might not want to spend the rest of my medical career wide awake at three A.M. attending some screaming drunk shackled to the bed while someone in the next bed over vomits copiously into a metal basin. It was beginning to get to me in ways I really didn't understand. Or ways I understood too well. It didn't take a genius to figure it out. The fact is that I have just seen too many cases of child abuse, sexual abuse, assaults, bad mothers and worse fathers, disastrous car wrecks, people dying who shouldn't die, people alive only by some whim of God's. I was turning into someone I didn't recognize, someone I didn't particularly like.

I have, when I go back home, some career decisions before me—a potential for a whole new life. I have been offered a chance to do a completely different kind of medicine. It involves—don't laugh—hair transplants. A friend of mine, a family practice physician, has offered me a partnership in her practice. She specializes in what charitably may be described as boutique medicine. Hair transplants, electrolysis, skin peels, that sort of thing. She is making a fortune as she sits, day in, day out, planting sproutlets of hair onto bald domes. "Just think," she told me, "no insurance hassles! No nights or weekends or holidays. You even have background music while you work."

"New Age?" I asked her doubtfully.

"Anything you want," she told me.

What do I want?

Perched on that step, a warm Coke in my hand, I contemplate an image of myself sitting in a quiet room performing one simple task at a time with pleasant music in the background, surrounded by polite professional nurses, and patients who don't vomit on my shoes. The image seems comforting in a way. I even think of a slogan for myself: "Stop doing good and start doing great!"

Simon appears out of the darkness, looking grim. "There is a child here," he tells me. "Very, very sick. Could you please come?"

I sigh and get up. Candle aloft, I light my way back down the path following Simon.

In the last tent a father is sitting on a mat with his child in his arms—a boy—maybe seven or eight. I kneel down beside them and lift up the candle in order to see. The child's head lolls back—his eyes are open and glazed yellow from jaundice. I look up and my eyes meet the father's eyes. His expression is unreadable.

I pull the child from his father's lap onto the matted floor. Automatically I reach for the IVs I keep in my bush jacket pocket. An 18-gauge is all I can find. I need something smaller. The child lies motionless; his matchstick limbs collapse away from him, completely flaccid. His face is sunken, hollow. He is clearly septic and desperately dehydrated.

"Simon," I whisper fiercely. "Quick, quick, get me some IVs and some ampicillin." Simon stays rooted to his spot, though, staring down at the child. I look again and then grope for a pulse. I try the wrist but there is nothing there. I fumble, trying to feel for the carotid.

Nothing. The child is dead.

"I see," I say to Simon, who must have known before I did. "Never mind."

Simon kneels to tell the father. The father looks down at the child. He hasn't known before this either, I realize. There was still hope. Now the hope is gone.

"How long has he been here?" I ask Simon fiercely.

"Since just after you left for dinner."

I thump the ground before the child. "Was the child alive when they got here?"

Simon leans over and speaks to the father softly in Hausa. They stop. Simon shrugs. "The father says, yes, he was alive."

"When did this child die?" It suddenly seemed important to know. I glance at my watch. It is now eleven and I left at six P.M. The father must have been here almost five hours, and during that time his son died in his arms here while he waited for the doctor. Would he have held his son in his arms until morning if I hadn't been here to round? How many hours had he been protecting something no longer his child but a corpse?

"I'm sorry," I say to the man. I don't dare touch him. Here women do not touch men.

He bows his head.

From out of the shadows comes a woman. She must have been sitting just outside the tent. The man looks up at her and says something. She, too, bows her head.

"It was Allah's will," I say in Hausa. Who knows if they understand me.

The mother kneels beside her son and lifts him up. She holds him for a moment gazing down at him, a Madonna in chiaroscuro, face as grave, solemn and still as if she were painted by some old master. Then she bends over, and with her husband's help she slips the child onto her back and steadies him. She takes the long winding sheet of broadcloth that all Nigerian women use to wrap their children into place on their backs. She wraps him close to her for the last time. Again his head lolls back drunkenly. The husband touches the wife's hand and they look down at me. The wind gutters the candle so I can't see well, but they seem to be blessing me, thanking me even, though they say nothing. Simon whispers something in Hausa and they look around dazed, like sleepwalkers. This is their grief. The man lifts his hand to me, a gesture of farewell, and they turn and vanish into the dark, noiselessly, as if they were never there.

There's a beat. Simon squats down next to me. "That was a bad one," he says.

I just sit there looking after them.

After a moment there is some rustling to the right of Simon. It is one of the other mothers, motioning to her sleeping daughter. The daughter has a rash on her face, and the mother holds her hands out toward the rash as if she is trying to sell us something valuable at a market. Staph infection, I think, then I look more closely. The rash is more like a wound and has a purplish hue, like nothing I have ever seen before. I wonder how many things I miss, mistreat, misunderstand, here in the tropics. A world of strange diseases. How many patients . . .

I realize I can't look again at another festering wound. I have reached my limit. "Tomorrow," I tell Simon. "I'll look at it tomorrow." I stumble out of the tent.

The trees, the stars, the night that had so charmed me a short time ago, now seem sinister and oppressive. I kick some IV tubing off the path. There are IV needles on the ground, used IV bags, waste everywhere. I am thinking of something I read somewhere. All grief is alike, someone had once written. Clearly, he didn't know grief; he hadn't seen it every day, day after day, the way I have. There is a taxonomy of grief; it is not one human feeling, one set of human actions. I try not to think of the grief I've seen expressed, but images come flooding back anyway. The young woman in America, one who had just lost her mother, wailing, beating on the walls, shrieking. The husband whose wife had just died in a freak auto accident. He just sat there in stunned disbelief. "But this really can't be . . . ," he kept murmuring. An old woman, crying after I told her that her husband of sixty-seven years was now dead. "I'm sorry," she kept saying to me, as she cried. "Please forgive me, I know you all did your best." She seemed more worried about me than about herself.

I have, in my memory, a whole catalogue of grief. Each entry differs as the human face differs.

And now this. African grief, Hausa grief, Islamic grief. All silence and darkness, no voice, no gesture, just a gathering up and heading out into the night. Did those parents love that boy any less than any other parents in the world? Did they suffer less? Did they see his death as I did—something absolutely unnecessary, useless, a chance encounter between two pieces of bad luck, one involving politics and the other the natural history of a disease?

I shake my head. Of course they don't see it that way. Thank God, thank God.

I find my warm Coke still out on the front steps. I sit back down and look around at the night, the darkness. All this death.

I think: You can't save everyone in the world. You must save yourself first.

I remember a snatch of a poem by—was it Auden?

> But here and now,
> Our oath is to the living world.

I turn the bottle opener over and over in my hand. W. H. Auden. What did he call death, "the cosmocrat"? Why is it that some poets understand death better than doctors do? I remember another set of lines:

> . . . I have seen
> the just and the unjust die in the day,
> all, willing or not, and some were willing.

I look down and notice my hands are wet. Stupidly I look up at the sky, but there is only the canopy of leaves. Then I realize I am crying, real tears. The funny thing is, I think, as I wipe the tears out of my eyes, I don't feel sad. In fact I really don't feel anything. And that, it occurs to me, is the problem. I never feel anything anymore. The death of a child—I shrug it off. A bad car crash where people come in dying or dead—nothing; it feels like nothing to me. It's not as if I don't care. I'm sure I do care or I wouldn't be here. But I'm not sure anymore what caring really feels like. It doesn't exist for me as an emotion. In fact, I think, as I turn the bottle cap over and over again, nothing exists for me as an emotion anymore. I try to remember the last time I felt sad or upset, worried or lonely or confused or even happy. The only emotion that seems to have remained a friend is anger. I still know how it is to be angry. All the other emotions just get in the way of being a doctor, of working in the ER, of working in Nigeria.

I can no longer feel things, I think, because I couldn't survive if I did. I can't mourn everyone who needs mourning; I can't grieve at every death. I can't feel outraged at a rape or at a child abused. I can't afford these feelings. What could I do with them except to pile them higher and higher? But what have I become? An automaton? A person who shrugs off the death of a child and all the other tragedies?

And with these thoughts it feels as if I have redeemed another feeling, but not the one I could ever have expected. I am flooded, suddenly, not with sorrow for that child or those parents or the woman in the bed next to the policeman's son, I am flooded by a kind of wistfulness about myself. Here I sit, as detached as ever, another tragedy under my belt. My youth is gone, spent haunting hospital corridors at all hours of the night, and now my middle age is spent in some washed-out back corner of a country where I have come to make some decisions about my life and have ended up, once again, awestruck by the suffering God can inflict.

Just as suddenly as that feeling of wistfulness came, I feel laughter rising up. I'm feeling sorry for myself, I think, smiling as I wipe the tears out of my eyes. The first true feeling I have had in a long time and what would that be? Self-pity, of course. I look out on the night. Everything is as still as death, as still as that child. I put my face down into my hands and draw a deep breath. I would rather feel anything else in the world, self-pity—anything—than feel the death of that child.

As I sit there, images from the ER come flooding back. I see them all, the crazy patients, the nurses, the cops, the paramedics. I hear the banshee wail of the ambulance in the night. Another trauma, another disaster. What I miss most, I realize, is the feel of the instruments, the snap you make with the latex sleeve when you put on a pair of sterile gloves. I miss peeling open the suture package and wrapping the suture around the index and middle finger of my left hand. Putting my hands over the hands of the residents and trying to make them make the right moves for suturing, for starting central lines.

I remember the last evening that I worked, the last ER shift before I left. It was a quiet night. I was reading a magazine in the nurses' station when the deadpan voice of Mark, the security guard, came crackling over the intercom:

"Attention, triage," he said wearily. "There's a full arrest in the parking lot."

A full arrest in the parking lot, I think, shaking my head. And I realize, as I wipe more tears out of my eyes, I am smiling.

Could I miss the ER? Could that really be home for me?

I stop myself. I am in Africa. A child has just died. What does the ER have to do with this? But I don't stop thinking about it. I can't. Do I miss it? I don't know, I can't tell. What would it take to have feelings again?

I think of hair transplants and that beautiful office, those professional nurses, the sober patients worried about nothing more than their hair. Kenny G playing softly in the background. What a nice life that could be. As I think of this, though, I can feel the tethering, the sense of being anchored and drawn down, back down, again and again, to those dark places, the places where children die and monsters are born. Probably, I can never go completely back to the surface again, where the bright sunlight is, where most people live. I remain entwined by the memories of days and nights in the ER, and those memories would never let me go, not even if I were drowning.

An owl flies overhead and beyond, down to the tents. The first tent is lit from within; the nurses are making their rounds. The light is amber through the canvas of the tent, the color of old gold. I have emptied my mind out—there is nothing left for me to think. I stand up, dust my pants off and lock up the pharmacy again. My candle has gone out, so I make my way back slowly down the path shuffling in the dark. It must be midnight, I think. Late, late. A few hours from now, not long at all, the world will begin to fill with light and from every minaret and mosque rooftop the crackling sound of some old loudspeaker will echo and reecho the *muezzin*, the Muslim call to prayer.

2

SUDDEN DEATH

What to Do When Someone Dies

IT'S FIVE A.M. WHEN YOU GET THE CALL. Ambulance 18. "We've got a full arrest from Lake Village Nursing Home." Everyone groans and you groan too. "Eighty-two-year-old female, severe short o' breath. Doc, she arrested, stopped breathing, just as we got here. She had a pulse but now we've got nothing . . ."

You can hear the banshee wail of the siren in the background.

"We've intubated her, and have a line established, normal saline and all. We'll be there in two."

You hit the transmit button. "I assume the patient is *not* DNR." Do Not Resuscitate.

"That's an affirmative, the nursing home says she's a full code."

A full code means the whole enchilada, chest compressions, intubation, the pharmaceutical resurrection cocktail.

You shake your head while Pam M., the nurse in charge tonight, raises a hand and says, "We know you have a choice when choosing your emergency department and we want to thank you for choosing Hope General Memorial Hospital." She drops her hand and walks away in disgust. Pam is rarely cynical like this, but Julie, who is standing to Pam's right, is the embodiment of peevishness. She throws a clipboard down on the desk. "Why do they even *bother* to do this? It's so stupid. Like we are going to bring back an eighty-nine-year-old full arrest. Get *real*."

"Eighty-two," you say, but you know she's right; everyone in the ER knows she's right. You glance at your watch and think, this shouldn't take long.

One of your classmates decided he wasn't cut out to be a doctor when, one night during his first week of internship, as he performed CPR on a patient, he found himself hoping that the patient would just die because he was too tired to take care of her if she lived. You, too, have had this thought more than once—the irony is that you never took it to mean you shouldn't be a doctor. You have always felt that death can sometimes be a release for everyone involved, not excluding yourself. Tonight, for example, you are hoping for something easy: a quick death.

There's an old saw: "It is the duty of a doctor to prolong life. It is not a doctor's duty to prolong the act of dying." You believe in it.

Everyone shuffles off to the code room. Pam, as charge nurse, commands the crash cart while you fiddle around trying to get suction to work. The sense of utter fatigue, that five A.M. slump that occurs at the end of every night shift, steals over you. You feel as if you are doing everything underwater—as if exhaustion has exaggerated the drag coefficient of air so that every movement, even breathing, has become a major effort. You abandon the suction equipment, fold your arms and sag against the cabinet, looking around, seeing nothing.

The ambulance doesn't take long to get here—you hear the backup signal, then the doors bang open. The paramedics, panting and sweating, sweep into the code room. One is doing chest compressions, the other is ventilating the patient. Firefighters maneuver the gurney.

"I told you guys to stay out of trouble," you grumble at Jack, one of the EMTs.

"Trouble loves us," he responds brightly. He's counting out

chest compressions Lawrence Welk style, "and a-one and a-two and . . ."

Everyone moves to take over from the paramedics, transferring the monitoring leads, switching off on CPR. The respiratory tech takes over the Ambu bag. Julie climbs up to replace Jack for chest compressions. "This is so stupid," she observes once more.

You look down at the patient and then close your eyes tight. Full code! you wonder to yourself. How could anyone think this patient should be full code? There is barely anything human left to her. She couldn't have weighed more than sixty pounds, each bird-like limb bent, arms to chest, knees to belly—the fetal position except she's been fossilized there. The paramedics had a hard time just doing CPR because they can't get her to lie flat on her back. As you lean over her you smell that distinct odor, the odor of old age and of nursing homes, that curdled milk and rotting blood smell with overtones of decayed feces. You know the rest too, without even looking. The peg tube in the stomach, maybe a colostomy, an indwelling Foley catheter draining silt, and, always, massive decubitus ulcers. (Decubitus: from the Latin *decumbo*, to lie down.) These are pressure sores, great potholes eroded through the skin—sometimes even down to bone. They occur when someone lies in one position in a urine-soaked bed for months or years. As this woman probably has.

From the Latin . . . actually, from the Greek. It was Eos, you think, Goddess of Dawn, that fell in love with a mortal. She went to Zeus to ask for eternal life for her lover but forgot to ask for eternal youth. Eos realized what she had done when her lover's hair turned gray. She left him and he went on alone to age and age and age into all eternity. Eventually he shriveled up and became so small he turned into a grasshopper.

You shrug at the thought. Your fate as well, perhaps.

Pam must be thinking of the same thing. "Just kill me when I get like this," she tells you.

"What'd she get?" you ask Jack, meaning drugwise.

"She got three of epi and three of atropine."

"Hold CPR," you say, hand up. The patient is now connected to your monitor and you want to see the rhythm.

Flat line. Zippo.

"I feel like I'm not doing CPR," Julie says, "I feel like I'm beating a dead horse." She folds her arms, glaring at you, daring you to have her restart CPR.

You glance back down at the patient and the glance confirms your first impression: it's criminal to go on.

You raise a hand. "Anyone object to terminating this code relatively early?"

Julie glares around the room. No one else moves.

You check your watch. 5:38 A.M. In the hour of the wolf.

Code called 5:38.

The nurses are drifting out of the room when Father Minke, the priest on call in the ER this month, peeks in. "Am I too late?" he asks.

"Well, Father." You are peeling off your gloves. "I guess it depends. She's been declared dead, if that makes any difference."

"Okay," he says, paging through his prayer book. You look at him again, quizzically. You didn't call him for this death.

"Father, what are you doing up this late?"

He *hmmms*, distracted.

"Father?"

He looks up at you. "I was watching TV," he says, as if that explains everything. He goes to the foot of the bed, opens up his prayer book and begins, in an almost imperceptible whisper, his bedside prayer for the dying and the dead.

Everyone gets this, regardless of creed, if Father Menke is in the mood.

You stump away, back into the ER. Your job is the secular side of death.

Step 1: When someone dies: fill out the paperwork. In this case, the eponymous "death pack." These are supposed to be in the drawer by the door. You poke around there until you finally unearth one. The envelope contains a set of forms and a conveniently provided toe tag. You must fill out the forms with information about the deceased (but you may give the toe tag to the tech so that *he* can put it on the body—that's why you went to medical school).

You open the pack and pull out the first form. Name, age, social security number. Cause of death? You think for a moment. What you usually write here is: cardiopulmonary arrest. After all, the heart has stopped beating and the body has stopped breathing. Someone, though, probably a pathologist, pointed out once that this was the *definition* of death, not a cause, so you sit there, pen tip tapping against the paper. What am I supposed to write? you think. Cause of death: Old age? Human nature? Cell apoptosis? God's will?

You write: cardiopulmonary arrest.

As you finish up the form, Bill, the ER tech of the day, comes in. He has an empty body bag in his hands.

"I wish someone would think to put this bag on the bed before they put the patient on it," he grumbles. "Do you know how hard it'll be to put the patient in it now?"

You hand him the toe tag and walk out. You are on your way to Step 2: Call the coroner.

When you call you actually talk to the night shift deputy coroner, a Mr. Loredo. You've talked to Mr. Loredo so many times that you recognize his deadpan voice in an instant. Mr. Loredo sounds the way you expect a deputy coroner working night shift to sound. He's not real happy to be there and he's not real happy you called. He has a nasal, monotone voice salted with a bit of country music. He gives you the impression that he has seen everything, and, in fact, Mr. Loredo may be one of the few people in the world that, given the nature of his job, actually *has* seen everything. Once Mr. Loredo asked you for the cause of death and you told him you thought it was secondary to a butcher knife, the blade of which had transected the left ventricle of the heart of the deceased. He said, without a beat, "When was the patient pronounced dead?" and he just went chugging along with his list of questions without pause until he got to the last one: "Any sign of foul play?" And you said, "Well, Mr. Loredo, I'm no detective, but the guy does have a knife sticking out of his chest."

Now, at last, he paused. "Okay," he said after a moment's reluctant reflection, "I guess that means he's a coroner's case."

Mr. Loredo's job is to ensure that nothing is a coroner's case. In fact you've heard that the best way to get away with murder in this state is to dump a body somewhere in these city limits and have someone find it when Mr. Loredo is on.

"Cause of death?" he asks you tonight.

You wonder for a moment what he would say if you told him, "Rabies." Then you think, he probably wouldn't say anything at all. He would just ask the next question. So you tell him with a shrug, "Cardiopulmonary arrest," as you scribble, scribble a note about the code for the closing chapter of this patient's chart. Your mind is already on:

Step 3: Notify the family. This is the hardest part of the job. Breaking the news. The bad news. As an ER doctor you get to give families the worst news they will ever receive and you get to do this almost every day. It's your job to say, "I'm sorry, but your mother, daughter, brother, husband, <insert name here>, has died."

After saying this you always stop and there are a couple of heartbeats while the news sinks in on the other side. Disaster; shipwreck. This is the time when people hate you as a doctor. You have failed, flunked, dropped the ball. You should be sued—you will be sued. You are a quack; if they had gone to the hospital down the street this never would have happened. And a part of you believes all this because no matter how sure thing the death was, some part of you really believes that because you are a doctor, you really can perform miracles. And actually you've seen this happen. Only not today. Today you *didn't* save a life. That nightmare you had during your second year of medical school has come true. You couldn't save a life because you *are* a fake; you are an incompetent fool who never should have been a doctor. Hippocrates would have laughed you out of this profession.

But it's not Hippocrates that calls you to judgment; it's God. After all, you just went one-on-one with Him and God won. Forget the patient; this is between you and Him. But then, you've always had a very special adversarial relationship with God, just like every other practicing physician you know.

So they hate you and you hate yourself even though this has really very little to do with you. But each death still leaves its mark on you, every telling, every "I'm sorry but he has died . . ." always leaves its little bruise and sometimes more than a bruise. Last week, for example, you had a classic "sudden cardiac death" patient, a fifty-two-year-old male with no history of medical problems, no previous cardiac symptoms, who suddenly collapsed at church. You took the radio call—which didn't sound promising. On scene, per paramedics, the patient was apneic—not breathing—and the monitor showed an "agonal" rhythm, the heart's electronic death rattle. By the time the team arrived at the hospital the patient was in asystole—flat line. He was also wearing a tuxedo. In fact, he was the first patient you ever tried to resuscitate who was wearing a tuxedo. You had to hack away at the black tuxedo jacket with your trauma scissors, cursing all the while, in order to get your monitor leads on his chest. He stayed in asystole too, never a hint of anything else. After twenty minutes of drugs, cardioversion and CPR, it was clear that this was all useless, so you raised a hand. "Let's call it a day," you said. Time pronounced: 4:14 P.M. Pam immediately turned to the paramedic. "The tuxedo," she said. "What gives?"

As it turned out, the patient was the father of the bride at a wedding. He had seen his daughter get married and then collapsed during the reception. The paramedics told you all this so you knew up front that, in this case, talking to the family was going to be a very bad scene. But still you weren't prepared. They were sitting in the grieving room, a tiny cubbyhole of a room back behind the security office. There was the patient's wife—the mother of the bride—wearing a beige dress, pearls and an orchid corsage; the groom was in another tuxedo, then the maid of honor, and, of course, the bride. A flower girl sat in the corner weeping, unnoticed and uncomforted. The rest of them sat there, stony faced, looking at you as you walked in the door. They expected the worst and they were dead on, but still you just stood there, looking at the corsage, the tuxedo and the pearls, anything but anybody's face. You had no idea what to say and you don't really remember what you finally came up with. Afterward you came out of the room quaking, and sat down out in the nurses' station in front of Pam, palms sweaty, hands shaking a little. *"I can't believe it,"* you told her, "I had to tell someone in a *bridal dress* that her father had died."

"Bummer," Pam had said.

But that was last week. Tonight, thank God, there is no wedding. This woman's death was a release if ever there was one. Still, you would give anything not to have to talk to the family. You are so tired you feel like your skin has been peeled away exposing every neuron to the open air.

"Who's the next of kin?" you ask Pam.

She pushes the chart toward you. "Daughter," she says. "In Phoenix."

You sigh, half glad that at the very least you don't have to talk to the woman face-to-face.

Usually you try not to notify a family on the phone, but tonight there doesn't look to be a choice. You paw through the chart and miscellaneous pieces of paper that have accrued during the course of this death until you find a phone number for the daughter. You dial the hospital operator and it takes her a long time to answer; she was probably asleep in her chair.

The call rings through, rings and rings until finally a sleepy voice asks, "Hello?"

"Hello, Mrs. . . . ." You shuffle frantically back through the stack of papers in front of you looking for the registration sheet. "Mrs. . . .

You had it just a moment ago. Finally you give up. "Are you Helen Jablonski's daughter?"

"Yes," she says, not sounding much more awake than before.

"This is the doctor calling from Hope General Memorial Hospital. I'm afraid I have some bad news for you."

"Hmmmm?" the woman murmurs, oblivious.

Always it comes up, how to put it into words. Most medical experts tell you not to use euphemism—don't use "passed away," or the even more delicate "gone." Use dead—died—has died. You personally have always like "passed away," especially with the death of someone very old. It seems to evoke a gentle slipping from one spiritual plane to another—something appropriate to the death of someone who has lived out their full term of life, as, you believe, this woman has.

You take a deep breath and say, "I'm afraid your mother has died."

There's a long pause; the tossup moment. Anything can happen now.

"Oh," she says, still sleepy. You're not sure she heard.

You take another breath. "I'm terribly sorry but your mother has passed away," you say again, to be sure she understands. "I'm the doctor in the emergency room and I'm afraid there wasn't much that we could do. The paramedics gave her medicines to restart her heart and put the breathing tube down her to breathe for her. We continued this in the hospital but we were unable to bring her back."

"Oh," she says again. There is a pause and she says, "Well, thanks for calling." And the line goes dead.

You stare at the receiver.

"What did she say?" Pam asks.

"She said thanks for calling and then she hung up."

"She hung up?" Pam asked. "But you have to find out what funeral home they want."

You look at Pam and shake your head. "You call," you say pushing the phone toward her. "I'm at the end of my rope."

You look up at the clock. You want to be busy doing something so that you wouldn't think about the resuscitation but you are too tired to move. Face it, you think helplessly, there isn't a time when you see an elderly patient like Mrs. Jablonski that you don't think of yourself there in her place.

Stop! you think. You close your eyes and discover that by rubbing them you generate dozens of colored lights that dance on the back of your eyelids. Then you open them again and discover the intern sitting in front of you, ready to present a patient. He looks to you so bright, so young, so ready for the future—even at five A.M.—that there is nothing else that you can do but close your eyes once more and let your face drop back down into your hands.

Congratulations: you have successfully declared someone dead. Now, as an encore, sometime during this shift or the next, you'll get to do it all over again.

The Farmer's Wife

I've had two or three patients who have reached up and gripped my hand and whispered, "Don't let me die, please don't let me die." One patient I took care of, a guy with a terrible cardiomyopathy, thirty-two years old, exactly my age then, was wide awake and alert but had a systolic blood pressure less than forty—no matter what I whipped his heart with. He, for sure, said, "Don't let me die," as I stood there, one hand on his carotid, staring up at the monitor, saying, "You're going to be fine, fine," while I was thinking, This is it. This is the end of the line. This guy is going to die. So dopamine, ephedrine, atropine, epinephrine, the whole drug box. Nothing worked and, by God, he died, staring me straight in the face until the very end, with terrified, accusatory eyes. I was letting him die, those eyes said, even though I was trying with every thing I had *not* to let him die.

And there was another one, another patient, fifty-five, a smoker, chest pain, vital signs okay. Normal ECG. I was standing by his bed talking to him, once again half watching the monitor, just out of habit. The patient had a perfectly normal sinus rhythm rate of 82 when he reached out suddenly, grabbed my hand and said, "I'm going to die." The monitor went straight line, asystole. I stood there a moment, stunned, while a nurse, who had seen it on the monitor in the nurses' station, came running over, shouting, "Hell's bells, we've got an arrest here!" I fumbled for the Ambu bag while the nurse started CPR. Thirty seconds later the patient reached out and popped me on the nose. I turned away with a yelp while the patient, freed of the face mask, shouted, "What happened? What happened?"

"I don't know," the nurse said, leaning over him, "but by any chance did you see a light at the end of a tunnel?"

But this is about the farmer's wife and the farmer. They were both very nice people and the daughter, who was with them, seemed very pleasant as well. The wife was my patient; she seemed like the kind of woman who became nervous when she wasn't cleaning. Sixty-four years old, according to the chart. She was overweight, of course, old Germanic stock, but otherwise healthy. Here with chest pain on a sleepy Sunday afternoon. So far I had seen mostly ankle sprains and mosquito bites.

"How would you describe the pain?" I asked and she paused for a moment, stumped.

People work very hard at describing their pain and can sometimes come up with strange, creative results. "It's a sort of rushing, gurgling pain." "It's a whooshing pain." "It's a kind of dry, sparkly pain." Other people don't have any kind of vocabulary to describe how they feel; they grope around even longer and come up with the (not uncommon) response, "It's a hurtin' kind of pain," which of course takes you nowhere but is the best that they can do.

"Well," she replied, "it's not really pain . . ." She groped for the right word while one hand hovered over her left chest. Finally she came up with a "pushing feeling." I stood wondering what this really meant when she made it easier by saying, "Sometimes it's like an elephant sitting on my chest."

"Sometimes?" I said.

"Like if I'm vacuuming or something. If I sit down it goes away."

"Do you have any pain now?"

"No, not now. I feel better. I think I can just go home. The pain's gone."

On the patient's right was her husband, on her left was, I presumed, her adult daughter. They stood humbly in the background, husband with his arms folded, daughter with hands clasped as they waited on the story.

"How long have you been having this elephant stuff?"

"About, well, for about a month now."

The husband came forward. "You didn't tell me anything about this."

Actually, it became clear, it was more like six months. At first the pain just came with exertion, but recently it had come on even with rest. She had been in to see her gynecologist two days ago and had mentioned it to him. He called another doctor, who wanted to put her in the hospital right away, but she really didn't feel that bad, she thought, and she hadn't had any pain for the last week or so (deny, deny), so she decided to go home. That was Friday. Today she had begun to feel the pain again, so she thought maybe she should come in just to make sure everything was okay.

"Everything was okay." That was the key. She didn't want to know what was wrong. She wanted me to tell her that everything was okay.

I finished the history and examined her. In her favor: she didn't smoke, drink heavily or have a strong family history of heart disease. On the other hand, she had never had her cholesterol checked and she had been overweight for years. Nothing on exam. Normal heart, normal lungs. Pulses normal throughout. Even so, the symptoms were classic. The patient had unstable angina, most likely due to coronary artery disease.

"I'm going to put you in the hospital," I told her.

She started. "You haven't even done any blood tests."

"It doesn't matter what the blood tests show," I said. "You have a very good chance of having heart disease, significant heart disease. You need to be in the hospital."

"There is no way," she said. "I have laundry at home in the dryer."

As I rolled my eyes, the husband came forward. "Now, Mother," he said. "Don't argue." He laid his hand on her shoulder and gave her a gentle shake. "You've got to listen to the doctor."

"You know if I leave it all night it'll do nothing but wrinkle." She turned back to me. "What if the tests are all normal?"

"The tests can be all normal and you can still have heart disease. Even if they *are* normal, I will recommend that you stay."

She looked around at her daughter and then at her husband. "That's impossible. Who's going to feed the cat?"

"I'll feed Binky," the husband said.

"You don't even know where I put the cat food."

"Mom," the daughter said kindly, "shut up."

The woman shook her head. Her face was set, but I could see she felt that by being ill she was betraying the two people beside her. They were her life.

Carolyn was standing behind the daughter with the ECG machine. "Hel-*lo*," she said loudly. "You know, when someone has chest pain it *is* important to get an ECG, and we're not going to *get* an ECG until you all move out of the way."

I took the woman's hand in mind and said, "You're going to be fine, dear. You are going to be very okay. I promise."

Carolyn shouldered the daughter out of the way, scowling at the family and at me. Carolyn was one of my favorite nurses. She was a brusque, no-nonsense kind of person—worse than me, even. On a bad day she could generate more patient complaints than anyone I knew, mostly by being crusty and blunt. (One patient referred to her as the "ER Gestapo.") But she was always there, always working, technically brilliant. If you ever needed an IV on a crashing patient or a deft hand with drugs, it was Carolyn who could deliver.

Now at the bedside, she pulled out a packet of ECG leads and began stripping them off one by one and sticking them on the woman's arms, legs and chest. Carolyn had been doing this for—how long? Fifteen years, maybe twenty. She stood over the woman applying electrode leads with infinite grace; no hesitations, no wasted motions. This is where trouble always starts on the TV shows about medicine; actors just can't quite get the rhythm down. The TV doctors fumble with their gloves, whereas the real doctors pull them on, one, two, with no wasted motion and a snap of a cuff as punctuation. There is magic to these practice moves—they have been worn smooth like a stone polished by water.

I crossed over and stood behind Carolyn, watching the wavering baseline finally settle out on the ECG. Heart rate 92; normal ECG.

"That's good, isn't it?" the woman said.

"Very good," I said and went back to squeeze her hand again. "You're going to be fine."

I turned, studying the ECG printout as I walked away. I had taken exactly two steps when Carolyn said sharply, *"Doctor!"*

I had several complicated thoughts as I paused, one foot still in the air. *Doctor!* Carolyn and I had been on a first-name basis for a long time. There were only two reasons why she would call me "Doctor!" One: she was angry at me. (This is a dead giveaway to watch your step. Nurses can make the word *Doctor* sound positively scatological.) Two: she was frightened. Now I was pretty sure she wasn't angry at me, which meant she was frightened. But of what? I mean, I was just there two seconds ago. I hadn't even walked three steps away.

I backtracked. "What's the matter?"

In the narrow moment when I had turned to walk away, all the color had drained out of the patient's face. She was now stark white, bloodless, her lips pressed thin in a rictus of pain.

"Hurts," was all she said. Her hand was on her chest.

What the hell had happened?

Carolyn raised her arms to shoo the family away. "You folks need to go out into the waiting room."

They both stood for a moment, husband to the right, daughter to the left, looking down at her.

"We'll have you back in a little bit. Just give us a few minutes here."

The husband reached out and squeezed his wife's hand, clucking at her. "You be good now," he said with a worried smile. "They're going to take good care of you." The wife responded with a grimace.

As soon as they had pushed through the doors to the waiting room, I barked at Carolyn. "We need another ECG." I leaned over the woman. "Are you having chest pain now?"

She nodded.

"What's the pain like?"

"Heavy, heavy like an elephant." She grabbed my hand, looking up at me. "I'm afraid," she said. She squeezed my hand tightly. "Please don't let me die."

I bent over for a quick listen to her chest. "Don't be ridiculous," I told her. I rechecked her pulses: radial, femoral, dorsalis, pedis. They were all present but fainter now, threadier. "Is this the same kind of pain you've been getting over the last few months?" I gazed up at the monitor, not waiting for her answer. Her heart rate had increased from the initial 80 to 112. I recycled the blood pressure cuff by poking at one of the monitor buttons. In a moment the numbers flashed up. Blood pressure 90/40. It had dropped precipitously since her arrival.

"We've got a little problem here," I said to Carolyn, who rolled her eyes; she was miles ahead of me.

The patient tugged at my hand. I looked down. "Please," she whispered. "They need me."

I barely heard her. I was watching Carolyn reapply the ECG leads across her chest, pulling the woman's flaccid breasts out of the way. Once again the screen faded to light and the baseline bucked and shivered before settling into place. This was a whole new ECG; it was difficult to imagine that it was related at all to the one we had just taken five minutes ago. This woman was having a heart attack of major proportions, a massive anterior wall infarction. The whole front wall of her heart had been deprived of blood—blood-carrying oxygen—because a clot had formed in one of the heart's major arteries. She must have been teetering on the verge of this for months; hence the angina. Her arteries had been narrowed with cholesterol and miscellaneous debris. Whenever she increased the oxygen demand on her heart, she would get ischemic pain because there was not enough blood flow. Now the inevitable clot had formed, blocking the entire artery. As a result, half of her heart was dying. It had all happened in a moment.

I stared up at the blood pressure reading on the screen, shaken by how low it was. We had to do something right away to open that blood vessel back up. Nitroglycerin is what I usually use first, but that drug would be a disaster with this blood pressure. Heparin, a venerable blood thinner, was also high on the list, but heparin only prevents clots from forming. It does not break up clots that have already formed. Lastly there was TPA. "TPA," I said aloud, relishing each letter. Tissue plasminogen activator, the "clot buster" drug. It was new then; I had only given it a couple of times before, but I had never given it to someone who looked like she needed it more.

I waved at Carolyn. "We need to get a loading dose of TPA up from the pharmacy."

"No joke," Carolyn said. She looked around the ER. "Where's Bill?" she asked at large. Bill was the tech; he needed to run to the pharmacy for us to get the drug.

"He's sleeping," the unit clerk sang out.

"Well, for Christ's sake wake him up."

I had my fingers on the woman's wrist, counting out her thready pulse, my own hands already slippery with sweat, my pulse racing ahead of hers. "Don't let me die," she had said. Never a good sign.

I thought of another possibility, an outside chance. This could also be a dissection, a tear in the lining of the blood vessel. Sometimes aortic dissections can present with ECG findings just like that of an acute anterior MI, but you give them TPA and it's a disaster. The patient usually hemorrhages to death (not that their chances are that great to begin with). I shook myself, remembering that her pulses were good, rare in a dissection, and her symptoms were classic for a heart attack, not a dissection. If I pursued this line of thinking, I might end up wasting the precious time we needed to treat her MI.

I barked at Carolyn. "Let's get some heparin going. *Now.*"

Carolyn put one hand on my shoulder and whispered, "Chill out." Then she leaned over the woman to start an IV. I watched in awe as, one-handed, she flicked the cap off the hub of the IV and slipped it, almost without even looking down, into a tiny vein on the back of this woman's hand. God love her.

I leaned over to the patient and said, as calmly as I could, "Ma'am, it looks like this pain is coming from your heart. We are going to give you several medicines. One of them is a new medicine that seems to work very well when someone has had a heart attack. It's called TPA, tissue plasminogen activator."

She gazed at me blankly and then finally raised a weak hand. "Whatever you need to do."

TPA was what we needed to do. This was the dawning of a new era in medicine, the era of "clot busting" drugs: streptokinase and, of course, TPA, the first effective drug therapy for heart attacks. Not a few years before, all we had to treat heart attack victims was painkillers and attentive nursing. Now there was a *real* treatment—inject these drugs and there was a chance the heart attack would go *away* with minimal damage to the heart. Cardiologists and ER doctors were falling all over themselves to get the TPA to any patient in whom there was even a remote possibility that it would help. (And the drug company that manufactured the drug, and sold it for $2,200 a pop, was falling all over itself to get the drug to the doctors.)

TPA works by breaking up—"lysing" in medicalese—blood clots after they are formed. Heparin, TPA's alter ego, prevents clots from forming but can't break them up after they are formed. TPA "lyses" clots that form in the main arteries of the heart, allowing the blood flow to return to normal and thereby salvaging heart muscle. Not surprisingly, this action also produces, as its worst side effect, uncontrolled bleeding. Patients can bleed from anywhere into anywhere, but the most serious side effect is bleeding into the brain. This happens a little less than 1 percent of the time, but when it does, the results can be devastating. GI bleed, stroke, death. Always in medicine there is the risk/benefit trade-off. Nothing comes for free. But in this woman's case benefit surely outweighed the risk. Surely, I thought uncertainly, surely.

When TPA does work, the results can be unexpected. The first sign is a collection of panic-inducing cardiac arrhythmias. My heart, a couple of times, has leaped through its own hoops as I tried to keep track, second by second, of the barrage of abnormal rhythms, one right after another, that finally, spontaneously and without warning, arrived at the heart's distinctive and most welcome normal sinus rhythm. The first patient I went through this with looked up at me and said, drum roll, *ta da,* "My chest pain is *gone.*"

His heart had reperfused. The blocked coronary artery had reopened.

There were four of us at the bedside now. The other nurses had abandoned their patients and rushed over to help. Someone pulled over the crash cart; someone else ran for the morphine and the heparin.

Now we spoke staccato—trade lingo.

"Bolus heparin?"

"Five thousand."

"How much an hour?"

"Thousand. Can we hang dopamine?"

"We can if you ask for it. Give me a twenty-gauge."

"Hey, call for a portable chest."

"Do you want a blood gas?"

"Not if we're giving TPA."

"You need more tubes?"

"I need a heparin flush and some tape here. Someone get me another I-VAC. This one is a dead marine."

"Yes on the dopamine."

"How fast?"

"Renal dose, two mics only, okay?" I turned and shouted across the room to the desk clerk. "Who's on call for cardiology?"

The unit clerk called back, "I'm checking, I'm checking."

I turned back to the patient. "Honey, how do you feel?" I didn't even listen to the answer. She looked terrible.

The unit clerk called back. "It's Gupta."

"Which one?"

"The short one. Rajiv."

"Well, call him. Tell him we have an acute anterior wall infarct here."

Carolyn waved a hand at me. "You want a gas?"

"I already said no."

"Are you sure?"

"Where's Bill and where's our drug?"

"It's coming, for Christ's sake."

PVCs appeared on the monitor. Premature ventricular beats—hiccups of the heart. Almost everyone has the occasional PVC, usually not dangerous in themselves, but not totally innocent either. I studied the monitor, watching as the green point of light swam across it, each heartbeat etched out on the gray screen; the regular atrial blip and ventricular ricochet, the chaotic extra beat here, there. Carolyn stood beside me, studying the monitor as well, scowling. I recycled the blood pressure cuff and glanced down at the patient.

The woman's face was still ashen gray. I realized I'd never paid much attention to that phrase, ashen gray; the color of no color.

Again I gazed up at the monitor, assuming the usual posture (hips slung forward, shoulders drooping, mouth dangling open) that physicians instinctively assume when they are befuddled by what's on the monitor screen.

Blood pressure: 78/40.

Pump failure. As simple as that. The heart muscle is a pump, and the blood pressure gives a glimpse of its pumping power. Right now though, so much heart muscle was without oxygen that the heart really couldn't pump enough to generate the kind of blood circulation one needed in order to sustain life. We needed to open up that blood vessel, lyse that clot, right now.

Bill, the technician, came in at a dead run from the pharmacy, plastic bag of TPA held aloft. He tossed it to Carolyn.

"Did you get Gupta?" I shouted at the desk clerk.

"Just now; I'm on the phone with his nurse. He's got a patient in the cath lab. He'll come when he's finished."

The luck of the draw. Gupta could have taken this woman to the cath lab if he was free. If the TPA didn't work, that was the next thing to try.

I stared up at the monitor, thinking. Maybe I should try to get someone other than Gupta here. But where else could I find a cardiologist on a Sunday afternoon?

"Is there anyone else we can call?"

"I'll try."

Carolyn hung the TPA. Average time to reperfusion, I had read, was twenty-seven minutes—when it worked. Did we have twenty-seven minutes?

I leaned back over the patient, clasping her hand in mine.

"On a scale of one to ten, where ten is the worst pain you ever had and one is just a tiny pain, what do you say your pain is?"

"Ten," she breathed. She looked too frightened to move.

"Honey, we've given you some medicine that will help you get better. You just have to hold on until it works."

She nodded, clutching at my hands, and closed her eyes. "Okay, okay," she whispered. I could barely hear her.

The radiology technician showed up with her portable x-ray machine. I stood next to the machine as she adjusted the giraffe-necked cone.

"Yikes," she whispered to me. "That woman looks like shit. What's her problem?"

"She's dying," I whispered back.

We sat the patient up in the bed for her x-ray. She looked like a broken puppet, head rolling, eyes staring off into nothing. I helped the technician tuck the cold, flat x-ray plate behind her and steadied her for a moment so she wouldn't pitch off to one side.

The technician stood back, the trigger in her hand. "X-ray!" she called out. "Shield 'em if you got 'em."

Buzz. Safety.

We pulled out the cassette and I recycled the blood pressure cuff: 80/50. We were losing ground. "We need to hang some saline," I told Carolyn. I probably should have ordered this before.

"How much?"

"Give her two hundred and we'll see."

"Shall we try some morphine?"

I looked at the monitor, checking the pressure. "We can touch her with a milligram, maybe." I was mentally reviewing everything I knew about the patient and everything we were doing. Was there something I missed? Was I wrong? Was this actually an aortic dissection, a rip in the wall of the body's main artery? Or maybe a pulmonary embolus, a massive clot in the lungs?

I ran my hands from her feet up to her groin, reexamining

her pulses. She had good femoral pulses. Belly was soft. I listened to her lungs. Crackles there, water on the lung. Heart failure, failure, failure.

The x-ray technician tapped my shoulder and thrust the chest x-ray up on the view box next to the bed. I peered at it, looking for answers. No heart enlargement, normal-looking aorta, no evidence of a dissection. This was a normal x-ray.

I leaned over her. "Pain any better?" I whispered.

She turned her face in my direction, but she seemed to be somewhere else. She looked as if the pain had consumed her.

"Gupta's on the phone," the clerk sang out.

I took one last glance at the monitor before I turned away. One PVC, two PVCs. No, God, she was in V-tach.

V-tach, ventricular tachycardia—a heartbeat triggered from deep within the ventricle. Sometimes there is a pulse with it— the rhythm can be life-sustaining, though usually not for long. Other times the heart just gives up, pumping no blood. When this occurs, the rhythm is the last brief burst of electrical activity the heart assumes before it dies.

I groped at the woman's neck, trying to find a pulse.

"Oh, shit," Carolyn said. She had just looked up at the monitor. "Christ."

"She's got a pulse. Honey, can you talk to me? Honey, honey?" To Carolyn: "Get the lidocaine." Lidocaine is a drug used to banish bad heart rhythms. "I think this may be from reperfusion."

The reperfusion arrhythmias, the jolt and shutter of an engine restarting. If we were lucky, this was a signal that her artery had opened back up with the TPA.

"Honey, can you talk to me?"

She barely moved her lips. "I feel so weak," she said.

"The pain, dear. On a scale of one to ten . . ."

"It's still a ten."

I again recycled the blood pressure cuff: 85/50. Holding, anyway. I checked the IV bag. She had gotten 120 cc.

Carolyn injected the lidocaine. "Do you want to shock her?" she said.

"Wait, give her a second."

A minute, two minutes. Still a good pulse but still V-tach—reperfusion arrhythmias usually don't last this long. And the patient usually stops having chest pain . . .

The V-tach rhythm stopped suddenly. Straight-line; no heartbeat. I had gotten no further than to put my hand to my mouth when the flat track of light wobbled, bucked once, twice, and settled into a sinus rhythm. Rate 110. The lidocaine had worked.

Blood pressure 92/50.

The chest pain was a little better, the patient told us. Eight on a scale of one to ten.

"Come on, God," I prayed. "Let the TPA do its stuff. Please, God, just this once."

"Let's touch her with a little more morphine," I said. "What about Gupta?" I shouted out to the desk clerk.

"He said he'd be here when he finished."

I stood watching the monitor—which stayed in a blessed sinus rhythm—no PVCs. The blood pressure cuff recycled: 74/32. Not good. And then I thought, hell, why lie? This was very bad. I was sure she had not reperfused.

I wheeled around to Carolyn. "Where the hell are the blood gas results?"

"You said you didn't *want* a blood gas."

"Oh, well . . . let's go up on the dopamine."

Dopamine is a drug that, in part, causes the heart to work harder, beat stronger. "Flogging the heart," it's called.

"What are you at?"

"Twenty mics."

"Higher," I said. "What about a Foley?"

Carolyn looked at me askance and said, not unkindly, "Yes, Doctor." She already had the kit out.

A Foley is a tube placed in the bladder to drain urine. (Who was Foley? I have always wondered, and what's it like to be immortalized as an aid to urination?) The urine draining from the Foley would give us a rough idea of how well the kidneys and, indirectly, other organs like the liver, the gut and the lungs were being fed oxygen. Good urine output meant good perfusion.

We struggled to get the Foley in. I stood holding the patient's right leg on my shoulder. This is the other part that never shows up on TV, the part of emergency medicine that involves groping around in various genitalia sticking rubber tubes into available orifices. The least glamorous job in the world.

There was a trickle of urine.

"Dust," Caroline said. "Nothing but dust."

Pump failure, pump failure: 76/40 and holding. What should I do? Kidney function gone to ground. Blood pressure terrible. If only she would reperfuse. If only Gupta would get here. If only we could find another cardiologist.

"Have you tried calling the other Gupta?" I shouted to the clerk.

"Yes, his office said he's in Duluth for a conference."

"Duluth," I repeated stupidly. "Well, then how about Rawlings?"

"He's not on call either, and his answering service said they were not allowed to call his house if he wasn't on call."

"Dear Jesus," I whispered, then leaned over the bed. "Honey, how are you doing?"

She spoke up in a little voice. "Chest still hurts." She seemed to get littler and littler with each passing moment, with each notch down in her blood pressure.

"On a scale of one to ten . . ." I didn't really want to know the answer.

"A little bit better."

Blood pressure 70/40. We were losing ground, really; with the dopamine and fluids it should come up at least a little. Why didn't the TPA work?

I looked down at the patient. On her right arm, where we had drawn some blood, there was a trickle of blood that wound down to her hand and dripped onto the floor. She was bleeding from her IV site, blood oozing onto the sheet. Couldn't get more anticoagulated than that, I thought.

The woman put out her hand to me. "No," she said. Her hand dropped.

"Christ." This was Carolyn. "She's in V-fib."

I looked up at the monitor. So she was. V-fib is a terminal rhythm; a heart that is not beating at all, but is quivering. The monitor displays this quivering as random noise, a squiggle. That's what we saw now.

Her reperfusion rhythm! I thought. I stood for a moment, rooted, hoping, praying. But the woman stayed in V-fib. This was not a reperfusion arrhythmia.

"Paddles," I said. "We need to defibrillate her."

Defibrillation; electrical medicine. The best way to understand it is to think of the heart as a collection of millions of electrical cells, usually well coordinated. Under circumstances of hypoxia—lack of oxygen—this coordination breaks down and chaos ensues. The most effective means of correcting this chaos is to trigger, all at once, the entire heart muscle, causing every cell to fire simultaneously. You do this by delivering a large electrical shock, a sort of stun gun, to the heart. It's called defibrillation. After defibrillation you hope that as the heart recovers from the shock, normal electrical activity can resume. It works well, sometimes. The energy charge starts at 200 joules, the kick from a very large mule, and is dialed up from there. Carolyn huddled over the defibrillator, pulling out the paddles. These paddles, two metal plates attached to plastic handles, carry the charge. She leaned over the bed rails and applied the paddles to the woman's chest.

"All clear," she shouted. We all leaned back. If anyone touched any metal on the bed while the shock was administered, they, too, would be defibrillated.

The patient's body jerked—arms and legs jumping. There followed that faint smell of burnt flesh that always goes with bad resuscitations. We all looked up, prayerfully, at the monitor. The bouncing electric point of light settled back into chaos.

"Again," I said.

Carolyn punched the power button and reapplied the paddles.

"Clear!"

The shock; the flaying arms and jerking legs. All of us stared again at the monitor.

A rhythm, we had a rhythm. And the best kind of rhythm: sinus. Rate 140.

I groped at her neck and then raised a triumphant fist. "We have a pulse here, guys."

Have we got a blood pressure?

Carolyn punched at the monitor to recycle the blood pressure pump, and we all stood staring at the screen. It felt like waiting for the slot machine to finish spinning and come to rest on the magic symbols. "Please, let there be a good blood pressure," I whispered. "Please, a blood pressure compatible with life. I don't want to lose this woman. Please, God, give her a chance."

The monitor came up with slash marks. Blood pressure too low to measure.

"Still, we have a pulse," Carolyn said. I looked down at the patient. Whereas she once held the hospital gown primly in place, she now lay nearly naked, breasts sprawling, eyes half open and sightless. Blood everywhere. She looked like a murder victim.

"Get Respiratory down here. I'm going to tube her," I said. Intubation, the breathing tube. "And we need to Doppler her pressure."

"Bretylium?" Carolyn asked. Bretylium was the next drug on the antiarrhymic hit list, for use after lidocaine.

"No," I told her.

"She's going to need it."

"She doesn't need it now."

"What about bicarb?" one of the other nurses asked.

She meant plain bicarbonate of soda. In the chemistry of acid-base, it is pure base. Fads in resuscitation research come and go, and last year everyone thought bicarb, judiciously administrated, saved lives. This year, though, it was yanked from every protocol. Rarely indicated, experts noted. In five years we will all be using it again.

"No, no," I said. "But let's get a gas."

"You said you didn't want a gas."

I looked down. "Well," I said, "I changed my mind."

The patient was deeply unconscious now. I intubated. The trachea was clear, easy to see. The respiratory therapist took over the airway, fussing with the Ambu bag, taping the tube into place.

The monitor was still sinus tach—rate 140, then 145, 150, 160—like an inevitable chord progression in music. Carolyn was trying to get a blood pressure with the Doppler when the rhythm collapsed back into V-fib.

"I told you she would need the bretylium," Caroline said.

We got ready to shock again. Carolyn unsheathed the paddles.

"Now, guys."

Shock, spasm. On the monitor: V-fib.

Julie, another crabby nurse (she was going through a divorce) punched at the monitor, saying, "I wish she would just *pick* a rhythm and *stay* with a rhythm. This back-and-forth shit has got to quit."

We shocked the patient back into a sinus rhythm again, but her heart rate was still high: 138. Carolyn triumphantly administered the bretylium. I stood going over the case again and again in my head. What had I missed, for God's sake, what had I missed? Think, *think*, what can it be?

There was no pulse with sinus rhythm now. This meant that the heart was generating electrical activity but the mechanical part of the heart, the working part, had shut down. We needed to pump the blood for her: CPR.

Julie, short and squat, pulled over the footstool, climbed up on it and started rocking up and down with her palms on the patient's chest. I looked back down at the woman's face. A trickle of blood ran from her mouth. It oozed down her neck and pooled on the sheet. She was still bleeding from her IV sites, and it looked like there was even blood in her urine bag. It seemed that she was bleeding from everywhere except her heart.

"Mother of God," Carolyn said, gazing at the monitor. "I don't believe this."

Hold CPR.

V-fib on the monitor.

Shock: 360 joules—the highest you could go—the end of the dial.

Asystole. Flat line. Dead end.

I knew this, expected it; the final station of the cross. The heart had now given up, flat line, no electrical activity at all.

"Epinephrine," I said wearily. This is adrenaline, used in the last-ditch pharmacological effort to jump-start a dying heart.

Carolyn yanked open the top drawer of the crash cart. We took the next step down the ACLS protocol, the ritual of resuscitation, modern last rites.

If someone could put her on a balloon pump . . . I thought, but the nearest balloon pump from here was a helicopter ride away. Transfixed, I stared at the monitor, which had now taken the place of the patient. Here the process of dying was displayed electronically. "Atropine," I said, nodding to myself.

Atropine, epi, atropine, epi. The litany for asystole. What else, I thought to myself: pneumothorax?—air in the lining of the lung? That can happen during an arrest. Pericardial tamponade?—an outpouring of blood into the sack that embraces the heart.

"*Please, don't let me die,*" she had said.

It came in small steps. The feeling of inevitability. She's dying, she's dying. She's already dead.

Not yet, not yet.

"Hold CPR."

Asystole. Flat line. Nothing.

"Restart CPR." Then I remembered; it really should have come to me before. "The external pacemaker," I said.

Julie moaned. "Oh, come on now, give it a rest."

I shook my head, glaring at her.

Julie looked away, shrugging her shoulders. "Jeesh."

Carolyn was already over by the wall of supplies, pulling open drawers and strewing random pieces of equipment. "Now, where are those damn electrodes," she kept muttering. And then: "Aha!" She returned waving two large, flat pads. "Every time I look for these, they are stored somewhere else."

An external pacemaker is a simple device, two giant electrodes, one placed on the anterior part of the chest and one on the posterior. A charge smaller than the one delivered with defibrillation is now passed from one pole or paddle to the other. With this, we hope like crazy, we can jump-start the heart. This is known as "capturing." You dial up the joules until you find a current strong enough to depolarize the heart muscle. I had used it several times under different circumstances in the past, but it had never worked for me in a patient in asystole.

"Hold CPR."

We all stood gazing at the monitor screen while Carolyn dialed up the current. There was the charge passing through the heart but no "capture." Nothing, nothing. Finally, at the highest current, the patient's chest wall muscles started contracting. We were capturing skeletal muscle but still—nothing from the heart.

No pulse.

"Restart CPR."

I became aware of someone standing next to me. It was Dr. Gupta, fresh from the cath lab. He was still wearing his surgical cap and paper booties. I grabbed the ECG off the top of the ECG cart and shoved it at him. "Anterior wall, massive infarct. She's been in and out of V-tach, V-fib . . . and now she's in . . ." I glanced at the monitor to double-check and saw, still, "asystole. I thought it was reperfusion, but I don't think she ever opened up."

Gupta *hmmm*ed noncommittally. "Yep," he said, staring at the monitor while Julie paused momentarily. "Looks like asystole to me."

"TPA hasn't worked."

"Well," he said, with a "these-things-happen" shrug of his shoulders.

"Do you think she has a chance in the cath lab?"

Gupta looked around as if I were mad. "She's in asystole," he said, looking at me quizzically as if to say, "She's dead. Why would I want to take her to the cath lab?"

I looked down at the woman, staring at the blood that still trickled from her mouth, dripping onto the floor. She was now bleeding from every puncture wound.

"Hold CPR."

Asystole. Nothing.

"Restart CPR."

Carolyn put a hand on my shoulder. "Nothing's working, honey."

I hung my head.

"It's time to wave her good-bye."

Julie stopped CPR and looked down at me—waiting.

I looked at my watch. "One more round of drugs," I said. I stood looking at the monitor, turning my back to the patient.

Epi, atropine.

"Hold CPR." I gazed up at the screen, trying to will her back. She must come back, she must.

Asystole on the monitor.

I looked at my watch and raised my hand in the air. "Okay, code called twelve thirty-five."

Julie stepped heavily down from the footstool and peeled off her gloves. Carolyn stood, arms crossed, staring at a wall. Gupta was looking at the first ECG we had gotten.

"Wow," he said. "Perfectly normal. Can you believe it?"

I stood watching the monitor until Carolyn disconnected it

from the patient. Nothing left. I turned away from them all, mumbling, "I've got to tell the family."

I walked slowly out through the back door to the waiting room thinking, Pump failure, pump failure, as I shuffled along. I was trying not to think about what could have happened. What if she had come in yesterday? Or the day before, when there would have been a cath lab available?

I stopped at the door to the waiting room and looked in through the window. There the husband and the daughter sat, not looking particularly anxious—after all, the last time he had seen his wife and she had seen her mother, the woman had simply been complaining of some chest pain.

Yesterday . . . , I thought.

I walked in, feet still dragging, and sat down beside the husband. He looked at me trustingly. I felt like I was about to shoot a puppy.

"Your wife had a massive heart attack," I told him. "Her heart lost the power needed to pump blood. She had problems with her heart rhythm as well, problems I couldn't correct." I took a deep breath and stared down at my hands. There was nothing more I could do except just *say* it.

"I'm sorry, sir, but your wife has died."

The air was empty for a moment. I couldn't even look at them.

"Well," the husband said in a wan voice. "I lost a partner."

"We tried everything we had," I told him. "We gave her TPA and everything else, but her heart . . . just failed her." I looked up.

His face was blank. He shook his head but said nothing. There weren't the words; there was nothing at this moment to say. Finally he held up one hand and with the other pulled his daughter close to him.

"I'm sorry," I said, just to say something. I had been in this room many times under similar circumstances, and I knew—or rather felt—that in all honesty, I had no more to offer this family than some professional sympathy for a heartbreak that would touch me only for a moment.

Neither of them spoke, neither cried. They just sat there huddled together. The daughter rocked her father back and forth, back and forth.

"Dad," she said. That was the only thing she said.

We sat for a moment in silence. This was not the first time I wished I had the religious faith of some evangelical Christian, someone who was certain, someone who *knew* about God and his plans—because *I* certainly didn't. The only thing left that I could do, now that I had notified the family, was just the miserable bureaucratic stuff: talk to the coroner, fill out the forms, complete the last medical record ever filed on this patient—all those temporal things where faith, thank God, was not an issue.

I have thought often about that family: the farmer's wife, the farmer and the daughter. I wondered about the two survivors. Who did the laundry now? Who fed the cat?

One day about a year later, I saw the whole family once more in an unlikely spot. I was in the Midwest for a medical conference on—naturally—clot-busting drugs. On the afternoon of the last day, I decided to take a break, go for a walk in the park across from the hotel. It was a brilliant winter day, almost spring, and people were out walking just to take in the sunshine. I had strolled up a hill to a reservoir when I saw them: the husband, the wife and the daughter. They were all younger now, much younger—the parents were no more than a few years out of high school. Already, though, the wife was doughy plump and the husband as thin as a rail. Their daughter, this daughter, was a blond girl in pigtails. She couldn't have been more than four or five. The husband and wife held hands as they walked while the daughter ran on ahead. The couple seemed to radiate a sort of serene security, a security in each other, in their daughter, in their life, that most people I knew could only dream of.

I was standing on a lip of land that dammed a small reservoir, a lakelet at the top of the hill. The couple was walking up toward me along a dirt path. The daughter reached the top first and she stood pointing at the lake, which was invisible from below, shouting, "Can you see? Can you see?" The parents waved, still holding hands, and kept moving slowly up the hill toward her. At one point, the husband stopped, pulled his wife up close and kissed her.

I closed my eyes. A happy marriage, I thought, and this thought produced a prayer. Please God, it ran, please protect that man and that woman from knowing the future. Please never let them see what I can—from where I stand—so clearly see: all happy marriages end in tragedy.

3

LESSONS IN EMERGENCY MEDICINE

How to Deliver a Baby

THIS IS YOUR FIRST real job as a doctor. After four years of medical school and most of an emergency medicine residency, you look like a doctor: handsome, chiseled profile, great abs. You know how to act like one ("Nurse, get me a tourniquet, *stat*."). But you've never had a chance to play one unsupervised. You are still in training, still a resident. (In emergency medicine that's four years of long days and even longer nights.) As a resident you have a degree to practice medicine, but all your moves are still closely supervised by "attendings," physicians who have finished their training and passed their board certification exams. You still have a way to go for that. But you do have a medical license—you can moonlight as a doctor, especially at jobs where you see simple things, like sore throats and colds. That's what's brought you here, to a tiny ER at tiny Grace Hospital. "It's a breeze," the ER director told you. "Kids with sniffles, sprained ankles. Most nights you just sleep."

The downside is that it's an hour and a half drive out here and you are in the middle of *nowhere*. This particular nowhere is located on the edge of a beaten-down industrial city, a steel town on the skids. This is your first night, and so far you've seen a weird collection of farmers and urban deadbeats. But that's okay. You are on your own now, making the decisions that will help you save lives. You are "the Man." Also you are getting paid something above the $10 an hour wage you make as a resident. Life is good. Now it has quieted down, and if all goes well, you can get back to the call room and get a few hours of sleep in. . . .

It's about 2:15 A.M.—you've just settled down to some Chinese takeout food—when you hear the shouting. It's a woman's voice, but you can't understand what she's saying. The shouting is followed by the voice of a nurse saying loudly, "Just breathe, just breathe."

Another nurse sticks her head in the door where she finds you, mid-chew, on your moo shu pork.

"You better get in here," she says. "This one is about ready to pop."

A delivery, you realize. A baby. You scowl at the nurse. "What is she doing here?" you say grumpily. "Get her up to Labor and Delivery." This is the routine in your training hospital. OB/GYN residents deliver babies. That's what they're there for.

The nurse smiles. She hadn't liked you from the moment you walked in the door. "We don't do OB at this hospital."

"What do you mean you don't do OB at this hospital?"

"Everybody goes to Lying-In on the other side of town."

You pause, stumped, and then you have a verbal tantrum. That's okay, though—all real doctors have them. "Well, why didn't she go across town to Lying-In?"

The nurse's smile broadens. She enjoys making you sweat. "Why don't you ask her?"

She turns away to go back to where the patient is. Her place is taken by another nurse, older but more kindly looking. You still haven't moved. "Well, you must have an OB/GYN doctor on call or something," you say to the kinder-looking nurse.

"I guess so," she says and leans out to call to the unit secretary. "Who's on for OB?"

"I think it's Dr. Panks," the unit secretary shouts back.

"No, he's retired," your nurse calls.

"Well, he's on the list."

"Dr. Panks?" shouts the nurse who hates you. She's calling from somewhere in the bowels of the ER. "Dr. Panks is up on the third floor. He had a big stroke two weeks ago. He's delivered his last baby."

"Honey," the nice nurse standing before you says. She puts her hand on your shoulder, and as she looks down at you, you suddenly see that she's thinking about how young you look. Then you realize how young you feel. "Honey," she says. "You'd better get in there."

And so you abandon your Chinese food and rise slowly from the chair. You're thinking, maybe this is just premature labor . . . maybe . . . just Braxton Hix contractions, the pseudocontractions of false labor . . . maybe, you know, very early labor, and there would be time to transfer her to another hospital.

It's not just that you've never *delivered* a baby—it's that you've barely even *seen* one delivered. You did do the mandatory OB-GYN rotation in medical school, but that rotation wasn't much. You were assigned to the university hospital, along with fifteen other medical students, during the time of a great managed care–induced upheaval. During the six weeks you were on rotation, only five patients delivered. You managed to be there for three of them, but of course the residents had first dibs on the delivery. There were so few deliveries that they weren't about to let the medical students do anything. Besides, there were so many medical students that you had trouble even finding a spot to stand so that you could see what was going on. Finally, on the last day of your rotation, a resident actually sat you down between the hoisted legs of a freshly delivered mother with a gaping episiotomy. The resident gave you thirty seconds of unintelligible instructions, some 5'0 Vicryl thread on a cutting needle and told you to get to work. You applied yourself vigorously, trying to maintain an expression that conveyed you knew what you were doing, but the fact was that this was your first clinical rotation and the only previous suturing you had done was on a dead pig. The resident watched you for almost forty-five seconds before grabbing the needle driver away from you, pushing you off the stool and setting to work himself. That was the full extent of your hands-on OB experience.

You did have several pediatric rotations during your fourth year, and six weeks in the neonatal intensive care unit. That was back in the days when you thought about becoming a pediatrician—actually, a neonatologist, specializing in high-tech infant care. There you have had a fair amount of experience. You are pretty sure you could resuscitate a baby, but getting that little sucker out into the bright lights and big city—that could be a problem.

As you slowly rise from the chair, you look into the kind face of the nurse before you. In a voice with a tremble and a high pitch, one you don't even recognize as your own, you say, "How . . . how . . . how far apart are the contractions?"

The nurse just jerks her thumb toward the acute room.

Get in there.

You walk down a hallway that seems impossibly long and impossibly dark. You can hear the woman wailing. "It hurts," she's screaming. "It hurts, oh God, it hurts." You think, Of course it hurts, you idiot. You're having a baby. In the room is the third nurse, younger and very pretty. "Breathe," she keeps telling the woman. "Just breathe."

"What the fuck does breathing have to do with it?" the patient screams back. "I'm having a fucking baby!"

The patient is a woman half-crouched on the end of the gurney. The nurse who hates you (at some point you learn her name is Helen) is standing over the patient, helping her struggle out of her pants. The patient is thin, gaunt almost, with dirty blond hair and a pendulous belly, striated with stretch marks, and stick-like arms and legs.

You are only two steps into the room when you smell it. Alcohol. She's drunk.

You may not know much about delivering babies, but you are training to be an ER doctor and you know a *lot* about alcohol.

She has half her clothes off when she pushes Helen away and screams, "Stop it, stop it! You're hurting me." You are struggling to get a pair of gloves on when Helen is knocked back into you. You step around her and use your only available weapon, your elbow, to push the woman back onto the examining table.

You lean over her. "You're *drunk*," you say.

"Yeah?" she says. More like a statement.

You look at her and somehow you can see the rest.

"How much crack have you smoked tonight?"

"That's none of your fucking business," she says in return.

You can see her with a crack pipe in her hand. It's a picture so vivid you have to close your eyes. A crack addict, for sure. That explains why she would be stupid enough to come to this hospital. Then you think, Oh my God, the first real delivery I've ever had and it's a crack baby.

She struggles up toward you, wailing, "I hu-ur-urt."

"Sit down," you yell back. There is a note of authority in your voice that you've never heard before, but it is almost masked by an equal amount of desperation.

"Sit down," you shout again. "I mean *lie* down."

"I can't," she wails. "I'm having a ba-aa-aa-by."

You shove her back down angrily. Helen is on one side and the pretty nurse, whose name is Carol, is on the other. You all struggle to get the damn pants off. Finally you get your first look at the vaginal area. The introitus, the vaginal entrance (or in this case the vaginal exit) is closed. The baby isn't exactly popping out, thank God. You at least can finish getting your gloves on.

"Anybody try to get fetal heart tones?" you ask in a sudden moment of clarity.

"I'll get the Doppler," Carol says.

You stare down at the woman's bulging abdomen. "How many babies have you had?" You are still shouting. You know you have to shout to get through to her; she is totally skanked.

"Seven," she wails. "Ohhhhhh, my God."

"When are you due?"

Carol, Doppler in hand, leans over her, applying jelly from a bottle to a spot just under navel.

"When are you due?"

"Please, Jesus," she says and starts panting. "Please Jesus, please Jesus, please Jesus."

Helen leans over her. "Do you have a doctor?" she asks. "Did you get prenatal care?"

"Lying-In," she moans. "I'm supposed to go there." She begins writhing her way through another contraction.

You've finally gotten sterile gloves on, but they are immediately contaminated when the woman tries to sit up again and you push her back down. Helen has the bottle of Betadine, an antiseptic, and begins pouring it over the woman's crotch. The patient starts shrieking again and rears up, knocking Carol out of the way. You push her back down again and put your face close to hers. "Don't move," you tell her in a fierce whisper. She looks up at you and, for a moment, is still.

You turn to Helen. "Do we have the stuff to resuscitate the kid? Laryngoscopes and stuff, in case this baby's in trouble?"

"I'll get the neonatal crash cart," she says.

"And the Isolette?" you ask the kind-looking nurse, who now just looks very frightened. The Isolette is a warming unit in which the baby is "gently cradled after its eventful passage into a new world," as the textbooks say.

"Okay." You brace yourself against the end of the gurney and lean forward. Her bent legs are on either side of you. You insert two fingers of your right hand through the lips of the vagina. They slide in a couple of centimeters and then you meet an obstruction. The baby's head . . . is it a head? Yes, it's a head. With your two fingers you explore the vaginal vault. You are feeling for the cervix, an anatomic landmark whose present condition can give you a clue as to just when this baby is going to pop out.

Ordinarily the cervix is about three centimeters long; it protrudes like a little short nose into the vaginal vault. During a delivery, as the baby is pushed out of the uterus, the cervix flattens, and the cervix's central opening dilates. This is what you are feeling for as you try to figure out how close that baby is to the real world and the rest of its life.

You sit on a stool next to her, grope around for a bit and finally peg this lady at about eight centimeters. She is going to deliver soon. No chance to get her to another hospital.

As you grope around inside the patient, she is moving all over the gurney. "Stop it," she keeps telling you. She rises somewhat to slap at your arm. "You're hurting me."

"*I'm* not hurting you," you say. "*You're* having a baby. That's what's hurting you."

"I know," she says, still wiggling all over. "But you don't have to be so rough."

"*Lie still!*" Helen thunders and for a moment again the patient lies still.

Helen has taken over the Doppler and is moving it across the woman's abdomen, still looking for fetal heart tones. "I'm not getting anything here," she says.

Carol bangs through the doors with a blue cart, the pediatric crash cart.

"She's eight centimeters dilated," you tell them. "Not quite there." You turn back to the patient. "When is your due date?"

"I don't know," she says, and she begins thrashing around again.

"What do you mean you don't?"

She looks you square in the face and spits out the words. "I mean I don't know because, you asshole, I don't know."

This stops you. The chaos is overwhelming. She doesn't know her own due date, you think to yourself. You stand there for a moment, a gloved hand buried deep inside this woman, baffled as to what to do next. Weird words and phrases fling themselves into your consciousness from some deeper place. They are words that dazzled you in medical school: *platypelloid pelvis, deflexed vertex, synclitic, anaclitic.* You must have known what they meant once, though now they seem incomprehensible. But as you try to remember, raising your free hand up to your forehead, there is a stab of bright light in your forehead. Déjà vu.

You dreamt this before, or maybe lived it. About a case of appendicitis. You were a first-year medical student, and you were standing in an OR suite with the dean of the medical school. He was ordering you to perform an appendectomy on a young boy laid out before you both on an operating table. You had instruments in your hand, but you were doubting yourself, saying, "But if I do surgery on him, I know I will kill him." The dean seemed to loom larger and larger before you until he towered over you. He was bellowing the whole time, "I don't care if you kill him or not, just do it." You remember now, if not the whole dream, at least the feeling it evoked, the terror. You remember then that feeling that you could hurt someone; they could be trustingly asleep and you would destroy them.

That feeling is here now, though it's not so overwhelming or paralyzing as it was in the dream. You look down at the patient and she seems very far away. You look around and that's when you see that everyone is moving very slowly—there is time, you think, there is time to think. You reposition your hand as the woman starts grunting, going through another contraction.

"You get anything?" you ask Helen, who is still trying to get fetal heart tones with the Doppler.

"Nothing," she tells you.

You turn to the other nurses. "Tell the unit clerk to get on the phone now. Call University and get the pediatric transport team. Tell them we have a baby . . . tell them we're about to have a baby that's high risk." You turn back to the woman. "Did you see anybody while you were pregnant—any doctor?" But the woman just wails in response.

You feel again for the span of the cervix. It seems wider now, bigger than even a moment before. The cervix itself seems stretched to a thin lip that rings the baby's head. You can feel the bones of the skull, unfused bony plates that override each other as they are squeezed through the birth canal. You can sense the compressive forces bearing down on that eggshell head. Oh, Jesus, you think. Oh Jesus, Jesus, Jesus. This woman is going to die, the baby is going to die, I am going to get sued and I'll never be able to work another shift in another ER anywhere in the world ever again.

There's a splat. Blood and amniotic fluid on the floor and on your shoes, a gusher of fluid from the vagina. Her bag of water has broken. You think, I've got to look for meconium staining, a sign of fetal distress, but suddenly the woman is louder than ever before.

"*I gotta push*," she shouts. "*I gotta push. I gotta push.*"

"*Don't push*," you shout back, sounding as desperate as she is.

"I gotta push. I gotta."

"Just pant, honey," Helen is telling the woman. "Pant, pant."

"Please, dear Jesus," you pray, and as you say this you can feel the head move forward, moved by a primordial force that could move the ages. The baby's head has left the uterus, descended into the vagina and is now burrowing its way out to light and air. The vaginal lips are opening, moving, spreading, embracing the glimpse of a massive egg, a scalp coated with black hair. The lips of the vagina are ovoid now, embracing this misshapen form. That's when you lose all sense of what is going on. You put your left hand over your heart and put out the right hand to do what may be the stupidest thing, to date, you have ever done as a doctor. You give the head a little shove to see if it will go back inside.

The answer is no; it's not going back in. The woman is bearing down like a mighty machine. You can actually see the misshapen egg, the baby's head, growing, pushing through the lips, a steadily enlarging globe. There is no going back.

You turn to Helen. "I need a bulb syringe," you say and when she looks at you blankly, you demonstrate with your hand. "The little, squishy, rubber thing. To aspirate with."

You are staring down at an ear now, the right ear of a baby that faces off to the left. You reposition your fingers past the vaginal lips and under the chin, which immediately pops out. The head rotates almost immediately and you stare down at the face of a very old man, eyes closed tight and lips pursed in suffering. Whatever it is looks very dead.

"Stop pushing," you yell at the woman, and this time you can hear that note of authority, real authority, edge back into your voice. "Just give me a second."

You take the bulb syringe and use it to suction the little nostrils and, very gently, the mouth. With your other hand you hold the body in the vagina.

"This is a tiny baby," you tell the nurses. "Get ready," although you have no idea for what.

You let go of the shoulder and wait a moment. The baby stays where it is—not moving at all. The mother goes through another set of contractions, another tidal wave, but the baby doesn't move, nothing.

You wait out the contraction, staring down at the baby. Shoulder dystocia, you think in awe, a phrase you never thought could someday terrify you. The baby has gotten hung up, shoulder trapped somehow within pelvis.

You wipe your forehead with what you can reach of your left shoulder and arm. You reposition your hands, poking an index and a middle finger of your left hand around the left side of the neck, sliding up under the shoulder. You sort of sweep your fingers inside the stretched lips of the vagina and the right shoulder pops out. But the other shoulder is still snagged somehow. You can't tell by what. You can't even get a finger over it—your hand keeps slipping and scooting around. That's when you look up at the nurses suddenly; you have forgotten they were there. There are three naked faces, mouths dangling open, staring down at you.

"Get me a sterile towel" is all you say, and you go back to trying to dig this baby out. You try with your fingers again, scooping up over the right shoulder. How long do you have? Not long. You try again. Nothing. Helen hands you a sterile towel by peeling open, banana-like, the paper edges of the sterile package. You shake it open and use it, first on your hands and then the head, neck and shoulder of the baby, so you can get a better grip. You try rotating the shoulders a little, twisting the body clockwise and then, in a rivulet of blood, the whole body slithers out so fast you almost lose your grip, and then you are sitting in a puddle of blood and amniotic fluid, the baby in your lap.

It is absolutely purple and it doesn't move, not a flicker. You hold it there gingerly for a moment, just staring at the thing on your lap, and then you reach up, fumbling around for the cord with your left hand.

"My baby," the woman is shouting. "Is it all right? Is it all right?"

With the index finger of your right hand you begin tapping on the baby's leg.

"He's got a pulse," you say. "Count my finger tapping."

They do. After fifteen seconds Carol says, "One-ten."

"My ba-aa-aa-bb-bb-y," the woman is shouting.

One-ten. Time expands a little as you stare down at the blue, flaccid form in your lap. You start drying it like mad, trying to stimulate it. "Hello," you say out loud. "Hel-lo, wake up, little guy." You milk the cord for a moment and then turn to the nurses. "I need a clamp and scalpel," you say. You go back to stimulating the baby, slapping it on the bottom of its feet, thumping it. Nothing. Helen hands you a scalpel and two plastic clamps—it takes you a moment to figure out how to work them. You clamp the umbilical cord and slice between the two clamps with the scalpel, producing even more blood. The baby is officially on its own now. Things don't look promising. You give it to the nurses to put it in the Isolette. Him in. It's a boy.

The APGAR score, you think ponderously as you rise and

step through the primordial ooze on the floor. You need to get a one-minute APGAR. APGAR measures five things—or, in medicalese, "indicators." Each indicator is given points: zero, one or two. Respiratory effort is one indicator. If the baby were breathing well he'd get a two. "Needs some stimulation to breathe but is doing so on his own," nets a one. This kid is a big zero. Pulse is another indicator. A heart rate over a hundred gets this guy two big points. What else, you think, what else? Color. Pink is two points. This baby was blue from head to toe. Another zero. Reflex irritability, how much the baby was wiggling around—here is another zip.

You can't remember the last indicator.

Top APGAR score is ten. This baby: two.

The mother is struggling up off the gurney. Carol holds her back. "What's the matter? What's the matter?" the mother is calling out.

"He's not breathing," you say, practically spitting the words.

"Oh God!" She flops back on the gurney and starts wailing. "Oh God, oh God."

"Hook up the oxygen," you tell the nurses. "And get me a face mask and an Ambu bag."

"The first moments following delivery," the textbook for your second-year pediatrics course counseled you, "is the crucial moment of life. The sudden inspiratory effort of the newborn opens the pulmonary tree and completely alters the circulatory system. The foramen..." The rest is lost in the dim reaches of your mind.

This baby wasn't doing any of this. Someone hands you a face mask that is too large. You throw it on the floor. "Smaller," you say. You get handed another one that fits better. We were "bagging," holding a face mask over the patient's nose and mouth, forcing air flow into the lungs by squeezing the attached oxygen-filled bag. Not the best way to breathe for someone—a lot of air goes into the gut—but for now it was the best we had.

You hold out a hand for the Ambu bag. What you know is

this: the first breath is the hardest, the one that requires the most effort. If you can open up this baby's lungs, if you can help him take that first big breath, he might be able to go from there.

It's like resuscitating with toys; everything is so small. You fit the mask over the baby's face and squeeze the bag a little, then a little more. You lift the baby's chin with your little finger in order to get a better seal with the mask and then try again with more force. You lift the bag and check the baby. He hasn't moved.

"I'm going to have to intubate," you say. That means putting the breathing tube down through the vocal cords in order to ventilate the lungs. "Somebody try for an IV."

"Oh, sweet Lord," Helen says and grabs up one of the baby's tiny fists. "I haven't done this in ten years."

"What? What?" the mother shouts. "What are you doing?"

"I need an endotracheal tube," you tell Carol. "A 3-0. What laryngoscopes?" You nudge her out of the way so you can get to the drawer in the crash cart with one hand while the other hand holds the bag in place. You sort through what you find and pluck out a handle and the smallest laryngoscope blade. You are surprised to see that your hands are steady. You've never intubated anything close to this small before.

It's simple, you tell yourself (and then answer immediately, "Hah!"). You just have to place this pencil-sized tube into the narrow breathing passage, the trachea, which is not much larger than the tube and has its opening tucked so out of the way it can sometimes be impossible to find. The easiest mistake to make is to put the breathing tube into the esophagus. This allows you to ventilate the stomach—no good for anyone.

You lean over the table with the tube and laryngoscope in hand. This baby is tiny, you think, as you look down. How small? Two kilos? Three? You look at the little hands, turning them over between your fingers. Doesn't look too premature though, you think. A very small, term baby.

Carol has her hand on the umbilical stump. "I've got a heart rate of eighty-two, I think."

"Somebody get the kid on the monitor." You flip open the laryngoscope. "What's going on about transport?"

Helen shouts to the unit clerk. "What's going on about the helicopter?"

The unit clerk shouts back. "They're saying they can't take any transports from us. The hospital hasn't paid transport bills for over a year."

"So what the hell are we supposed to do?" you shout out.

"I'm trying to get somebody at Lying-In to do ground transport. They are checking with the neonatal critical team now."

"Goddamn it," you say out loud, but at least the clerk is trying. You return to the baby. With your left hand you slip the laryngoscope into the mouth, over the tongue, to the back of the throat and beyond. You can see the epiglottis, a flap of skin that seals off the trachea when food is passed through the mouth to the esophagus. You have to get the tip of the tube up under the epiglottis, then through the vocal cords. It's so hard with something this tiny. The anatomy doesn't seem right; nothing like in the textbook. You keep losing your grip. The doll's head rolls to the right, out of position. You lose where you are and have to reposition and start all over.

Idiot, idiot, idiot, you whisper to yourself. In the distance, far, far away you hear the mother shouting again. Out of the corner of your eye you see her waving her hands. The kind nurse, the one whose name you still don't know, is standing over her, trying to calm her.

Placenta, you think, she's delivering the placenta. The rest is a blur. You hunker back down over the child and look again. You can't see well, you can't really see at all, so you poke and hope, guiding the tube in the general direction of the vocal cords, the voice box. The tube slides forward, then stops, hung up on something. You try again, passing again. Same thing. You straighten up and start to bag the infant again. This isn't working.

Think, think, you tell yourself. If you were alone, you'd butt your head against the wall; that's how frustrated you are.

Helen is still working on the IV, and she is not having much luck. She has to pass a tiny needle into a vein not much larger than a hair. Right now she is down on her knees, her head bowed over the baby's blue fist, tapping, tapping at it, looking for another IV site. She blew the last one.

"Give me a smaller tube," you tell Carol.

"What size?"

"Two point five."

"We don't . . . No, wait."

She hands you a package and you break it open. A size 2.5 endotracheal tube. You bow back over the baby, and once again you insert the laryngoscope and lift the jaw forward, looking for the larynx and the vocal cords, but you don't see much more than you did before.

Blind again. You slip the tube down toward where you had it before, and this time it slides easily forward.

You gasp and straighten up, struggling to fit the Ambu bag onto the tip of the ET tube. One breath, two, another, and you watch as the stomach rises and falls.

"Somebody check for lung sounds," you hiss.

Carol does. "No. I think it's in the stomach."

You pull the tube out and lean again, taking the laryngoscope back up. *Think,* you tell yourself, *think.*

Carol stands looking up at the monitor. "We've got a heart rate of about forty here."

You kneel again and slip the laryngoscope over the tongue and down beyond. This time you lift the tongue at a different angle, rocking the laryngoscope handle a little bit.

"Somebody give me some cricoid pressure," you say—pressure on the neck to help bring the vocal cords into view.

You think you can see better now; there is, perhaps, the treasure at the end of the rainbow. You slip the tube forward and in it goes, unhindered. You straighten up, give the Ambu bag a few squeezes and watch the chest rise and fall. The chest—not the belly.

"Listen for me," you tell Carol.

She does. "Sounds good," she says.

You look up at the kind nurse and say, "We need blood from the umbilical cord. Just put it in a red-top tube. We can run it as a blood gas." You turn back to Helen, who has abandoned her second catheter and is working on a third. "I'll try a scalp vein," you say.

You look up at the monitor. The heart rate has already jumped from 40 to 64.

You need access. IV access. Scalp veins are often the biggest, most accessible veins neonates have. You get at them by putting a tourniquet around the top of the baby's head, usually a rubber band, and using a type of needle with two plastic wings, called a butterfly. You are working, brushing the slick seal-like hair out of the way, searching for a vein, when Helen says, "Look."

You look up at the baby. There is a flush, barely pink across the chest and the abdomen. Wait, no. It's just your wishful thinking.

But no. It's really there. A near-rose color that is not your imagination. You look up at the monitor, heart rate 105, and you stand there, flatfooted for a moment, gazing at the monitor in wonder, until from the corner of your eye you see something shifting, moving. You look back down at the baby and you see it again. The hand is twitching and grasping a little on its own. The fingers of the left hand are curling, twitching, and now you see that the flush across the chest, a color, once barely vermilion, is now almost rose. A radiant rose. The kid is oxygenating. The carotid pulse is easily palpable. The kid is coming around, you think, and as he turns pinker and pinker you stand waiting for more movements of the hands. You find yourself praying, waiting, hoping for another twitch, but there is nothing.

You turn back to the scalp vein and begin fussily pawing through the IV cart, looking for a 23-gauge butterfly. "Do you have anything small enough to take a blood pressure?" you ask as you paw. "Have we got the cord blood back? And I need a fluid setup; we've got to get this baby's volume up."

You are working under the infrared light of the Isolette. It's there to keep the baby warm, but instead it heats you. Now you've gotten to the point where you are dripping sweat on the baby. You wipe your forehead with your arm again, but it really doesn't seem to do any good.

"What are you doing to my baby?" the mother says behind you, over and over again.

Everybody continues to ignore her. You are a little beyond the five-minute mark now. You need to take another APGAR score. It's higher now but still not that great. Heart rate over 100, that remains a two; color, that's a one—the baby has pinked up some but not all the way. Reflex irritability? You're not sure that hand twitching qualifies even as a one. The baby has made no attempt to breathe on his own, no other movement. Why? you wonder. Was the hypoxia, the missing oxygen, during birth that bad? So bad that it destroyed brain function? But the pulse was strong when the baby was delivered. There was oxygen there. You wouldn't have expected him to suffer that much brain damage.

So there it is: five-minute APGAR score barely four.

Something else is wrong, you think. Something else has to be going on. This baby is pink, ventilating well, but still totally flaccid.

"I want to hold my baby," the mother says.

"Yeah, yeah. In a minute," you say mechanically. This baby should be alive and kicking. There is something more, something more. *Think,* you say again to yourself. This baby is going to die, or worse, live to be a vegetable. You can't finish the thought.

"What do you think is wrong?" Carol asks. "Why isn't he moving?"

"I don't know," you bark out. You've given up the search for the needle. "Can I get a 23-gauge butterfly for this baby's head?"

Somebody hands you one.

You shout out to the desk clerk, "Any word about transport?"

"University called a few minutes ago. The team is coming back from Spit Bay. As soon as they unload they'll be here. They said to just hold on."

Hold on, you think to yourself. Right.

You turn to the kind nurse. "What about the cord blood?" you ask.

She holds up a tube.

"Did you get two?"

"No," she says, "just one."

"Did you send it?"

She bites her lip and looks down at the tube. "You want it sent?"

"I wouldn't have asked for it if I didn't want it sent." You say this nastily but instantly regret it. How often has this nurse been involved in a delivery from hell?

She looks devastated as she turns away with the tube in her hand.

. . . and she cares, you think to yourself. That's why you just so successfully made her feel bad. She wants this baby to live just like you do.

You turn back to the matter at hand, the IV. Helen has handed you a rubber band, and you stretch it over the crown of the baby's head. The veins pop up, good veins. You scrub a patch of baby scalp with an alcohol swab and then take the 23-gauge butterfly, pinching its plastic wings between your fingers, piercing the skin, aiming for a blue thread, a blue rivulet crossing the hairline.

You poke and miss, poke and miss. You can feel the nurses hovering over you while the hot light of the Isolette shines its full fury on the back of your neck. You feel burnt, roasted alive and exasperated. The vein in question just rolls and rolls away.

But you are good at this. You can do anything with your hands; you know that. You can get IVs into patients when nobody else can. Even just holding the butterfly between your fingers is soothing and comforting. Therefore you're not really surprised when on your fourth pass you score and a little spout of blood backs up into the tubing.

You are taping the IV into place as X-ray rolls up. Blood, blood, blood, you are thinking to yourself.

The x-ray tech looks down on the Isolette. "Ah," he says, "just a little fellow."

You look down on the baby again. His left hand is still twitching. A focal seizure? you wonder, but it seems more purposeful than that. It looks like a hand trying to reach out to feel. Blood, blood, blood, you chant to yourself. Or rather something within you seems to chant, something beyond your consciousness.

"What are you doing now?" the mother asks from her gurney.

"X-ray," you say tersely. You can't even look at her. Blood, you are thinking. Blood. Sugar. Blood. Sugar. Blood sugar. What is this kid's blood sugar?

You remember now. You learned it for an exam, but more important, you saw it happen once at the university. It was a precipitous, disastrous delivery that resulted in an acutely asphyxiated baby. They intubated the kid just like now but also got a blood sugar. It came back zero, nothing at all, a surprise to everyone and yet not a surprise. Babies have only a small amount of sugar stored away for use during times of disasters. That particular delivery was so stressful to the child that he had used up all his glycogen stores—his reserve of glucose. He had nothing left.

Maybe now . . .

"We need a blood sugar," you tell Helen.

She raises a finger as if to indicate: "Good idea."

What else? you think. What else? You are racking your brains. Fluids? Electrolytes?

You are helping the x-ray tech position the little guy on the x-ray plate when Helen taps your shoulder. She raises the glucometer up so you can read the screen.

The digital readout says: 12.

"Twelve," you say. "His blood sugar is twelve?" Normal is 80–110.

The baby is severely hypoglycemic. He has no blood sugar.

The answer to this baby's problem could be as simple as a little bit of sugar.

"Glucose," you tell Helen with a kind of wonder. "The kid needs glucose."

The nurses scramble for an ampule of dextrose while somewhere in your mind the chant sets up again. Dilution, dilution, you think, then you realize you need to dilute the sugar.

Helen mixes a syringe, half glucose and half sterile water. You stand over the baby watching as she slowly administers simple sugar water. You have never seen anything like it. The bluish-gray blush that had lingered at the baby's fingertips dissolves before your eyes. Then the left hand starts twitching again, but the movement is more complex this time. The child is reaching out. Then the other hand moves, twitching, spasming, and it reaches out as well. Both arms are up in the air and the legs are starting to kick and in a moment you realize you are seeing what you had always thought was one of the saddest sights in medicine: a baby crying, but crying with an endotracheal tube in place so that he cries without making a sound.

Now, it is a wonderful, wonderful sight.

"How's my baby?" the mother asks.

You don't even turn around; you just cross your arms and continue looking down at the baby. The kind nurse, whose name you never learn, turns to her and says, "He's doing good."

You wipe your forehead, which is sopping wet again, and then look at your watch. You don't really see the time. It's as if you've been outside time ever since this woman came through the door. You look up at the monitor. Heart rate 150. Normal baby heart rate.

"What about transport?" you shout out to the clerk.

"They're unloading now. They said they'd be here in about forty minutes."

"Forty?" you say. You were thinking something more like five. You look back down at the baby, all wiggly now, and pink. You can't wait to get him out of the ER before something else happens. But there's pride there. You can't help thinking what you are thinking, which is, *I did this.* Then you think aloud, "I should check the x-ray."

It's up on the light box. You amble over and look up at it, squinting. You look first for the endotracheal tube, which has a little radiopaque stripe. It is well above the corina, the bifurcation point of the trachea. You look at the lungs and a casual glance at what's next, the ribs, the stomach. No mysteries revealed.

"We need a copy of this x-ray," you say, still looking up at it. Marveling at it. "To go with the kid."

The clerk from in front shouts back, "I gotta Doctor Hu or Hue or something, on the phone. He wants to hear about the patient." Simultaneously Helen says, "The heart rate is dropping."

You pick up the phone on the wall and have a distracted four-minute conversation with a doctor who speaks almost incomprehensible English and doesn't seem to understand you any more than you understand him. Meanwhile you stand there, staring across at the monitor. The heart rate drops as you watch. Once 150, it is now 130.

The unit secretary steps into the room with the results of the cord blood gas. You look down at them, frowning, but the results are really pretty good. The baby is acidotic—a touch on the acidic side—not too surprising, considering the nature of the delivery. The electrolytes, sodium, potassium, etc., are all okay. In short, nothing that needs correcting right now.

You look back up at the monitor, which now gives a heart rate of 120. You look at the baby, and maybe this is just your hyperstimulated imagination, but the baby looks a little bluer again. As you stand there in front of the monitor, you watch the heart rate drop: 120 . . . 119 . . . 117 . . . 114. The baby is more restless as well, little hands raised in the air, fingers reaching out, folding, then reaching once more.

113 . . . 110 . . . 108 . . .

This is not your imagination.

But still you stand there, lead-footed, gazing up at the monitor, your jaw slack, mouth dry, glancing occasionally down at the baby only to look immediately back up at the monitor, hoping. You unloop your stethoscope and start from the beginning, listening to heart sounds, lung sounds. You recheck the endotracheal tube—it could easily have slipped out of place, but no, the lung sounds are okay. The heart sounds a little more distant maybe—maybe—not sure. Could be. For sure, though, the hands are mottled, blue, frankly blue, almost vermilion, cyanotic.

"We should check another sugar," you say, uncertainly. "Get a new set of electrolytes," but you are thinking, No this cannot be. We brought this baby back. The baby was looking good.

105 . . . 104 . . . 102.

. . . 99 . . . 98.

"What's wrong?" Helen wants to know. "What's happening? Why is his pulse rate dropping?"

"Is my baby all right?" the mother calls from her gurney. "My baby . . ."

You say nothing but lean over, plant your hands on the mat on either side of the baby and stare down at him. The baby looks slightly shriveled and much bluer for sure now. You prod the chest with a finger. The child stirs, arms waving still but more feebly.

97 . . . 94 . . .

Your head hurts. It more than hurts, it feels as if someone took a hammer to the back of your skull, and a screwdriver to pry out each eye. You suddenly realize how tired you are—it's almost four A.M. now—and how ill-prepared you really are to be here. Six hours ago you thought you were on the top of the medical heap, at the peak of medical conditioning. Now you see your future as a long road of disasters striped with dense shadows of ignorance. You see the heart attack patient who goes sour, septic patients, asthmatic patients. All little catastrophes out there just waiting for you, and maybe you just won't know what to do.

"What is going on?" the mother asks. "Can I hold my baby?" You ignore her.

"Excuse me, but it *is* my baby. I do have a right to hold it."

Still, everyone ignores her. You continue to stand there thinking nothing. Nothing comes to mind. You have no idea what is happening. He was *there* just a minute ago. He looked so normal.

"Blood sugar 130," Helen tells you.

It's not the blood sugar.

What? What??

You fumble for the pulse, first at the arm, but when you can't find it there you go to the big femoral artery located right at the crease of the leg. Nothing. There's nothing there.

Heart rate 80 now. No way to ignore this. Now it's 78 . . . 76 . . .

A disaster. You move your hand up to the neck, to the carotid again, groping for a pulse.

"What's the matter with my baby?" the mother shouts. "What's going on?"

You turn your back to her. "Jesus," you say aloud. Face it. The baby's heart rate is now 72 and you can't find a pulse. The baby has no pulse.

The baby is dying.

Through clenched teeth you tell Helen, "I can't get a pulse. We gotta start CPR."

Helen is watching the monitor too. She looks as thunderstruck as you feel. "But he was okay," she says. "*He was okay.*"

"We need atropine," you say. You too are thinking, *But he was okay.* "And get some epi ready."

Meanwhile Carol, the only one of the group who seems to be able to unstick herself from the floor, positions herself at the end of the Isolette. This may be the most soul-crushing thing you have ever seen. To give CPR to a baby this small, Carol holds the baby with each hand around his chest and squeezes the chest with her thumbs. The baby is completely limp. It looks dead.

"What are you doing with my baby?" the woman shouts. "What? What?" She struggles up from the gurney. "You are hurting my baby."

She struggles up again out of the gurney and claws at your back, trying to catch at the belt on the lab coat.

"What are you doing to my baby?" She swings at you. "You're hurting my baby."

"I'm hurting him?" you say, wheeling on her. "I'm hurting your baby?"

"You're killing him," she screams back crazily. She must still be totally wired from the cocaine. "You are killing my baby."

"Shut up," you say, stepping over to the gurney. You bring a hand up. Your first impulse is to slap her, slap some sense into her, but instead you point your finger so that it is nearly touching her nose. You start speaking very quietly; this is just you and her.

"*I* killed your baby? *I'm the one that killed your baby?* I'm not the one who did crack my entire pregnancy, my entire life. *I* didn't get drunk every night and not give a damn about whether I was pregnant or not. *I* didn't have so little fucking idea of what I was doing that I never saw a doctor the whole time I was pregnant. *I* didn't stumble into a hospital that has no way to take care of me and has absolutely no way to care for a baby that's this sick. *I* didn't try to bring a child into the world that I have spent the last nine months fucking up. *I* didn't kill your baby. *You* killed your baby. You may as well have stuck a fucking gun in its face and pulled the trigger."

You have been, as you talk, getting louder and louder, and by now everyone is standing frozen, looking at the two of you. Even Carol is staring at you wide-eyed, still pumping away at the baby's chest.

You prod the woman's chest with your outstretched hand. "Now, you sit there and stay quiet, because *you* were the one who was killing your baby and *I'm* the one that's trying to save its life. *Okay?*"

You stomp back to the Isolette. No one looks at you.

"Hold CPR," you growl.

The monitor shows a heart rate of 75.

"Epinephrine," you say, entranced by the monitor. *Think*, you say to yourself, *think, think, think.*

"I don't know what's the matter with this damn pop-off valve," the respiratory therapist who must have arrived in the middle of all this chaos mutters. You just barely hear her.

The pop-off valve protects the lungs by venting the respiratory circuit should the airway pressures get too high.

"You are bagging too hard," Helen tells her.

You look at Helen and then at the respiratory therapist. The answer is so simple it makes you want to cry.

"Pneumothorax," you say in awe.

Everyone looks at you, blank-faced. Then they look to the respiratory therapist who, oblivious to it all, is still fussing with the pop-off valve.

"Pneumothorax. The kid's got a pneumothorax." But as you say this suddenly you are not sure. It's possible, but there are other potential causes, all of which at this panic-stricken moment escape your mind. A pneumothorax is one thing, though, that could explain what is happening. It is also something you could fix.

You backtrack over to the view box and peer up at the x-ray. Was it there and you missed it? You search the image and think there is perhaps a little line there, in the apex of the left lung. Perhaps. Not clear.

A pneumothorax occurs when air is trapped in the lining of the lung. This can happen if the lung lining ruptures for any reason, and artificial ventilation is a very common reason. A simple pneumothorax causes the lung to collapse, making it harder for the patient to breathe. There is also a special kind of pneumothorax called a tension pneumothorax that can be more dangerous than that. Tension pneumothoraxes have a paradoxical effect. Every time the patient breathes, the amount of air in the lining of the lung *increases*, causing the lung to collapse more and more. Eventually the lung will collapse down to a useless stump. The more the patient struggles to breathe, the worse the pneumothorax becomes. The patient becomes cyanotic—blue. Having lost blood pressure, the heart can no longer pump blood.

If the condition is not corrected, the patient will die. Right in front of you.

The pressure created by the Ambu bag can easily cause the lung wall to rupture and a pneumothorax to develop. Maybe that's what happened here.

Treating it is simple. You must vent the lining of the lung so that the air can escape and the lung can, at least partially, reinflate. This can be done most easily by "needling" the chest, which is exactly what it sounds like. You stick a needle in the chest wall between two ribs (second and third at the mid-clavicular line). The lung will remain partially collapsed, but the pressure in the lining of the lung will be gone. The patient can breathe again.

"Give me a twenty-gauge needle," you tell Helen.

Carol is still doing CPR. You watch her for a moment and you doubt yourself, doubt the monitor, the Ambu bag, the needle. And yet, fiercely, you know you are right. There can be no other explanation.

Besides, you think, if it is something else, then the baby will be dead anyway.

"Hold CPR."

You listen to the lung fields as the respiratory therapist bags. There are breathing sounds on both sides—that doesn't rule out a pneumothorax, though. The chest is so resonant that it's easy to be misled. You listen closely. It does seem to you that the lung sounds on the left side are a little softer than the ones on the right. "There," you say aloud and point with the needle. You are talking to yourself, trying to steady yourself, steady your nerves.

A 20-gauge needle—a little longer than this baby's finger. You unsheathe it from its hub and brace your fingers against the baby's chest wall. It's all of one piece, aiming, inserting, pushing deep through the muscles, and then a slight pop. You are either in the lining of the lung or in the lung itself. The difference is literally life and death.

Air, you swear to God you feel air.

"Restart CPR?" Carol asks you.

You raise a hand. "No, wait," you say. Everyone turns to the monitor. The heart rate is 65 . . .

65 . . . 64 . . . 64 . . . 64 . . . 68 . . . 69 . . .

There it is, the comeback. In a couple of heartbeats the rate is over 70, over 80, 85.

"Pneumothorax . . ." Carol sighs. "A tension pneumothorax."

As you palpate the baby's neck, you feel, clearly, unequivocally, a carotid pulse, a brisk carotid pulse. Let's face it, in your heart you hear a choir of angels.

"Jesus," is all you can say. "Jesus, Jesus, Jesus."

You are finished, done for. You look at your watch and cannot believe that all this took only forty-five minutes. It has been the longest forty-five minutes of your life.

But you can't linger this way. "We need another chest x-ray in here," you shout out. "And transport, what's the status of transport?"

"En route," the clerk yells back. "They should be here in ten."

"I need that doctor for report. Get him back on the line, would you?"

You look around at the acute room, which looks like a disaster area. Blood, mucus, amniotic fluid, are everywhere. The mother is huddled on the bed, her knees still up, legs parted, the way you left her after the delivery. She is weeping quietly.

You need to put a chest tube in; this will vent the lung better than the needle. For now this is fine. You are not worried about anything. Right now, the baby is alive, moving, wiggling those little hands in the air. A live baby. And what they say is true, you do feel like God—no, not God, really—just like a manifestly great human being. Carol, the pretty nurse, looks beautiful now and she is glowing at you. Even Helen, the nurse who hates you, is glowing a bit, though not specifically in your direction.

You've finished. You've won. The problems that remain—a premature baby with severe hypoxia at birth and a crack habit from the moment of conception—these are not your problems. Nothing can take the edge off this glow.

Congratulations. You have just saved a life.

4

Born under a Bad Sign

RULE #1: There is no real preface to disaster. One minute I was drinking some silt-like, end-of-the-pot coffee from a Styrofoam cup. The next minute I was palpating the belly of an immensely pregnant sixteen-year-old girl in active labor, contractions two minutes apart.

Sterile gloves. Betadine. A quick check to find out how far labor had progressed.

The girl lay on the hospital gurney, legs bent, belly distended, her little stick arms draped doll-like over the bars of the gurney as she awaited the next contraction.

"Something's wrong," she said. But what did she know? This was her first baby, after all.

"Nothing's wrong," I told her evenly. "You're just having a baby."

I was near the end of my residency, and by now, nothing fazed me. I had become a medical automaton shorn of wasteful emotions, emotions like concern, compassion, surprise. An example: two days before, a man had walked into triage with a knife buried to its hilt in his skull, he *walked* in, and the most I felt was a sort of risible annoyance—now I'd have to call neurosurgery and that asshole resident on call always gave us such a runaround.

So I shrugged when the nurse, Darla, announced she couldn't find a fetal heartbeat. I wasn't worried . . .

... but I should have been. I was moonlighting that day at a local hospital where backup was limited, usually, to either a very busy or a very sleepy doctor on the other end of a phone. This was not like my training grounds, a teaching hospital where, when things went bad, you could call every kind of specialist known to man. I had been told up front by the director that obstetrics coverage was at least a half hour away (and not to even *think* of trying to find a plastic surgeon).

I had to slide my hand in past the wrist before I felt anything. What I finally felt, though, was ... I wasn't sure what it was. It felt like a string of grapes.

That's odd, I thought. I stood there a moment repeating to myself, Grapes, grapes, grapes. I then brought my hand out, looked at it, checking to see if there was something wrong with it, and then I returned to the vaginal vault. Even though I told myself I couldn't be feeling them, the grapes remained. Why would there be grapes in the vagina? Some primitive part of my brain, some subcortical region, knew before it reached any level of actual consciousness, and my heart started pounding unmercifully as I thought still, Why? Why? And then suddenly I was fully aware of why.

These were toes.

I hadn't lost contact with all emotions. There remained one feeling that could still overwhelm me, one sensation that began now at the back of my neck and radiated into my throat and my heart. This was the only emotion available to an exhausted, overstressed resident.

The emotion was fear.

The baby was breech—that is, upside down. Instead of the head presenting first as in a normal pregnancy, here the buttocks were presenting first—not only that, but with this one the foot had descended. I felt around—I could feel only one. The other must have been hung up in the uterus.

"I've got a foot here," I told the nurse. "This is a footling breech." I turned to the patient. "Who's your obstetrician?"

The girl looked at me, frightened. "I don't have one."

"You never saw a doctor during your pregnancy?"

"I was supposed to see one next week."

The hell she was. She was full term. She should have seen somebody seven months ago.

There *was* one other emotion available for rapid access. Anger. The quick judgment of an overextended doctor. The patient had had a high-risk pregnancy and never knew it. I turned to the unit clerk, who was standing next to the door, arms folded. She'd seen it all. "Whoever's on for OB, call 'em now."

The clerk ran back to the desk. I crawled up on the gurney and knelt closer to the patient. The girl went through another contraction, and now that her nightmare had come true, she started sobbing. In addition, she grabbed my arm in a vise-like grip. I had to pry her fingers off one at a time.

"Look, I can't help you unless you help me," I told her.

"I am helping you. I'm just scared."

This last statement was accompanied by a wail so pitiful, even I softened a little. "You're going to be okay," I told her grudgingly.

If this were a normal delivery and if labor progressed, I would go ahead and deliver the baby in the ER room; but breech deliveries are extremely difficult. I was way out of my league.

And we still couldn't get fetal heart tones.

"I've called up to the obstetrics ward," the unit clerk shouted from the desk. "No doc there! I'm calling the on-call guy now."

I took over the Doppler and vainly mapped out the woman's abdomen. There was nothing but the rhythmic plash of blood in the mother's aorta. I tuned the Doppler back over to Darla, shaking my head.

In a moment the unit clerk shouted back again. "I've got the obstetrician's wife. She says he's in the shower. He'll get dressed and be there as soon as he can, but it's going to be a good half hour."

"What are you going to do?" one of the nurses asked me. I was still up on the gurney, sitting on my haunches.

"I don't know," I said.

The other nurse shushed us. "I've got something," she said, and we all listened for the Doppler tones, the rapid, whiplash sound of a normal fetal heartbeat. All we heard, though, was just a slow swish, slower than the mother's pulse. Everyone counted silently, gazing at their watches. Seventy-eight, half of what it should be. Fetal distress.

What I remembered, hazily, was this: the biggest problem with breech deliveries is the head. The head is the largest part of the baby; during a regular labor it is delivered first. If it hangs up in the birth canal, labor doesn't progress. Ultimately, the child may require a C-section delivery, a comparatively simple procedure. In breech babies, however, the rest of the baby is delivered first; the head is delivered last. If the head hangs up, you have a child half in and half out of the birth canal. To deliver the baby, you have to open the pelvis and cut down through the uterus and the cervix—a massively complicated procedure—and only if you are lucky is the baby delivered alive.

Should I wait for OB or try the delivery?

If the head hangs up, the baby's dead and I'm dead, I thought. I would be hung out to dry by anybody who reviewed the case.

With prolonged fetal distress, though, every minute is a catastrophe.

Darla counted again. "Fifty-six," she announced. A half hour is a long time for a baby with that slow a heartbeat. And it was dropping.

I put my gloved hand back up the birth canal. I wasn't sure, but it seemed that the leg had descended farther, and I could now feel the buttocks beyond.

"Do something!" the girl shrieked.

So close, so close. Another monumental contraction, and then it seemed to me that the baby slipped down another notch. Think, I told myself.

"Well," I said, "let's do it."

The trick with breech deliveries is to corkscrew the baby out, turning it slowly so that first one hip is delivered and then the other, then one shoulder and then the other. I held gentle traction on the legs and the baby began the slow rotation. It didn't require much traction; this baby was ready to come out.

The unit clerk called from the desk. "I've got OB back on the line. He's on his car phone."

"Tell him we've got fetal distress and that labor is progressing. I'm trying to deliver the baby."

Consultation. "He wants to know how far along you are."

"Tell him we've delivered one hip. What should I do next?"

More consultation. "He says to deliver the other hip."

I wiped my forehead with my wrist. "Oh, tell him *thank you.*"

The other hip slipped through. I had my hands on the baby's waist and kept pulling gently. Two OB nurses with an Isolette appeared at the door.

"Well," one of them said, "another fine mess."

Both the baby's legs were out, and the baby kept descending with traction. I could get my fingers up near the shoulders and hooked one of them, easing it down. One shoulder popped out, a turn, then the other. Textbook.

I got my fingers up to the neck, and that is when I felt the cord adjacent to it. I couldn't feel a pulse.

"He's hung up on the cord," I told Darla. "I don't know how."

"Can you push it back up?" Darla said. "I mean . . ."

"I don't think so. The bulk of the traffic is moving in the other direction."

The lower half of the baby dangled like a doll, blue-black and lifeless. I got my hands over the shoulders and began again, pulling gently. I could feel the walls of the cervix give a little, the baby slide out a little more and a little more. The bones of the skull progressively overlapped as the baby's head descended farther and farther. It stopped. I tried a little more traction, nothing, and so eased up. The moment I released my grip on the shoulders, the baby's head, as if on its own volition, popped out.

We all stared down. It was a normal, if very blue, baby, a boy.

Everyone began frantically to prepare for the next step, the resuscitation, but while we were fumbling with the resuscitation equipment, the bag-valve-masks, the endotracheal tube, the Isolette, the baby made it easy for us. He took one deep breath and started howling.

"My baby!" the mother said.

That night I lay in bed, staring at the ceiling, too exhausted to sleep. And too angry. It was the worst kind of anger—anger at myself. Yes, I delivered the baby and all went well, but what if it hadn't? I would have been hung out to dry by any obstetrician. This was a sin, a terrible error of judgment. According to the medical world, a sin of commission is far worse than a sin of omission. If I hadn't delivered the baby and it was dead at C-section, nobody could really criticize me. After all, how was I going to deliver a breech baby? But if I had attempted the delivery and the baby's head had hung up in the birth canal, it would have been a medical catastrophe. The baby would probably have died, and I would be defenseless. It didn't matter that I was trying to save the child's life; I would have been caught up in the medical process of blame. I had taken too great a chance . . . but thank God, thank God . . .

My thoughts wandered, and for some reason I thought of a question people occasionally ask me: have I ever seen a miraculous occurrence after a death in the Emergency Department? After all, what better place for dissatisfied specters to haunt? I always say no—monitors haven't flown across the room, resuscitation tables have not levitated, no ghostly presences have been felt by me. But I have seen enough miracles and near-miracles happen to the living to wonder if God just might suspend the rules of chance and physics, occasionally, that lives might be touched, here and there, at least once in a while, by grace. Especially in the ER, most especially on Friday or Saturday night, when it is really busy: an overlooked x-ray pops up at the last minute, just before the patient is discharged, and changes the diagnosis radically; an ECG is glanced at for the second time; a family member mentions something in passing. And now a breech delivery in the ER ends with the birth of a beautiful baby boy. For myself, while I mainly concede a strict Cartesian universe in which truth can be determined only with controlled clinical trials, that night I thanked God from the deepest part of my heart for saving my sorry ass once again. I thanked Him for letting the odds go the patient's way—for that flicker, that brief glimpse, of grace.

Six days later I had another delivery. Moonlighting, same hospital.

A woman, thirty-five years old and seven months pregnant with her first baby, presented to the triage desk complaining of abdominal pain. Premature contractions? The nurse signed her in and sent her into the waiting room.

While in the waiting room, the woman's bag of water broke suddenly, and she began to leak amniotic fluid onto the floor. The nurse rushed her back into the ER proper and came to get me.

I still had not recovered from last week's delivery. I kept having dreams about reaching out and feeling toes, feeling feet. I craved a normal, head-first ER delivery, all panic and chaos, climaxing with the delivery of an irate, squalling, but otherwise just great baby. I wanted the expectedly unexpected—a healthy woman whose labor had proceeded more quickly than foreseen.

I was thinking this as I pulled on my gloves and the nurse said the ritual, "You're going to feel something cold and wet." I slipped my hands into the vaginal canal and I felt . . .

. . . I didn't know what I felt. There was the cervix and the os, or opening, and there was something sticking out from it. It felt like a piece of wood, like a little tree log extending into the vagina.

This was in the days before near-universal ultrasounds in pregnant women, so that surprises such as twins could occur. But I had never had a surprise of this magnitude.

"What the hell . . . ," I said. There was a rivulet of fluid, and then this *thing* slithered out onto the cart.

It was a fetal body, its skinny neck topped off by a great bubble of membranes with a wrinkled, gray, gelatinous mass under it. Two gigantic bulging eyes—like the eyes of an enormous fly—stared blindly at the ceiling. Long gray folds of flesh draped down to the grinning mouth.

"Jesus Holy Christ," the nurse hissed.

"*Anencephalic* . . . " I whispered. I stared down at this monster. I could not believe what I was seeing. "It's an *anencephalic* baby." The gelatinous mass was the brain.

Stedman's, the venerable medical dictionary, defines anencephaly as the "markedly defective development of the brain, together with the absence of the bones of the cranial vault. The cerebral and cerebellar hemispheres are usually wanting with only a rudimentary brain stem and some traces of basal ganglia present. Colloquially, individuals with this malformation are sometimes called 'frog babies.'"

To me, the baby's head looked exactly like the head of a giant housefly.

"Is it my baby? My baby?" the woman cried.

The nurse and I looked down, too stunned to move.

"Is the baby alive?"

I was so stunned I hadn't even checked for a pulse. I put my hand down on the umbilical cord. There was a pulse.

I saw it all laid out before me: the neonatal resuscitation, intubating the baby so it could breathe (it hadn't so much as made a gasp in front of us), IV in the umbilical stump, the drugs, the fluids, a helicopter ride to a neonatal intensive care unit, the days, weeks, even months in the unit, the hundreds of thousands of dollars, the grim prognosis, the inevitable heart-wrenching end. I thought about all of this, and I said:

"No, dear. I'm afraid your baby is dead."

The woman struggled up a little.

"Is it a girl?"

I looked down. I hadn't even noticed. "No, he's a boy."

"Can I see him?"

The nurse and I looked at each other. The nurse shook her head.

"No, dear," I said. "Later, later."

I cut the cord and delivered the placenta. The pulse was gone in a minute or so. There was never even a hint of the baby's taking a breath. Nothing.

That night, I went home to bed and, as usual, stared at the ceiling and reviewed what had happened. What I had thought would haunt me didn't, really. When I closed my eyes, I didn't see the ethics of the life-and-death decision I had made laid out before me so I could worry over it. It somehow didn't bother me, although probably it should have. What I saw instead was that baby—that inhuman fly baby. I couldn't get out of my mind how terrifying and evil it looked. But then I thought about the mother. This woman had tried to conceive for ten years and now, finally, she was pregnant. After I had delivered the placenta, she had sat on the cart in the pelvic room, weeping, saying, "It's all my fault. I'm bad, I'm bad. It's all my fault, and I wanted that baby so much," while Darla, the nurse, held her and rocked her and tried to comfort her. Meanwhile, the rest of us all sat out at the desk trying to figure out whether we should call the coroner and report a death or just send the body straight to pathology as a stillbirth (coroner, it turned out).

Now I couldn't sleep. I kept going back and forth between the image of the fly baby and the weeping mother until finally I got out of bed and foraged for some beer from the refrigerator. I sat down by the window and looked out over the city. It was late; a few cars passed by, a dog barked. Somewhere in the distance a car alarm went off and then almost immediately stopped. Efficient thieves. A cat picked its way across the street, otherwise nothing. Except, of course, somewhere in this city, someplace I couldn't see from my window, that mother was crying and still blaming herself.

So much for grace.

After that I grew up as a doctor and began supervising residents who now had to make their own tough calls and then go home and stare at the ceiling at night. I, on the other hand, got lots of practice shaking my head in disbelief.

One afternoon, a resident sat going over a case with me. The patient, a twenty-year-old woman, had presented a week before with new onset seizures. She had no past medical problems. Her second seizure occurred in the ER as she was being loaded with Dilantin. The ER physician then admitted her to the hospital under the family-practice physician on call. The patient did well, had no further seizures and was sent home seventy-two hours later. Now she had returned with a low-grade fever, burning when she urinated and some crampy lower abdominal pain.

The resident drummed the clipboard nervously with his pen. "I think she has a urinary tract infection," he said.

"I'll buy that." I shrugged. I was only half listening to the presentation.

A nurse shouted from the patient's room on the other side of the ER:

"She's *crowning!*"

The resident and I looked at each other.

Someone else shouted, *"She's in labor! She's having a baby!"*

We rushed across the ER and back into the cubicle where this young woman lay, knees drawn up and open wide and the dark dome of a baby's head just visible between the lips of the vagina.

It is always now, when you are trying to put them on, that gloves assume a life of their own; fingers won't go in right or the glove tears into shreds. The woman was moaning and beating the aluminum bed rails with her hands as I wrestled with the glove. I finally got one on and slid my fingers down, beside the baby's head, under the strained skin of the vaginal opening. This must be the girl's first baby, I thought grimly. The vaginal walls had never been stretched, and the vaginal opening was too small for the baby's head to pass through. She needed an episiotomy, an incision to open up the edge of the vagina—usually done with sterile scissors. I shouted for someone to find the OB tray. The risk was that if the skin wasn't cut, it might tear—a mess.

The baby's head strained against the skin, which was purplish now as it bulged. It seemed like an hour or so (it always does) before the nurse returned with the obstetrics tray. The other ER attending began tearing it open to get at the neonatal resuscitation equipment for the baby. I fumbled with the scissors he handed me.

Most obstetric physicians I had trained under taught us that the vaginal wall at this point during delivery is entirely anesthetized. But most of these doctors were men. Every woman who has so much as felt the cold steel of scissors or scalpel on her skin has gone through the ceiling. This time was no different. The woman screamed and beat the cart railing while I cut into the flesh. The vaginal entrance opened wider and the baby practically popped out into my hands.

The baby was dead.

It was clear it had been dead for a while—no pulse, no respiratory effort, but it was more than this. The skin was macerated and yellow and the fingertips and toes had started to necrose. The baby was very dead, perhaps a week or more.

"What is it?" the girl shouted. "What's wrong with me?"

"It's a baby," I said, peeling off my gloves. "And I'm sorry, but it's dead."

What else could I say?

"A baby!" the woman shouted. "I'm pregnant?"

"You *were* pregnant," the nurse said evenly. I glanced up; I understood her look. How could anyone be so stupid?

"How can I be pregnant? I've had my periods!"

"It's a miracle," the nurse said dryly.

"I can't be pregnant," the girl said. "I would know that, wouldn't I?"

I shut my eyes and pressed my fingers against them. Something was wrong. "Wait a minute." I turned on the resident. "What was this woman here for last week?"

"Seizures. First-time seizures."

"A week ago?"

"Six days."

I looked at the baby. It looked about six days dead. I looked back at the resident. "*Eclampsia.*" I nearly whistled it. "She was *eclamptic.*"

It was interesting to watch this transformation pass like a pinball into the various potential scoring places of the resident's brain before it finally dinged. Pay dirt.

"*Eclampsia.* Oh, my God."

This was very bad. When this woman had presented six days ago, she was seizing not because of an underlying seizure disorder but because she was pregnant, unbeknownst to her and everyone else. She was having a complication of her pregnancy. Eclampsia is a condition in pregnancy that involves the mother's toxic reaction to the fetus. It usually occurs in the last month of pregnancy.

The initial symptoms are an elevated blood pressure, leg swelling and protein in the urine. That is preeclampsia. When the patient has a seizure, that is true eclampsia—a full-blown catastrophe requiring immediate delivery of the fetus, otherwise the baby's life, and sometimes the mother's life, is in severe jeopardy. That's what happened here. The patient had come in to the hospital seizing and nobody had thought to get a pregnancy test. A lethal mistake—but one, I'm afraid, any doctor might make. A busy Friday night—trauma in the next room, people stacked up in the hallway—and another seizure patient . . .

And there goes the grace theory right out the window.

I looked up from the chart to the girl. She wasn't particularly large, but she was fleshy—fleshy enough, apparently, to hide a first pregnancy even at term.

I'm a scumbag; worse than the worst lawyer. My only thought now was lawsuit, damage control.

The girl was here with her parents. I told someone to put them in the grieving room, the room where we put families whose relatives have died, and I would be right out.

So there I was and there they were, West Virginia hillbillies of the first water. Mother, middle-aged, dressed in pants she bought twenty pounds ago; father, skinny, almost scrawny, with a raggedy black beard that didn't quite mask a protruding chin, cigarette pack in his shirt pocket, dirty undershirt visible underneath, tattoos: anchor, naked woman.

"Your daughter was pregnant," I said simply. "We've delivered the baby, but I'm afraid the baby is dead."

"How's Suzy?" Mom asked.

"Suzy's okay. Suzy's fine."

They both sat for a minute taking this in, then the father scratched at his beard and rubbed his nose. Mom cleared her throat. "I thought she was putting some weight on, and I asked her one time . . . but . . . ." She trailed off. She was thinking. "How long has the baby been dead?"

"I don't know," I said.

"She had that seizure last week. Did that seizure have anything to do with the pregnancy?"

"I'm not sure," I lied.

They thought for a minute more, then the mother nodded. She was analyzing the situation. "She told me she was still having her periods."

Wishful thinking. "Apparently she wasn't."

"Can I see Suzy?" the father asked. The mother thought for another minute, then said: "Can I see the baby?"

Wrongful death. The worst kind of malpractice case. Accusations started flying the next day.

Family Medicine, which had admitted her into the hospital for observation the week before, claimed that it was the ER physician's responsibility to make the diagnosis. After all, the ER saw her first, while she was seizing, no less. The ER doctors countered that Family Medicine had the patient for two days. They should have caught it. It became a pissing contest conducted in the shadow of a recent local malpractice suit: An internist saw a patient once for a few minutes, a patient under the care of a neurosurgeon for a neurosurgical problem. The internist was sued for a poor neurosurgical outcome even though he had taken no active part in caring for the patient. The plaintiff was awarded $1.5 million (in addition to the several million dollars from both the neurosurgeon and the anesthesiologist). Professional prejudice aside, this was clearly excessive. But it was reality; we all lived and worked in this shadow. I was at risk as well for a number of things: not attempting to resuscitate the baby, for the episiotomy, for any gynecological problem the woman might develop.

I knew all this that night. When the ER finally slowed down enough for me to think, I sat and reviewed my decisions. I walked through the thrash a couple of times in my mind. There was absolutely nothing I would have done differently. There was never a question in my mind that the woman needed an episiotomy and that the baby was clearly dead. Nothing would have brought that baby back. But I could already hear some lawyer at a deposition asking me if it was possible that the baby did not die the week before during the seizure but had actually died because I did not attempt resuscitation.

It stayed quiet. At some point I picked up a book one of the nurses was reading, *The Healers*, by someone with an intensely Anglo-Saxon name. The cover showed a beautiful nurse, with a nurse's cap, of course, staring deep into the eyes of a handsome young doctor in a white lab coat. The blurb on the back said:

Beautiful neurologist Dr. Nan LeBaron and Emergency Room chief Dr. Steven P. Winstead III [where do they get these names?] are fighting for their medical lives. They are codefendants in a malpractice suit after their best efforts failed to save a patient's life. But neither of them can deny the physical chemistry that flares between them. . . .

Inside there was a listing of "The Lovesick Women of the Emergency Ward."

Ann is on the brink of realizing her dream of power at Chandler Medical Center, only to find herself back in the arms of a doctor who could turn it into a nightmare.

Lisa has one last chance to break the hold that drugs have on her body and that a diabolically domineering dealer has on her flesh.

Avon discovers that wearing her white uniform will not make people in power forget the color of her skin.

Rosa is torn between her determination to be the perfect doctor and her desires as a woman.

Meredith can deal with patients' mental disorders but not her own guilt about her heritage.

This is Chandler Medical Center, where contagious scandal stalks the corridors in crisp and spotless uniforms and hides behind a medical mask. . . .

I opened the book at random:

Chapter 6

Patrick studied the exposed surface of the brain where the skull had opened. . . .

How did it open, I wondered idly as I tossed the book aside. Like a clam?

I glanced around the doctor's desk where we wrote our reports. There were multiple Styrofoam cups of cold coffee; crumpled pop cans; a two-year-old *Physicians Desk Reference* with the cover torn off; magazines (an old *New England Journal, Sports Illustrated, Glamour*); someone's half-eaten sandwich covered by a paper plate with MINE written on it; a cheap stethoscope missing an earpiece, a reflex hammer with a broken handle—stark fluorescent light, worn linoleum floor.

Reality.

5

HOW TO CRACK A CHEST

"THIS IS AMBULANCE THIRTEEN. We're bringing in a John Doe—trauma victim, boarded and collared. We've got a pulse of one-sixty and a BP of eighty over palp. He's disoriented but . . ."

"What kind of trauma?"

"Uhhh . . . we're not sure."

"What do you mean you're not sure?"

"Well, there's a lot of trauma here."

"I don't get you."

"You will."

The patient was a mess. Some kind of large-caliber weapon had taken out his right shoulder and much of his lower left leg. He had several stab wounds to the chest and a crushed pelvis. You pronounced him dead within ten minutes of arrival. It took longer to reconstruct what had happened to him. It seemed he had been shot, stabbed and run over several times by a car.

The resident whistled. "Someone wanted that sucker *dead*."

Donna, one of the nurses, leaned over the gurney and said, "Yeah, they wanted him dead *stat*."

Stat. In the ER, after a few seasons of watching various versions of the job on television, everyone started running around ordering things "stat." It was an ER in-joke: Get me that IV STAT! Make some coffee STAT!! Get out of that chair! I need to sit in it STAT!!!

You all watched that stuff on the TV in the nurses' lounge on the occasional slow nights in the ER. The quick-thinking paramedics! the compassionate nurses! the dedicated doctors! The most hilarious part was watching the procedures—actors intubating, suturing, doing brain surgery. ("I want that chest cracked STAT!" someone shouted from the rear.)

One show had the paramedics bring in a trauma victim. Within seconds, the TV doctors had made the decision: they needed to perform a thoracotomy on a patient—that is, "crack his chest."

Cracking a chest—the mother of all procedures—involves opening the chest wall to get at the heart and other vital organs. It is the most dramatic and least effective procedure in medicine. Occasionally, though, it can save a life.

On TV everyone looked as if they were playing the piano or some board game. The actors—all dressed up as doctors—lined up around the hospital bed, the patient groaning thoughtfully as they stared down at some middle distance where a chest, presumably, was really, truly being opened.

"Can you see the aorta?" one superserious senior-statesman doctor asks. Everyone is standing as if they were innocent bystanders who had happened upon a minor traffic accident.

"Yes, I see it."

"Now take this and clamp it."

"I can't. I tried to, but I can't."

"Then let's have this other [more photogenic] physician do it."

"There, I did it. Do we have a blood pressure?"

"Yes, we now have a normal blood pressure. You can take him upstairs to his room, Nurse."

That is the fantasy. This is the reality. It's five-thirty in the morning. You are standing in the trauma room when two breathless, frightened-looking paramedics sweep in with your next patient strapped to their gurney. They had radioed ahead, but the scene was such a thrash that they could only transmit three pieces of information: gunshot wound to the chest, two bullet holes, thready pulse.

Three or four firefighters accompany the paramedics. The bad news: one of them is doing CPR; another is holding the man's endotracheal tube in place. That means the patient doesn't have a heartbeat and is not breathing on his own—signs of bad trauma.

"We lost the pulse," one paramedic says. "He had one when we left the scene, but we've lost it. We've got nothing."

Donna, charge nurse for the evening, says, "Okay. *Party time.*"

You are in the midst of the golden hour, the hour that follows a trauma or other medical emergency. Each minute of the golden hour is a last chance, the last chance to do a procedure or temporize an injury, to patch the patient back together enough to at least get him to the OR, where the surgeons can do a definitive repair. The golden hour, though, started thirty minutes ago, when this patient was shot. It takes that long for EMS to arrive, stabilize and transport to the hospital. Not much gold left over.

J. T., the other physician on, has followed the stretcher into the acute room. "Gunshot wound to the chest? Five in the morning?" he says. He's shaking his head. "It's gotta be drugs."

You catch a quick glimpse of a boy's face, a bloodsoaked T-shirt and a pair of oversized jeans. But before you can really examine him, you and everyone else on the team must do these things:

Check the airway. The paramedics have intubated the patient, but is the tube in the right place?

Check for a pulse.

Hook patient up to the monitor, establish heart rhythm. Connect patient to blood pressure cuff and pulse oximeter (which checks the amount of oxygen in the blood).

Start IV lines, big ones, to get fluids into the patient. The paramedics have started one, but Donna, looking down at it, says, "It's blown." The patient will need several peripheral lines and, optimally, a central line—an oversized IV plugged right into one of the main veins. First, you'll give him regular IV fluid—blood comes later, if the patient lives that long.

J. T. pulls the central line kit out of a closet. He points to it, looking at you, and you nod.

Next you must cut the patient's clothes off to look for hidden injuries. If the universal symbol of a physician is the caduceus, then the universal symbol of an emergency medicine physician would be the trauma shears. These are tough-looking scissors used to rip open the clothing of drunks, car crash victims and critically ill patients. (Note: There is always room for surprises here—most recently you saw a well-respected male judge in the ER with severe chest pain and discovered that he was wearing under his business suit black satin underwear, garter belt and pantyhose.)

You help cut off the jeans. All that's revealed tonight is bloody underpants.

Get blood samples: for hematocrit, chemistries, drug screen, blood typing, HIV testing.

Call for four units of type O blood. Tell them you want another four of type specific, pronto.

Call the thoracic surgeon on call; alert the OR. You've got a gunshot wound to the chest.

Only now can you get a quick look at the patient.

"Hold CPR," you say. The firefighter pauses and wipes the sweat off his forehead.

You check what's on the monitor. There is a sinus rhythm: rate 128. Recheck pulse. Donna does that.

"I got nothing here, gang," she says.

The firefighter looks up at you.

"Restart CPR?" he asks.

"No, stop for a minute."

Now for the first time you look at the injury. The patient has two bullet holes clustered over the sternum, right where the paramedic had placed his hands for CPR. Blood is trickling from each one. Are they entrance wounds? exit wounds? You can never be sure.

"Restart CPR," you say.

You look up at the patient's face. It is hard to see with the endotracheal tube in place and blood smeared everywhere, but he looks to be a kid, maybe sixteen at the most, with a ratty goatee and acne. You look him over. He's dressed like a punk—his enormous pants, now filleted open, are barely hooked up over his hipbones. There is a homemade tattoo on his right arm that looks like a dragon or maybe a serpent. Someone has carved an outline into the skin with something sharp and then filled it in with ink. It's amateur gang stuff, not something you see too often here. This is a quieter part of a quiet town; the last drug-related shooting you saw was over a year ago when you did a few shifts in the big city. But, ER doctor that you are, you have a working familiarity with the local kids who hang out on the curbs outside the convenience stores, the tough guys who think they're hot stuff, who think they can play hardball as well as the big-city boys. You peer over at the kid's face. At least you don't recognize him.

"You're right," you say to J. T. "It's gotta be drugs."

J. T. is setting up to start the central line in the groin. He has a pair of sterile gloves on so that, to stay sterile, he has to push his glasses into place with the back of his wrist as he looks up at you. "You going to crack this kid's chest?" he asks.

You don't answer him. You are still thinking—two gunshot wounds to the chest . . . You need to look at his back to see whether the bullets went all the way through the body.

"Let's roll him over," is all you say.

Donna and the paramedic help you roll the patient. There are two exit wounds in the back. They are angled off toward the left side of the chest wall and downward. One of them is angled far enough that it probably went into the abdominal cavity. If these are exit wounds, then whoever shot the kid was standing to the right with his shooting arm angled down.

Through-and-through chest wounds, vital signs in the field but lost by the time the patient arrived at the ER.

Precious seconds are ticking by while you stand there trying to think of a good reason not to open this kid's chest.

Open a chest. Is there anything you can do other than to open this kid's chest?

No, it's his only chance.

There is no time to get a surgeon in here. So you, the ER doctor, must open the chest wall to expose the heart. If there is a hole in the heart, you sew it closed; if the heart is not beating hard enough, you try open heart massage, squeezing the heart manually; if there is uncontrolled bleeding in the lower half of the body, you cross-clamp the aorta. All you are trying to do is buy enough time to get the surgeon here and the patient to the OR.

The prime candidate for a thoracotomy, the technical term for cracking a chest, is someone with penetrating trauma to the chest who had vital signs at some point in the field or in the ER. Just like this kid.

Of course, you will have to open his chest.

"Get the thoracotomy tray," you tell Donna. "Get me some gloves. Anyone get through to the thoracic surgeon?"

"You know," Donna mutters, ignoring what you say, "these *stupid* kids go out and get shot and expect *us* to save their lives . . ."

There's no time to make more than a pretense of sterility, but you do make two concessions to the era of AIDS: you put on a pair of clear goggles, oversized to fit over your glasses. Then you double-glove.

Above you, J. T. is getting the fluid warmer set up and the blood transfusions started. Bill, the tech, has taken over doing CPR, such as it is. His hands keep slipping off the chest because of the blood.

Two bags of normal saline are already running wide open via snaky IV tubes into veins in the patient's arms.

Donna finds the tray and brings it over. It's wrapped in a gray shroud-colored drape and enclosed in plastic wrap to keep it sterile.

You open the kit. There is a haphazard array of clamps and retractors, needle drivers and towel clips, most of which you won't need. As you paw through the instruments, you remember some of the eponyms; the names are a parade of the great physicians of the past: Mayo, Metzenbaum, Fienchetto, DeBakey.

There is only a scalpel handle in the tray. No blades.

Even you, the calmest of doctors, look around impatiently. "Where the hell are the scalpel blades? What the hell are they thinking of? I need a ten-blade over here."

There's a momentary echo within you, from those TV shows. "I need it *stat*."

You cast a weather eye up at the monitor. There is still a heart rhythm registering there—the electrical part of the heart is still working. J. T. feels again at the angle of the jaw for a carotid pulse.

"Anything?" you ask.

"Nada."

Bill is still doing CPR with his hands over the bullet holes. Before you motion him away, you look around, taking a big, deep breath. Beyond you all, out in the hallway, the radiology technician is leaning against his portable x-ray machine, watching all of you with judicious interest.

Someone hands you a 10-blade.

Now the approach. You've drawn this picture a hundred times for the medical students. A sketch of the chest: the nipple, the inframammary fold. Then you trace on your little diagram the imaginary incision site, between the fourth and fifth rib, you explain to the bored medical students.

Now, as you stand there, scalpel in hand, you think back to the first thoracotomy you saw. You were a medical student; it was your first clinical rotation, surgery. The team had been called down to see a man in the ER who had been stabbed in the epigastrium—just under the sternum. He had lost his blood pressure by the time you and the senior surgical resident arrived. The resident called for the thoracotomy tray and tore the chest open in record time. Before you even got your bearings on the anatomy of the procedure, there was the man's heart. You could see it beating, or rather, you could see it intermittantly flopping around like a fish on dry land. You remember now that weird hot-and-cold feeling; and you knew you were going down an instant before you did so. You woke up to a circle of faces and someone poking a finger on your right hand, checking your blood sugar. Ultimately, the man died. They always died. What was the figure you were quoted once? One out of a hundred? That was probably optimistic.

One out of a hundred, you think, as you look down at this kid's chest. There's the chest wall, the inframammary fold, but this time it's not a drawing; it's live flesh, a skinny boy's chest with hairlets sprouting around the nipple. This is it. *Now*, you tell yourself, pointing the scalpel blade down. You trace the start of an arc. Nothing happens; the flesh stays pristine. You try again. Nothing. You pause, thinking, *nightmare!* Then realize you have the scalpel turned upside down.

You try once more and this time the flesh parts. You make your cut from the midpoint of the chest, the sternum, all the way around the chest wall. You go through skin, the epidermis, the dermis, into a layer of subcutaneous tissue, the knife passing through the flesh as if were warm butter. (This is the physical pleasure of a fresh blade.) Small red blood vessels spring open, dotting the yellow fat red.

"Metzenbaum," you say to Donna. These are scissors, long and curvate. You use these to cut through the rib muscles. To position them you have to push one blade through the muscles of the chest wall, entering the pleural space. As you do that, the lung collapses away from you, deflating and falling back into the chest cavity. With a couple of hefty snips you have your first glimpse into the chest cavity. You can't see anything but blood.

Fienchetto is the next physician's ghost you call upon. He is responsible for the rib spreaders. This is a device with two parallel bars connected to a simple gear. A handle turns the gear, causing the two metal bars to separate.

The metal bars each have a U-shaped edge. You hook the top bar edge under the fourth rib and the bottom bar edge over the fifth rib, and then you start turning the crank. As you do, you hear a cracking sound, like kindling catching fire—that's the sound of rib bones breaking.

You have to break four or five ribs before you can see enough to do any good. This was where those guys on TV were when they peered timidly and discreetly into the human chest. (Yes, yes, I see the aorta, one of them had said woodenly.) The truth is, you can't see anything. Nothing is textbook, because all those textbook drawings were based on someone who was definitively dead, not half dead and still bleeding like this patient. Right now, all you can see is blood pouring from the hole you have made in the chest wall.

But wait. You give the bleeding a moment. After the initial tidal wave of blood, it subsides. You mop around with some gauze sponges. After a moment, with your face down inches from the chest wall, after more swabbing, you see a liverish, collapsed lung and beside it, something else quivering in the dark.

There it is, the naked heart.

The trouble is that it doesn't look as it should. This kid's heart should be about the size and shape of a big man's fist. Instead what you see is something much larger, something that looks like a small head of cabbage.

"Sponges," you say aloud. "Is anybody getting blood started on this kid?"

"Keep your shirt on," Donna says.

"Well, someone hand me some more sponges."

They are stuffed into your outstretched hand. You mop around some more, surprised that the blood you've blotted doesn't reaccumulate all that fast. There it is: a quivering purple ball, not looking even remotely like a heart. But it is the heart, and as you see it, you realize what has happened; you see why this patient has no blood pressure.

The heart is a muscle, or rather a complex set of muscles, surrounded by a tough, two-layered membrane called the pericardium. At least one of the bullets has gone through the pericardium into, and probably through, the heart. Blood from the hole in the heart has leaked out now into the pericardial lining, turning it into a bulging sack.

With each beat of the heart more blood is pumped into the sac. Because the sac is not elastic (it has the feel and resistance of a plastic bag) the heart must occupy a smaller and smaller volume. As the blood collects in the sac, the heart reaches a point where there is no room to receive blood. That's where it is right now.

"We've got pericardial tamponade here, folks," you announce.

You look up for the first time in several minutes. There are two units of type O-negative blood—blood from "universal donors," along with several bags of normal saline. You know that half the blood pumped into this kid is going straight to the pericardial sac. Until you drain the pericardium, that is exactly where the blood will stay.

"The thoracic guy," you say. "I hate to bring this up again, but if we don't have a surgeon, then I may as well quit now."

"We've got him on his car phone," Donna tells you. "He's en route."

So you've got pericardial tamponade. You will have to open up the pericardial sac and drain the blood that has collected there. Then you will have to find the hole in the heart and in some way try to stop the bleeding. That is this boy's only chance.

But there is the problem of the phrenic nerve. The phrenic nerve powers the diaphragm. If it gets cut, the patient never takes a breath using his left lung again. The nerve descends from the brain stem along a tortuous path that you hope never to be asked to memorize again. The important part for you is that it runs along the left side of the pericardium, right about where you have to put the incision to drain the blood. Some supreme medical language guru has designated this hole as a "pericardial window," a window you can use to drain out all that blood collected within the pericardium.

But you have to find the phrenic nerve, so you won't accidently transect it, and there's nothing but blood here. You are looking for a narrow ribbon, a yellowish stripe, but all you can see is more blood, more blood. Seconds are ticking by; you can feel each one of them slip past you. Finally you say, "I think that's the nerve," pointing, although no one else can see and you are not really convinced. It doesn't matter. You have to move.

You make a small, experimental stab at a place just in front of whatever that was you saw running down the pericardium. There's nothing. You snip again and suddenly, there is blood everywhere.

"Whoa," J. T. says.

Blood splashes against your goggles and all over your jacket. You've unloosened a torrent of blood that quickly fills the chest cavity and overflows onto the floor. It looks as if every ounce of blood that should have been in the kid's body had leaked into the pericardial sac.

"Sponges, for Christ's sake."

Still the blood keeps coming. You start mopping with what you have, but you can't keep up. All pretense to sterility is gone now. You are up to your coat sleeves in the blood in this boy's chest. The blood has cascaded down onto the floor. There are two inches of blood where you are standing. Your shoes are soaked with it.

You get your fingers down into the pericardium and start removing blood clots, which you sop up using the sponges Donna keeps throwing at you. The bullet holes had caused blood to leak from the heart to the pericardial sac and then, more slowly, from the pericardial sac into the chest. You keep mopping and mopping and now, finally, you can see a little bit. In fact you actually think you do see the phrenic nerve there, a yellowish-looking stripe. You extend your incision cephalad (toward the head). You are looking for bullet holes.

"Do you see anything?" J. T. asks from the opposite side of the table.

"I see nothing," you tell him. "But one of those bullets must have nailed the left ventricle. At the very least."

More blood, more blood.

"More four-by-fours. Please."

Someone hands them to you.

There is the hole you have just made in the pericardium, now almost the length of the heart. Beyond, something is twitching. You put your first two fingers of your left hand up against it and gaze up at the monitor. You can feel a faint throb of muscle with each electrical pulse on the screen. It's hard to believe through all this, but it looks as if the heart is still trying to beat.

You've got almost your whole hand on the heart now, and with those first two fingers you reach around the back side of the heart. Gently, and when that doesn't work, not so gently, you deliver the heart through the hole in the pericardium. The heart remains attached at its base to the plumbing, the aorta, the pulmonary artery, but the ventricles have now been swung free, pulled up into the incision site, and the heart rests in your hand, quivering.

Here it is, the naked heart. And even though you've seen this before, even though you think it should be no big deal, it feels absolutely unearthly. The Aztecs did this, plucking the still-beating heart from a victim's chest.

J. T. has come around behind you. You don't have to say anything. He takes the heart, places it between his hands and begins squeezing it by clapping his hands slowly together. This is open heart massage. Again there is blood everywhere. It must be coming from the bullet holes.

Where are the holes?

You move J. T.'s hands away and replace them with your own. You don't look for the holes; you feel for them. Two bullets in the chest. Did they both nail the heart?

You find one hole, then another, both anterior and, you think, both into the left ventricle. Gently you feel around the back side of the heart, and there you find the two exit holes. They are positioned so they appear to have exited from the left ventricle.

"I think I got the holes," you tell J. T. "Here, get your fingers in here."

J. T. loops his right hand around the heart and with your help plugs his middle three fingers through the hole you've got your fingers on. He presses his thumb over the fifth.

"I feel like I'm holding a bowling bowl here," he tells you.

"Well, just don't let go," you answer back. To Donna, "Get me some 0' silk. Lots of it."

There are special techniques, special sutures to place in these situations, but you can't remember exactly how to do them. You'll have to improvise.

J. T. is now trying to do cardiac massage with his fingers still in place. He squeezes with his left hand, his right fingers still jammed into the bullet holes.

Donna opens packages of 0' silk by banana-peeling them over your thoracotomy tray.

You look around again and feel for the first time the tension in the room. Everyone there, including two police officers over by the ER door, is focused on one thing only, this man's open chest and the beating heart that you and J. T. hold in your hands.

You look down. I can't do this, you think.

But it all comes mechanically. You find yourself with a package of silk suture in your hands.

"I'm going to do this bullet hole first," you tell J. T. "Let me anchor a tie." You throw one quick stitch using the clumsy straight needle. It goes more easily than you thought.

"Okay," you tell J. T. "Slowly, take your fingers out."

"Christ," he says. Now there's blood everywhere. You can't see anything.

"Sponges, guys. We need sponges."

J. T. sticks his fingers back in the hole. You take another loop and then try to get one more, when J. T. suddenly says, "You got me."

You look up at him. "Wha?"

"You got me with the needle."

"Oh, for Christ's sake," you say. But then you realize what that could mean. You stop dead what you are doing. "You need to scrub that."

"That's okay," J. T. says.

"No way," you tell him. You are thinking now of one thing: HIV. "You know the risk is less if you scrub that wound. And this kid is a setup."

There was a time when we all were not so afraid of blood. . . .

"It's all right," J. T. says.

"No, it's not all right."

J. T. doesn't even let you finish this brief sentence. "Just keep going."

"I'm not going to risk your health over this."

"Listen," J. T. says angrily. J. T. never gets angry. You look up. He looks angry as well.

"I let go," he tells you, "*then this kid dies*. Now sew up the goddamn hole."

You duck your face back down, ashamed, and reapply yourself to the suture material. Your hands are shaking.

It's almost impossible to see. There's blood that just reaccumulates with every swipe of gauze. You make a guess for the next two loops, hoping you don't stick J. T. again. How could you have done anything so stupid?

You make a final loop. As you do, J. T. eases his fingers out of the way. The loops hold; there is a little leakage of blood but not much. You've nailed one of the bullet holes.

You cut the silk with the Metzenbaum, and J. T. gently massages the heart.

"I think we've got some blood circulating here," J. T. tells you. "Heart feels fuller."

So all the fluid you are pouring into this kid is starting to do some good.

"We've got a carotid pulse with compressions, guys," Donna says, her hand on the kid's neck.

"I've got this one," you say to J. T. "Go change your gloves and wash your hands. Donna can do this."

Donna speaks from over your shoulder. "There's *no way* you are getting *me* to come *one inch closer* to that heart than I already am."

"Just keep going," J. T. says.

There is, you see, a technique to this. For the next hole you move J. T's fingers gently out of the way and pinch the hole shut with two fingers of your left hand. It's easier to sew now, although you can't stop that shaking. At least you are less likely to pop J. T. again.

You can see better now that neither of these entrance wounds is bleeding. You can keep the field somewhat clear of blood. The second one goes more easily than the first.

"Nice," J. T. tells you. He lifts the heart somewhat to give you better access to the back side and you both bend down, peering at the holes J. T. has plugged with his fingers.

You realize now that if either of the bullets passed through the heart's septum, the wall between the left and the right ventricle, on its way out of the heart, you are sunk. There is no easy way to get at a hole *inside* the heart. Still, it looks as if they both exited through the bottom part of the left ventricle. Maybe this cat still had a few lives left.

You use the same technique to close the posterior lacerations. You pinch the bullet hole shut with your left hand and whipstitch with your right.

Once you close the last laceration, you let the heart fall away from your hand. The field stays fairly clear of blood. J. T. takes his hand away as well.

The heart just sits there quivering. It doesn't make sense until J. T. says flatly, "V-fib."

The heart is fibrillating.

You are such a creature of habit that you don't believe it until you look up at the monitor and see the green electronic squiggle of ventricular fibrillation marching out across the screen.

"Well," you say, "get the paddles."

To defibrillate the heart, you pass an electrical charge through it, stunning the entire myocardium—the heart muscle cells—all at once. If the circumstances are right and you are very, very lucky, then the heart may restart itself in a normal rhythm. Usually in ambulances and ERs and such, you do closed-chest defibrillation. You pass the charge to the heart through the entire chest wall. Now, though, you have the heart entirely available, open right here in front of you. You can apply the electrical charge across the heart itself, so you need less voltage.

You use two long-handled paddles and position the two paddles so that the heart is between them. It's like holding a wad of Jell-O between two metal fly swatters.

J. T. attaches the paddles to the defibrillator cords. You take the handles and sandwich the heart between the two metal pads.

Twenty joules. Not much. Even so there is the sudden smell of burning flesh that arrives seconds after the first shock.

Everyone looks at the monitor. V-fib still.

"Again," you say.

Another shock. More burning flesh.

"Epinephrine," J. T. says. Adrenaline. "I'm going to give it intracardiac."

Donna hands him the syringe. J. T. unsheathes the needle and jams it into the muscle of the heart. You can't give adrenaline any faster way.

J. T. goes back to cardiac massage. Everyone stands for a moment looking up at the monitor.

"Let's shock again," he says.

You are ready with the paddles. J. T. slides the heart between them. Another shock, this time at 40 joules.

There is the flash and that terrible smell again. Out of habit, nobody watches the actual heart; everyone looks up at the monitor.

There is—after some jiggly artifact—normal sinus rhythm: rate 99.

"Just like on TV," J. T. says.

You all look down at the heart, which is doing this weird shimmy as it contracts. *It's beating!* you think.

It is only now that you recognize that someone is shouting out in the hallway.

"Where's my patient? Where's my patient?"

The trauma doors swing open, and in comes Dr. Wu, the thoracic surgeon on call. He's a small, fierce-looking man, now wrapped in a wet trench coat. It must be raining, you think. Somewhere out there is a real world of night and rain.

"What are you doing?" Dr. Wu shouts before he even gets up to the bed. Dr. Wu is a character and not a pleasant one. He yells at the nurses and the patients, given any excuse. He throws instruments in the OR, he hectors the medical students, and when a patient goes sour, he shouts at anyone in his path. (He meets a mixed response to this, since no one can understand his English when he gets angry.)

However, he is a very good surgeon. You would want him to do your bypass surgery should it come to that.

Jesus, you think suddenly, and turn to Donna.

"Lidocaine. Bolus and drip." That's to keep the heart from going back into fibrillation. You could kick yourself; you almost forgot. That one mistake could negate everything you've done so far.

You present the case to Dr. Wu as he peers down into the chest cavity. "A sixteen-year-old kid. Two through-and-through gunshot wounds to the chest. Both nailed the left ventricle. See." You show him.

"You sutured!" Dr. Wu shouts.

"We had to do something."

"Pledgets!" he shouts. "You sutured and you did not use pledgets!"

"Pledgets?" you reply stupidly.

"Cotton pledgets! You must have cotton pledgets to sew the heart. Where are pledgets?"

Donna, who is afraid of no one, wheels on him. "Dr. Wu, this is the ER, not the OR. We don't have pledgets down here, so get over it."

Dr. Wu, sensing a dead end, immediately switches to another problem. "Who called OR? Is OR there? Where is Anesthesia? Why isn't Anesthesia ready? You people have gotten nothing done."

"Dr. Wu . . . ," you say.

Donna is after him, though. "I'm sorry we haven't gotten anything done, but we were busy trying to save this kid's life by sewing up the holes in his chest. And if you quit having a temper tantrum because you got called in on an emergency case, then maybe you could help us out."

Dr. Wu wheels around, his mouth open, ready to say something. He looks at Donna, closes his mouth, nods and tries again. Finally, he spits out the only thing, apparently, that he can think of. "I am going to scrub. Bring the patient to the OR."

"Fine," Donna says, arms folded. "You do that."

You go back to the patient, basically thrilled to see Dr. Wu here no matter what his mood. At least he didn't ask you to cross-clamp the aorta.

That was the procedure that the photogenic doctors on TV were trying to enact. ("Do you see the aorta?" "Yes, yes, I see it clearly!") The reality is this open chest, a bare beating heart and blood everywhere. To cross-clamp the aorta, you have to find it, and this means you have to root around in the darkest recesses of the chest. You remember the last time you did it—three years ago. That was another kid, nineteen, who was stabbed in the belly—complete transection of the aorta. After you resuscitated him, the young man went up to the OR. The surgeon repaired the aorta—a miracle—then the kid spent a month dying in the ICU. You remember talking to his gaunt, frightened parents, breaking the news. And then there was the death, finally, thankfully. Never again, you told yourself, no more miracles. And here you are again.

You realize that you faded out there for a moment. Donna is looking at you. "What now?" she asks.

The only simple part. "We take him up to the OR."

"What about his blood pressure?" J. T. asks. You look up at the monitor. Systolic blood pressure of 60. Normal is over 100.

What now? You think and you realize you just don't care. You just want to get him to the OR.

"Let's restart cardiac massage," you tell J. T. "At least until we get him upstairs."

It takes a while to get everything ready. You have to transfer all the monitor leads to portable monitoring equipment, change the oxygen supply, sign and break down the chart. Meanwhile, J. T. is standing there, pumping the heart patiently. You change gloves and take over.

The little procession bangs out the door and down the hallway. You take over clutching at the heart. Clenching, unclenching, clenching, unclenching.

You have to take the front elevators. It's still before six A.M., so the back elevators aren't working yet. (They shut them down between midnight and six A.M. to save money.) You have to take one of the visitors' elevators up.

The bed just barely squeezes into the elevator cubicle. Everyone presses in around it. Bill presses the button for the fourth floor. This all seems pretty anticlimactic compared to what came before.

As the elevator levitates, you stand looking up at the ceiling, pumping away at the heart. Something occurs to you. A weird thought and you say aloud, "Maybe this kid will live." Even you can hear the touch of disbelief in your voice. "Of course he's going to live," Donna says. "He's nothing but a stupid, punk kid who was out where he wasn't supposed to be, doing what he wasn't supposed to be doing. These guys always make it."

You look sideways at her. It seems that as cynical as you have become over the years, you haven't gotten cynical enough to go that far, to feel that way. Then you remember J. T. and the needle stick. You nailed J. T. with the needle. No matter what happens to this patient, no matter how well he does, you would unravel the whole procedure just to take that needle stick back.

At the third floor the elevator stops. Everyone groans as the doors open; the OR is on the fourth. Standing in front of the door is a middle-aged woman, obviously waiting to get on the elevator. She doesn't look like one of the employees; she's dressed too nicely. Maybe she is an early morning visitor here to see one of the patients. What she sees with the elevator doors now open is a patient on a gurney with his chest pried open and you mashing on his bare heart while a motley crew of exhausted-looking health care professionals look on. Her mouth O's. She stands there frozen for the thirty seconds the door remains open. It closes again, and you ascend the last few feet to the fourth floor and the OR.

More anticlimax. Dr. Jan M. Radjike, the on-call anesthesiologist, wanders over, looking sleepy. Next to him an OR nurse stands waiting for you, arms folded, looking peeved. You feel for the first time a sense of relief, mixed with disappointment. Here is where you will pass the torch; you will go no further. The bypass pump technician waddles up. He scans the scene coolly; after all, he sees open chests and naked, flailing hearts every day. There are other nurses now as well, padding around in their blue surgical booties, surgical caps in place. Everyone looks grumpy and sleepy. No one wants to face this case first thing in the morning.

Chances are, you think to yourself, one in a hundred. And that's assuming you have an OR team that's awake. You shake your head.

"Ready or not," the bypass tech says as he takes over heart massage.

And it's over. Just like that.

J. T. and you take the elevator back down. The hospital is waking up now. You check your watch: 6:14. The golden hour is over.

Now for the parents. They turn out to be two ordinary people, raincoats pulled over their pajamas, who look too stunned to be grief-stricken. Your job is to "lay crepe," that is, to prepare them for the likely death of their son while pointing out that technically the boy is still alive. One in a hundred, you think.

"If there's a miracle in the OR . . . ," the mother says. All families cling to that word *miracle*. They think miracles are an everyday thing in medicine, whereas you, knowing the odds, feel as if you are only leading them astray. You try to explain but quickly you see that you are not getting through. The only thing that matters to them now is the word *miracle*.

So that's the story. You dig it up sometimes when you need it: the story of the sixteen-year-old kid who came in with two gunshot wounds through the left ventricle. Went to the OR with you doing open heart massage in the elevator. You are cheating when you tell it, but you are not alone. Doctors don't often tell stories about the patients they *didn't* save, or mistakes they may have made, or medical events they didn't understand. You are like that too, since, over the course of your career, you've opened a hundred chests or more, but you never tell the stories of the vast majority of them. You just tell the story of one or two you managed to save.

It's a sleepy afternoon, maybe a year later, maybe more. You are sitting writing on a chart. (Scientists have proved that ER physicians spend 50 percent of their time writing on charts. This is another thing they don't show on TV). Donna is standing above you, discharging a patient. "Now," she says to him, pointing to the bottom of the discharge instructions. "Put your initials here."

"I don't have initials," the patient says to her seriously. "I only have a name."

You put your face down into your hand so that the patient

can't see you laughing. To get away, you stand up and go over to the chart rack and pick up the next player. Chest pain in someone seventeen years old. Practically no one with chest pain at the age of seventeen has any significant health problem. The only clinical skill needed is getting rid of the patient both quickly and gracefully.

The nurse had already gotten an ECG. You go into the room and ask the pasty-faced young kid there a few questions. Your first sense, strangely enough—that sixth sense you use a lot to make a diagnosis—is, "But this kid is okay. He's a nice kid." You're not sure why that is relevant here, but the kid understands. He looks up at you, cocks his head and says, "Do you remember me?"

You have just taken down his gown to reveal a wide swath of scar from the breast bone to the axilla, the scar still a little raw. There's also the upper terminus of a healed celiotomy incision, a remnant of an abdominal exploration.

The miracle here is not whether you remember him or not. It's that he remembers you. You wonder for a moment about those end-of-life things, the light at the end of the tunnel. You imagine the patient's spirit watching a resuscitation over the medical team's shoulders as everyone frantically tries to save that body's life. How else could he ever have remembered you? But you don't say anything about that. If the kid was at all sane, he would think *you* were crazy. You just close your eyes, pass a blind hand over the trail of the scar, the palm flat on the chest, palpating for the apical impulse, as you say, "How could I ever forget?"

6

THE GOLDEN MOMENT

I.

ONCE I WAS TRAPPED IN A BAD TRAFFIC JAM. Up on the hill ahead was a three-car accident. One car was overturned and burning. The scene was packed with fire trucks, ambulances and patrol cars. I eased out onto the shoulder and ran a quarter mile along it beside the traffic. I was almost at the accident scene when a motorcycle cop pulled me over.

He ambled up to my car in typical cop swagger style. "What the hell . . . ," he said to me as he leaned down toward the window.

"Listen, Frank," I said, "you want *me* to be *at* where I am going."

The officer took a closer look at me. "Hey, Doc," he said flatly. He waved a hand to dismiss me.

"How bad is this?" I asked him, but he was already walking back to his motorbike. He slapped the rear fender of my car. "They're gonna need you," he told me over his shoulder. That was all.

The ER staff and cops are natural allies. Only people from the ER *know* what cops know. Only cops and ER doctors and nurses know about *provocation*—that special in-your-face quality people in the street can have. It's the intuitive ability, perhaps the only talent these guys have ever displayed in their lives, to worm their way into your hidden store of hatred. Often it is hatred that you never knew you had and would otherwise never have suspected was there. It's invisible, even to the people who have a vested interest in finding it—ex-wives, lawyers, teenagers. Only a mean drunk in the middle of the night knows it's there and knows how to make you burn because of it.

Not long ago we had a patient come in with a gunshot wound to the abdomen. The bullet had entered the epigastric area, the midpoint of the belly, and exited out the right flank, well away from the spinal cord. A fixable injury. But it didn't take us long to figure out why the man had been shot.

The nurse asked him: "How old are you?"

"Look, don't waste my time asking a bunch of stupid questions," the guy said.

We were searching his pants for his driver's license and came up with over $9,000 in hundred-dollar bills stashed in his coat pocket.

"Do you have any health problems?" the nurse asked.

"No, I don't have any goddamn health problems."

The surgical residents started to arrive. The first surgeon to walk in was the second-year resident. He looked at the guy and said, "Who shot you?"

"That's none of your business," the patient growled.

"Do you have any health problems? Take any medicines?"

"What the hell is this with all these questions? I just told somebody about my general state of health, and I told somebody about all the fucking medication I take. I'm not going to sit here answering the same fucking questions over and over."

"Sir, there are going to be a lot of us taking care of you. We're all going to be working hard to make sure you are okay, so you have to answer us."

"Bullshit, that's total bullshit. There is no reason why you have to ask me a bunch of stupid questions."

The surgery resident persisted. "When was the last time you ate?" (Anesthesia always wants to know.)

The patient exploded. "What the fuck difference does it make about the last time I ate? You're here to fix me, not ask me a bunch of stupid questions. So fix me, goddamn it, and don't fuck around."

"Listen," I said into his ear. "We're trying to save your goddamn life."

"You just do your *job* and fix me. That's all you have to do."

"Hey, guy," one of the security guards said. He had been standing watching all this from the doorway. "Take it easy."

The patient looked him over. "Oh, so you are the tough guy. You are the big man. You think you can take me on, big boy. You can just kiss my ass."

That's when Sheldon, one of the beat cops, came in. He walked over to where the patient lay and looked down on him. "What happened?" he asked the patient.

The patient looked at him. "What the fuck does it look like happened?" He stretched out his arms. "I've fucking been shot."

Sheldon scanned the room. He must have figured out the scene pretty quickly: an asshole patient surrounded by a bunch of stony-faced, seething health care professionals.

"Well," Sheldon said, patting his shoulder. "It looks like it couldn't have happened to a nicer guy."

The next night we took care of another solid citizen. This time Sheldon had brought him in, an eighteen-year-old kid picked up for selling cocaine. Sometime during the thrash of an arrest, he had eaten the evidence. Sheldon had brought him in for us to lavage the guy out and work the rest of our ER magic.

"You need the stomach contents for evidence?" I asked him.

"No," Sheldon said. "We're not doing anything with this." He looked at me, genuinely concerned. "I just want to make sure the kid's okay."

I looked at him quizzically.

"I know him," Sheldon said. "He's a good kid, basically. Just really stupid."

Sheldon was one of the nicest cops I had ever met. He was a tall, immaculately bald black man, broad-shouldered, narrow-hipped. He had a big man's presence and ease. Sheldon never had to menace; he could take control of a situation just by walking into the room. He never lost his temper; never succumbed to provocation like the rest of us.

Sheldon's usual partner was Dino Dupuchio, short and excitable. He played small, yappy terrier to Sheldon's Saint Bernard. A gentleman, though. When he was on night shift rotation, every night about three A.M. he would bring us donuts from DonutLand and then sit around with us showing us pictures of his kids.

That night their suspect, in addition to swallowing crack, had also smoked some "wet"—a combination of PCP and marijuana. ("Nice mix of drugs," Donna said, "the marijuana sort of takes the edge off the psychosis.") He lay limp and "unresponsive" on the cart, eyelids fluttering, playing possum, while we got everything started to hose him down.

"We got to get that cocaine out of you, dear," I told him. "We're going to have to put a big tube down your throat."

He lay inert, eyelids still fluttering.

Donna opened up the lavage kit, got out the Ewald tube—a tube with a diameter a little smaller than a garden hose—and said to Sheldon, "What's his name?"

"Benny."

"Benny. You are going to feel something sliding down your nose."

Donna got the tube about three inches into his nostril when Benny woke up a madman. He reached up and pulled the tube out of his nose and then swung at Donna, sending her back against the wall. He took off toward the end of the bed at top speed, but his right wrist stayed tethered by handcuffs to the frame of the bed. Sheldon was on him in a second. He swung him back up on the bed while the rest of us grabbed at various body parts trying to hold the kid down. Even with Sheldon there it took five of us.

"Come on, Benny," Sheldon kept saying. "Now let's be reasonable here."

Bill put Benny's head in an "ER headlock." An elbow is placed on the patient's carotid, the forearm across the mandible, the other hand levered down on the first arm's wrist, providing extra torque. If the patient continues to misbehave, then a little more pressure is applied with the elbow.

Under Bill's arm, Benny was screaming something, maybe the same thing, over and over.

"What's he saying?" I asked Bill.

Bill lifted his arm up and we all stopped to listen.

"Let me go," Benny shouted. *"You're messing up my hair."*

Sheldon put his head down close to Benny's ear and said, "Come on, Benny, you made us do this. If you had behaved responsibly, we wouldn't be in this position."

Benny stopped fighting and now stared out beyond us, lost to us. Just another addled addict.

Sheldon leaned over him and began singing,

> Night and day
> You are the one . . .
> here in the old familiar . . .

Sheldon looked up at us. "Cole Porter," he said. "Always settles them down."

"Keep singing," Donna said.

It took a minute, but finally Benny put his head back down on the bed and appeared to be sleeping comfortably.

Donna picked up the Ewald tube and waved it at Sheldon. "Care to accompany me while I put this tube down?"

"Of course," Sheldon said, getting a good grip on Benny's face.

Donna looked at Sheldon standing there, a man's face torqued between his two bear-like palms. "Keep this up and I'm never letting you come to my party again."

II.

I once rode in the zone car around District Five, our hospital district. It was a Friday night.

"Let's have no end-of-shift arrests tonight," one of the two officers said. "I was doing paperwork until ten A.M. this morning."

"Deal."

The scenery we drove through was aging urban: run-down gas stations, ratty quick-stop stores guarded by iron grillwork, shuttered quondam factories, empty lots, Dollar Dave's Easy Auto—no credit, no problem—DonutLand donut shop, a strip joint, a twenty-four-hour Laundromat, Uneeda Car Repair. I recognized the homeless guy pushing a grocery cart up the hill: Anthony Gouchette. I had seen him a hundred times.

It was a quiet evening.

If I had waited a week, I would have been there this particular night. I can imagine myself sitting in the backseat, invisible, seeing it all. Two officers, experienced guys, were roaming the streets. They had just stopped at McDonald's and now were coming up Berwin Avenue. It had been a rare summer day, now deeply shadowed, nearly night. Saturday evening traffic ran the long way up the hill, cars braking once they saw the shadow of the dark cherry top of the police car behind them. The officer behind the wheel eased the car out into the middle lane, behind a white Toyota Corolla. The Toyota slowed.

"Left brake light out," the officer driving said.

"I, personally, can live with that," his partner countered.

"I, on the other hand, want do some fishing."

"Then you call base."

"No, you call. I called last time."

The officer behind the wheel turned the light on. The Toyota throbbed red, blue, red, blue.

They went through a green light at Maxwell; the car pulled over just beyond it, stopping in front of Dave's Easy Auto. The first officer took his flashlight, undid his seat belt and adjusted his holster. He opened the door to step out.

His partner took a bite out of his drive-in burger, than tapped his shoulder pack experimentally with his other hand as he watched his partner slam the door.

The first officer began the cop walk, saunter speed, up to the Toyota, flashlight held overhand at shoulder level. As he did, the driver opened the door—instant problem—and stepped out of the car. For the second officer it was hard to see because of the glare of the oncoming cars, but the driver appeared to be a white male, thirtyish, in a Tecate beer T-shirt. The driver took a step forward, and that was when the second officer saw the gun—a rifle—no, an assault rifle with a scope. The man with the Tecate T-shirt pointed the gun forward at the first officer. It was at waist level when he fired the first and then a second shot. The first officer took a step forward and reached for his gun as the man from the Toyota went down on one knee and fired an unknown number of additional shots. As the second officer came out of the car, gun cocked, the shooter stood up, aiming at the second officer. The second officer then fired three shots, all aimed at the man's chest. The man fell to the ground.

The first officer had fallen as well. The second officer shouted, "Officer down!" into his shoulder pack. He ran around to the side of the car, where he found his partner lying in a pool of blood—one hand to his neck.

The first officer reached his other hand out. "No," was all he said.

The "red phone" rang. It was a dedicated line connected to City Emergency Services. We almost always used the radio connection, so that when this phone rang it was usually a wrong number.

"You've reached Ambulance Med Command," I said into the receiver. I was the closest to the phone.

"We've got an officer down, coming to you by squad car."

"Who is this?"

"This is police dispatch."

"What did you say?"

"Shooting. An officer is down. No other details available."

"Are the paramedics going to radio—"

"That's a negative, Med Command. Transport in squad car."

I dropped the phone, fumbled for it and hung up. "Mary," I said to the unit clerk, "page Surgery." And don't get all worked up, I told myself. The last "police shooting" we'd had, I had activated the entire hospital trauma system for an officer who had sustained an abrasion on his palm.

"This is a trauma alert," I said over the intercom. *"We need a nurse to the trauma room and a gurney in the ambulance bay. Repeat—that's a nurse in trauma and a gurney in the ambulance bay."*

Mary, the unit clerk, looked up from filing her nails. It had been a mysteriously slow evening for a Saturday.

"What's up?" she asked.

"Officer shot, coming in by squad car."

"Uh-oh," she said. "I better page public relations."

"And page the surgeon overhead. Where *is* everybody?"

"Mental health break," Mary said.

That meant everyone was out in the ambulance bay already. Smoking.

"And what lucky surgeon do we have on tonight?"

It was Don "the Doberman" Doberstine, AKA Dr. Love. Good surgeon, though.

Bill had already started pulling the gurney out of the trauma room. He rolled it behind me as I walked through the ambulance bay doors. Outside in the warm summer evening Tracy and Donna stood smoking and complaining.

"Hey," Tracy said to me. "It's actually nice out here."

"Not anymore."

"What?" Donna asked flatly.

"Policeman reported down. Shot. That's all I know."

"Who's bringing him in?"

I shrugged. "I think he's coming in the squad car. City Emergency didn't know anything. They just said he was down."

As I said that, there was the wail of a police siren off in the distance.

I looked at my watch. It was 8:12 P.M. The police car turned down the drive. In a moment I could even see the frightened face of the officer behind the wheel. I felt nauseated first—it took a moment more before I consciously registered that it was Dino behind the wheel.

"Oh my God," Tracy said, *sotto voce.*

Dino pulled to a hasty stop and leaped out. *"It was a routine traffic stop . . ."* he shouted. He had blood on his uniform, blood on his hands.

We all ran to the passenger side. There an officer sat, head lolling back, covered in blood.

It was Sheldon.

Inside the car there seemed to be blood everywhere—on the ceiling, on the windshield, an inch or more on the floor, where a fast-food burger, still half wrapped in paper, sat soaked with blood.

Everyone pulled, trying to get Sheldon out of the car and onto the gurney. Dino pushed from the inside. Sheldon was completely limp, not helping us at all. He had a wound of some kind in his neck and his uniform was soaked in blood.

"What happened?" I shouted to Dino.

"The guy had a fucking bazooka. I think he got him once in the neck and then twice in the belly."

"Come on," I yelled at Bill, who was in the process of yelling something at me.

This is where TV gets it right. The simultaneousness of a

thrash. Everyone started yelling orders at everyone else; we all pushed and pulled Sheldon onto the gurney and ran, tripped and stumbled toward the door. I only managed to grope momentarily for a pulse and got nothing more than my hand covered with blood. There was a bullet hole in the neck.

"CPR," I shouted. "We need CPR. I can't get a pulse. Mary, Mary, tell the Doberman to get his ass down here now. Tell him this time it's real."

The respiratory therapist met us in the trauma room, took one look at Sheldon and panicked. "Oh, Jesus, it's a cop." She grabbed for the Ambu bag and the mask. She dropped the mask, retrieved it from the floor, fumbled trying to connect it to the Ambu bag and then dropped it again.

"Bill," I said, "there's no pulse here. Start CPR."

I needed to intubate. We had almost everything laid out, but I hadn't hooked up the suction yet. I cursed myself. I should have been in here setting things up before the squad car arrived. I grabbed up my supplies: the laryngoscope and its blade, the endotracheal tube, a stylet to put down the tube to stiffen it while I intubated. How many times had I done this? I had no idea— but how many times had I done it on someone I knew?—never. I balked for a moment as I stood there looking down. This was Sheldon's face. I can't be intubating Sheldon. I can't do this. Then with my left hand I adjusted his jaw in order to get the laryngoscope in. His face stayed slack, even as I got my thumb in to open the jaw. I wanted to slap him. "Sheldon, wake up. Wake up, Sheldon."

Instead I slipped the laryngoscope blade into his mouth, lifted his tongue and mandible up out of the way and slid the tube in place. I inflated the cuff to make an airtight seal. The respiratory therapist attacked the Ambu bag and began squeezing like mad. Good breath sounds.

My fingers kept slipping out of place, though, because of the blood. As I looked beyond the endotracheal tube, I saw the bullet hole in the neck and thought—No, no, it's too lateral to have caused any serious damage—too lateral to have struck the carotid. If it had hit the carotid we might as well just stop now.

I looked up. Bill was doing CPR, bearing down on Sheldon's chest. Up, down, up, down. Tracy was hacking at his uniform with a pair of trauma scissors while Carol struggled to get the ECG leads in place. I checked for a pulse again. When Bill gave CPR, I thought it was there, faintly, but when Bill stopped, it stopped.

I started calling out injuries for the charting nurse to record. "We've got a through-and-through neck wound, right side. It looks like it went lateral to the carotid."

Bill paused from CPR so we could yank at the Velcro straps and undo Sheldon's bulletproof vest. "No chest wounds," I went on. "It looks like two gunshot wounds, entrance wounds, to the abdomen. One in the left upper quadrant and one just above the umbilicus." I motioned for Bill to stop CPR and help me roll Sheldon. "We've got what looks like one exit wound here. Right flank."

Two gunshot wounds in the middle of the abdomen; nothing in the chest, no blood pressure. He must be bleeding out into his abdomen, I thought. The bullet must have struck the abdominal aorta. We might be able to stop the bleeding by cross-clamping the aorta within the chest, tying off the artery until the surgeons could repair it. That would mean a thoracotomy.

I palpated Sheldon's belly. It was distended and dull to the tapping of my finger.

"Restart CPR," I told Bill.

"Someone take these bloods," Carol said. "I've drawn enough to cross-match for four."

Our volunteer, a diminutive, nerdish creature—actually premed at a local college—stood out of the line of fire, one hand raised to his white face and his open mouth—*The Scream* embodied. I pointed at him. "Tell Mary we need four units of type-specific blood now, now, now."

He fled out through the ER doors, passing the Doberman and the second-year surgical resident, who were coming in.

"What's this?" the Doberman asked, stopping before the bed.

I leaned over Sheldon, the back of my hand to my forehead. "Thirty-seven-year-old male, shooting."

The Doberman looked at the patient, puzzled. He must have been sleeping and was only now waking up. "But this guy is a police officer," he said.

". . . shot in the gut and the neck. I don't think the neck one got the carotid." I pointed out the neck wound and then I looked up at the Doberman, looking for reassurance. "But I'm sure whoever shot him nailed his abdominal aorta. We gotta open his chest. That's his only chance."

"Blood pressure?" he asked.

"Not here; not now."

"Oh, Jesus. How many shots to the abdomen?"

I raised my fingers. "Two. One exit wound."

The Doberman looked down at Sheldon's chest and sighed. "Vitals in the field?"

"We dunno. His partner brought him in." I put my hand on Sheldon's chest. "I know him," I told the Doberman. "We've got to get him back."

Even I could hear the pleading in my voice. I looked at him, then at the surgical resident, who was panting with puppy-like eagerness at the thought of cracking a chest.

The Doberman slid his hands over Sheldon's chest and then along his belly, pausing to press deeply over the bullet holes. He looked up at me, shaking his head.

"We could try to cross-clamp the aorta," I went on.

The Doberman cast a weathered eye up to the monitor and then down the length of the patient. "Well," he said, "if that's what you want, somebody should hand me the thoracotomy tray." He turned to the resident. "You start a central line."

The resident, pissed because he wasn't doing the thoracotomy, slunk off for the kit.

Donna passed me a bottle of Betadine—brown and viscous disinfectant—used everywhere in the ER. I anointed the chest with it, a token gesture. This procedure would be anything but sterile.

Donna pointed out that the desk clerk was saying my name over the loudspeaker.

"What!!"

"EMS phone. They're calling about another trauma."

Somebody handed me the phone receiver. "Yeah?"

"This is EMS twelve, Doc. We've got a twenty-eight-year-old gunshot to the abdomen here. He's awake and alert but he's only got a pressure of ninety over palp—"

"Just bring him in—"

"Doc, he's the shooter."

I put my head down. "Just bring him in. We'll see you when you get here."

The Doberman had the thoracotomy tray opened up and was pawing through the instruments, the scalpels, the Fienchetto, Mayo scissors, twenty towel clamps (enough to crack ten chests). Carol handed me a package of sterile gloves, and I opened it up and slid them on—more ceremonial sterility.

"The shooter is coming in," I announced to everyone.

Nobody said anything. Donna was working on another IV; Tracy was helping the surgical resident start the central line. The respiratory therapist was bagging Sheldon. The Doberman and I bent over his chest.

He traced a long curve with the scalpel, a sketch mark embossed in skin, and then followed the same path, going deeper this time. Another cut went down to the ribs. Then the Mayo scissors; the lung collapsed back into the cavern of the chest, only to swell and fall in tandem with the squeezing of the Ambu bag. Now the Fienchetto. We worked clumsily to try to fit the rib spreaders into place.

I glanced up for a second and saw the surgery resident working the central line, a picture of total concentration. You can never be like that as an ER physician—totally focused—you always have to have your mind placed in a hundred different spots.

I looked back down at the chest, Sheldon's chest. *Think,* I told myself. *This is Sheldon.*

The Doberman finally wedged the Fienchetto in place and began cranking the handle. There was the sound of splintering bones as the ribs inched apart. Finally, when the Doberman had cleared about four inches, he got down, nose to chest wall, peering deep into the thoracic cavity. "Nothing," he said. He gingerly stuck his right hand between the bars of the Fienchetto.

"I've got the heart here," the Doberman said. "I can feel it pretty well." He had his hand deep into the chest by now. "It feels really, really . . . empty."

That's when the paramedics from ambulance 18, our home squad, hustled in with the ambulance stretcher. No CPR, thank God. Following them, improbably enough, was Sheldon's partner, Dino, literally snarling as he came in after the stretcher. The security guard trailed impotently behind him.

"*I want this sucker dead,*" Dino shouted, pointing at the shooter. "*This guy needs to be one dead motherfucker.*"

I came over to the curtain. "Who let him in here?" I yelled to security.

Dino bore down on me. He pointed behind me, into trauma bay one, where his partner was, and shouted, "*That's the man you need to save,*" while I shouted back, "*Dino, get the fuck out of this ER.*"

Dino was up nose to nose with me. "That asshole is toast, man. I shot that bastard, and if he doesn't die I hold you responsible."

I shouted back, still trying to override him. "*Get the hell out of here. I want you out. Security, get Dino out of here.*"

The security guard put his arm in front of Dino's chest nearly cradling him with it. "Dino, what the hell do you think you're going to do? Shoot him again? You need to cool it. Let these guys do their job."

I put my hand out as well, my palm resting up against his bulletproof vest. "Dino, don't make me have to throw you out of here."

Dino stopped shouting and looked beyond me distractedly. What he saw now in trauma bay one was his partner supine on the gurney, his chest wall split open, his heart pulled up and visible to all while the Doberman rooted around in the inner recesses of the thoracic cavity. Dino swayed as if he was about to go down.

That's when I turned my back on him and walked away. I had to; I had to work on the second trauma.

"Hey, buddy, what's your name? What's your name, guy? I know you're awake. Don't try to pull the possum stuff on me. Tell me your name." That was Carol shaking the shooter's arm. I walked over and looked down. He was a skinny white guy, with a face pockmarked with acne, who somehow through all the recent events managed to still be wearing his baseball cap. He seemed very much alive. I caught his right wrist in my hand. Good strong pulse.

"Do we have anything on this guy? A name, anything?" I asked EMS.

"He's got his license in his wallet," the paramedic said. "We got he's Jay Stryczek."

"Could you spell that?" Carol said. She unfolded the trauma form before her and began filling it out.

I grabbed at the sheet to help EMS transfer the patient from the gurney to the hospital cart. "What's the report?"

"Triple gunshot wound to the abdomen. Three entrance wounds, it looks like, no exits. Pressure of eighty when we got there. We started two IVs normal saline, last pressure of one twenty over sixty-four."

"Good work," I said mechanically.

The paramedic beamed. He had saved this guy's life.

I leaned over the patient. "Jay," I said loudly, "do you take any medicines?"

Slowly, almost imperceptibly, he shook his head.

Carol was the professional one. She put him on the monitor, fixed the IVs, labeled the blood. At this point my hands were shaking so badly that the only thing I could trust myself with were the trauma shears. I scissored open his pants, pulled his belt off, then sliced through his blood-soaked Tecate beer T-shirt.

The automated blood pressure cuff pumped up and I stopped, gazing up to watch the numbers dial through on the monitor. I felt as if I were watching a slot machine. And the winning numbers were: 84/30. This guy was hurtin'.

"He's going to need more fluids," Carol said.

"We need another IV for starters. I'll put in a central line."

I began my survey. Airway, good; breathing, yes; circulation—well, he was hypotensive but he wasn't going to die in the next twenty minutes. I ran my hand over his chest, which was bloody but otherwise unscathed, and then let both hands travel down to his belly. There were three bullet holes. One in the right upper quadrant, dead center of the liver, one in the epigastrium that had probably nailed his stomach and one just above the symphysis pubis. The part of me that was a doctor took over. I thought of the gunshot wounds in terms of anatomy and the bullet's potential pathway. Three bullet holes to the belly. No exits, EMS had said, although I needed to roll him to make sure. If the patient was standing erect and the bullets hit him straight on, most of the damage would be to the abdominal organs, the liver, the bowel, the spleen (which bleeds like crazy). If he was falling backward when he was hit, the bullets would have pierced the diaphragm, dropped a lung or even hit a ventricle of the heart. If he was falling forward when he was shot, the bullets would have traveled down into the pelvis, hit the bladder, the prostate. The trump card, of course, was the spine. The rest of it, bellywise, was pretty fixable. If the bullet had hit the spine, however, that could mean a lifetime of paralysis—wheelchairs, indwelling urine bags, crater-like bedsores—all at best.

I surveyed the patient's now naked body.

"Wiggle your toes," I demanded of him.

After a moment's thought he wiggled the toes on both feet vigorously.

I shook my head. Something inside of me was disappointed.

I abandoned him as Carol bent down to start another IV and went back over to where Sheldon lay. The surgery resident had finished the central line, and two units of blood plus several liters of normal saline were washing into Sheldon's circulatory system. The resident stood on Sheldon's left side now, both hands wrapped around Sheldon's heart, squeezing gently as he gave open heart massage. Underneath him, working in the narrow hole between the ribs, the Doberman had both forearms half buried in the chest cavity. He had his face down there as well, nose practically inside the chest as he tried to see. He had put on a face mask, but now one of the straps had come loose from around his ear, and the mask flapped uselessly against his cheek and jaw. There was blood in his hair. He looked up at me, and I could see his lips were pressed tightly shut, forming one thin line of concentration.

"I've got it," he said finally. "I've got it clamped." He eased his hands out of the chest and looked up at me. "How's the other guy doing?"

"He's currently alive."

"Which is more than I can say for your cop friend here." The Doberman looked around. "Have we got maximum fluids going, team? That's the only chance this dude has."

"Should I keep up with heart massage?" the resident asked while, simultaneously, Tracy said: "Oh, no, no, no. Oh, no. Do you see?"

"What?" We all looked around and then down at Tracy's hand. She was pointing at the bullet hole in Sheldon's neck. Blood had been oozing from the neck wound before but now it poured out, a wide stream of blood that swelled wider every time the resident squeezed the heart.

The Doberman threw the needle driver he had in his hand down on the floor. "Aw, jeez," he said, "for crying out loud. That bullet nailed the carotid, man. This guy was a goner before we even started." He yanked off his face mask.

"Okay," Carol said. She was standing pumping up a pressure bag on one of the units of blood. She had been silently crying throughout the code, and now she was trying to snuffle herself back together. "So what now?"

"Nothing now. This guy is dead."

"So you want to call the code?"

"Yeah, code called. Okay?"

Everyone just stopped what they were doing, mid-gesture. The Doberman turned away, peeling off his gloves. The resident, still giving open cardiac massage, looking around nervously, not sure if he, too, should just stop. Finally he pushed the heart back down through the rib cage into the chest cavity and reached in to give it a nervous pat before he, too, turned away.

"What about the other guy?" the Doberman asked. We both looked over to the other trauma bay, where Carol was taping a second IV into place. Except for Carol, the guy was lying there alone. "Do we have more to work with?"

"Yeah, if the cops don't tear him limb from limb."

So the Doberman went over to save the life of the guy in trauma bay two. I couldn't follow him. Not just yet. I walked up to the head of the cart and looked down on Sheldon's neck wound, still oozing blood. I remembered that I was sure the bullet had gone too lateral to have hit the carotid. When I looked down now, though, it was clear that the entrance wound was right over the carotid; there was no way the bullet could have missed it. I thought of the blood in the car, all that blood on Dino, the stillness of Sheldon's face. Why had I lied to myself? Clearly Sheldon had bled out from a carotid injury before he had ever arrived at the ER, but just as clearly, I hadn't been able to face it. That's why we cracked his chest. I wanted to believe that he still had a chance. But he never did.

Tracy, standing next to me, was staring down at her bloody

gloves. She looked gray and unsteady. "Sheldon's dead," she said miserably. She looked so young to me at that moment, like someone who still believed that just because we tried with all our might to save someone, he would be saved. "I can't believe it. What did we do wrong?"

"We didn't do anything wrong. He was dead at the scene."

Tracy leaned back so that her back was against the wall behind her. Slowly, limply, she slid to a seated position on the floor.

"Are you going to faint?" I asked, a ridiculous question.

"No," she said. "I think I'm going to cry."

The evening supervisor came up and looked down at where Tracy was sitting.

"Are you all right?" she asked Tracy.

"No," Tracy said.

"The wife is here," the supervisor announced. "Someone needs to talk to her."

There was a moment of silence. Finally I said, "I will."

The supervisor quizzed me as we walked away.

"How's the guy who did the shooting?"

"He's doing terrific," I told her glumly.

Outside the trauma room there were at least twenty police officers, ranging in rank from the foot soldiers to the brass-bedecked big guys. Dino came forward out of the pack, his head down. "How is he?" he asked my shoes.

"He's dead, Dino."

Dino stood there for a moment still looking at my shoes. Finally he said, "How's the assailant?"

"He's going to surgery. I don't know any more than that."

Dino turned away, shaking his head. "I meant to kill him," he said.

I reached a hand out to comfort him, but all I could feel was the bulletproof vest as I patted him on the back. "We did everything we could."

Dino stopped. He turned back around to look at me for the first time. That's when I saw that he was not grieving; he was furious. "What do you mean you did everything you could? My partner is dead and the guy that shot him is still alive."

"Dino," I said, "Sheldon died at the scene. The guy got him in the carotid. He bled out in the car."

Dino turned away again.

"Don't do this, Dino."

With his back to me, he said, "So you let the fucking shooter live. Well, fuck this hospital and fuck you."

Now I was angry. I came after him, grabbed his arm and turned him around. "I can't help that," I yelled at him. "I was just doing my job. People come here; I try to save their lives. *It doesn't work any other way.*"

I looked around at the other cops standing around us. Most of them I knew. I saw them every day; I gave them penicillin for their sore throats, physicals for their kids, back-to-work excuses for their wives, a dozen little courtesies. But I saw none of this reflected in their eyes as I looked around at them now. All I could see was suspicion and blame. One of theirs was shot and I did not save him. It was my fault. I didn't perform the expected medical miracle and save Sheldon. It was everyone's fault.

I just walked away. I couldn't take the way they looked at me. They all moved silently to let me through. When I passed by the district commander, though, he held my shoulder for a moment. "Okay," the commander said. "I know you did your best."

"I've got to go talk with his wife," I mumbled.

"Do you want me to go with you?"

"No," I said. "Just let me go alone."

It was that same long, dark corridor. At the end was a single door. I slipped into the room. A woman wearing a flowered sweatshirt was sitting alone on the couch, crying. When she heard me come in, she tried to pull herself together. She wiped her face with a wad of shredded tissue, sniffling, but it was impossible, so she just went back to crying again.

I sat for a while on the chair opposite her, hands steepled, elbows on my knees, trying to think what to say. Where had I done this before? Bosnia, Nigeria, the South Side of Chicago. A death is always the same.

Finally she looked up at me. "He did not have to do this," she said. "He's got a couple of businesses with his dad. I don't know if you knew that. We don't need the money." She paused. "He just liked being a cop."

I stared back down at my hands.

"Why did he do it?" she asked me.

I looked up.

"Why did he shoot? Why did that man shoot my husband?"

I thought of what Dino had said when he first jumped out of the car. "It was a routine traffic stop," he shouted. It had never occurred to me to ask more.

"I dunno," I told her. I wanted to tell her that the last time I saw her husband alive he was singing Cole Porter for a patient he had brought in, singing for all of us, really, but I was distracted by another thought. Imagine ten thousand deaths just like this. That's what Bosnia was. That was Nigeria.

"He died on the scene," I told her in a flat voice that did not sound like my own. "The shooter nailed his carotid. He bled out before he got here."

Why was I telling her this? I wondered to myself.

Sheldon's wife reached out and took my hand.

"I knew your husband well," I continued. "He was the nicest guy . . . I just can't believe this."

"I know," the wife said, crying. She patted my hand to comfort me. "Everybody knows."

The headline in the paper the next day read:

"Policeman Killed, Motorist Injured in Roadside Shootout." Below it, in smaller type, it read: "Mother of victim states son was a victim of harassment."

"Oh, give me a break," Bill said. "Give me a fucking break."

It was the next afternoon shift, a quiet one. We all sat there glumly listening as Bill scanned the newspaper article. "'Jay

Stryczek, twenty-eight, convicted of armed robbery times two, wanted for parole violation' . . . I see he is a topnotch citizen . . . 'critical condition from abdominal injuries. . . . Sheldon Tennant, thirty-seven, thirteen years on the force, pronounced dead on arrival' at this hospital. Was he really dead on arrival?"

"Close enough," Donna said.

". . . 'leaves behind a wife and three children.' It doesn't say anywhere in here about why the guy shot him, though."

"Yeah, well the big question," Donna said, "is whether the guy is gonna live or not." She turned to me. "Have you heard?"

I shrugged. "No, but then dirt never dies."

"We could have saved the county a whole lot of time, trouble and money if we had just accidentally let that guy go to ground."

"Listen to this," Bill went on. "The mother, Stryczek's mother, said: 'They stopped my son for no reason. He was observing the speed limit. They had no reason to stop him like they did.'"

I walked away. I couldn't listen anymore.

I talked with the district commander a few days later to catch up on the case.

"Well, Stryczek woke up enough yesterday that we asked him a few questions," he told me. "I don't know about the quality of the answers."

"Did he say why he did it?"

The commander shrugged. "He said he didn't wanna go back to jail."

"That was the reason?"

"He said he was sick and tired of living in a jail cell and he just didn't want to go back."

"Sounds like a suicide mission."

"Yeah, the only problem was—we missed."

The trial started one blistering July day, thirteen months after Jay Stryczek was discharged in stable condition to the county jail.

Why he did it, what he was thinking in the few seconds that the scene went down, turned out to be the crucial issue. There was no question that Jay Stryczek had killed a police officer. The question was whether it was first-degree murder—maximum penalty the electric chair—or second-degree murder, maximum penalty life imprisonment. The deciding factor involved intent. To convict of first-degree murder, the prosecution had to prove that the murder was planned and that death was the intent. To do that, Jay Stryczek must have intended to kill a police officer when he grabbed his assault rifle and stepped out of the car.

"Of course he intended to use the gun," Bill said. "Why would he have picked it up and gotten out of the car with it?"

"Well, it doesn't matter what the truth was, all that matters is what the jury believes."

"Yes, but who could possibly imagine getting out of a car with an assault rifle for any other reason?"

I shrugged. "No idea."

The trial lasted two weeks, during which the defense argued that Stryczek had gotten out of the car with the gun in order to "menace" the police officers—that there was no intent to injure, that the gun went off accidentally.

The day the verdict was to be announced, someone brought a little portable TV into the ER. We monitored the news channel throughout the shift, and when the newscaster announced that the jury was ready to read the verdict, all of the staff clustered around the set. I stood off to the side, leaning against the wall, arms folded, watching, thinking. Remembering.

I wish I could say that the strongest memory I had of Sheldon was when he sang Cole Porter to that whacked-out PCP player while he held him in a headlock. But it's not. My thoughts always go back to a place I never was, inside a patrol car that had just pulled over a guy with a bad taillight. I keep thinking it's me at the wheel, groping around, reaching for the flashlight, the sound of the door as it opens, the crunch of boots on gravel. After all . . .

Imagine it was you.

As you walk forward toward the car in question, you see everything happen in slow motion; the car stops, the door opens, there's the shadow of the man with a dullish angular reflection at his side, something that moves with his arm. The man himself is standing now before the door, legs apart, braced, not moving forward, not moving at all, and you see a gesture, as if the man had a gun, a shotgun. No, a rifle. No, you think, what a mess. And then: No, this cannot be. That's the point when you raise your hand to your gun and as you do, you think, I'm too late. And, Not now, not to me. This cannot happen to me. I have a family and plans, a future, a clear and wide, wide future. My life can't end just like this.

7

HOW TO WRITE A PRESCRIPTION

A PATIENT SITS before you, gazing at you, while on your desk, under your pen, is a square of paper. Printed at the top is your name, followed by "M.D." Or the name of a hospital, say "General Hope Memorial." A line for your signature is on the bottom (underneath a caption: "May substitute ___yes ___no"). This is the blank prescription.

The patient is waiting for you to write for something that will make him feel better. This is your job. You start scrawling something on the form, something from another place, another time. You and the pharmacist both know what's being written here, but the patient won't understand a thing. He may think the message is secretly encoded using bad handwriting. But it's not, or not only.

The hallmark of the paper, the confirmation of the scrip's authenticity, is the use of Latin (with an indelible shadow of Greek). This is not the Latin of modern science; this is the Latin of hellbane and devil's wort, powdered mandrake root and eye of newt. You may be writing for a drug invented no earlier than yesterday, but the language of the prescription will echo from the most distant past of medicine. And the human impulse behind the prescription will be the same now as then—a mixture of hope and wishful thinking, science and sorcery.

You begin by writing the name of the drug you want (using a ballpoint pen with the name of some unbelievably expensive antibiotic printed across the clip, gift of a drug rep). Traditionally, all drugs have two names. The first is the scientific name—the generic name. Usually this reflects the chemical properties of the drug, shortened in some way. For example, the drug 7-choro-1, 3-dihydro-1-methyl-5-phenyl-2H-1, 4-benzodiazepin-2-1, has a name no one but a chemist could remember. Its generic name is easier: "diazepam." But it has another name as well. That's the proprietary, or trade, name, the drug company's patented name for the drug. For this drug the proprietary name is "Valium." This most people have heard of, the name with the most resonance. But all of them are the same drug.

What's in a name? Well, after all the bad press Valium received during its ascendance, drug companies rushed to make congeners, related drugs with small variations in the chemical structure, each one requiring a new name. Solid citizens who wouldn't dream of taking Valium now pop its fellow drugs, identical in almost every way, including addictive properties.

You glance up. Your patient is still waiting for his prescription. Let's say he is waiting for a scrip for acetaminophen with codeine, trade name Tylenol #3. You can write down either name (but usually only medical students remember the generic names). Being a doctor, of course, you don't worry too much about the spelling. Bad handwriting helps hide many errors—although you can't be *too* cavalier. The hapless street addict who presented his (presumably forged) scrip for morphine written as "MOFENE," followed by "totel 10 dollers," did not get his drug.

After the name you write the number of pills to dispense, say "#30." Below this you write the mysterious word *sig*. Latin again. It is an abbreviation for *signa*—(imperative of the Latin *signo*, to set a mark upon). Hardly a physician knows what this word stands for, though they may write it twenty times a day. Used in prescriptions since the Middle Ages, it introduces the part of a prescription containing directions to the patient—not that many patients would be able to decipher what follows. (The Latin hallmark is everywhere and nowhere.)

The next step. You must write down the number of pills to be taken at any one time, but you can't write this in Arabic numbers. Tradition demands you use lowercase Roman numerals: i, ii, iv, etc. Next, you write how the drug should be taken—that is, by what route. You must write this in abbreviated Latin, of course, even though it would be just as easy to write what you want in English. The typical abbreviations include: po (*peroral*, by mouth); pr (*per rectum*, by rectum); ou (*oculus uterique*, each eye); sl (*sublingual*, under the tongue—where a rich rete of capillaries sweeps the drug almost immediately into the bloodstream).

After this, another mysterious signifier—the code for the number of times a day the drug should be taken: bid means *bis in die*, twice a day; tid, *ter in die*, three times a day; qd, *quaque die*, every day; or, as in the case of this particular prescription, you will append "prn." This is Latin for *pro re nata*, loosely, according to need. Now you are finished. Well, almost. There is one more thing, something which yanks you back to the twentieth century. Tylenol #3 (T#3) is a controlled substance. This means you need to include your DEA number with the scrip. The DEA number is your assigned designation from the U.S. Drug Enforcement Agency. Your particular number allows the Feds and state officials to monitor your prescription habits, albeit in a shadowy way. Get frisky with the prescriptions for Percocet and somewhere someone is supposed to notice.

What makes T#3 a controlled substance? Controlled substances are those drugs designated by the DEA as having addictive potential. There are five classes of controlled substances. Class V (note: not 5) are medications that have minimal abuse potential and are sold without a prescription. Examples are over-the-counter cough syrups with minuscule amounts of codeine. Class IV drugs are prescription drugs believed, by the federal government anyway, to have relatively low abuse potential. These include Darvon, Talwin, Valium, and Xanax. Class III drugs are considered more addictive; they include anabolic steroids and hydrocodone. Class II contains the strongest analgesics—pain medicine—that can generally be written for: morphine, methadone, methamphetamine. These are drugs thought to be medically useful but also to have very high addictive potential. Finally, Class I drugs are usually available only to researchers. These are drugs which are considered both to be highly addictive and to have no beneficial medical use: heroin is a Class I drug. So is marijuana.

So you put down your two letters and the following seven-digit number. Now you are finished.

But what does a prescription for 30 T#3 mean? Well, different things to different people. For some patients, the ones with the occasional headache, this prescription is something to fill, use once, then put in the back of the medicine cabinet, where it will sit forgotten for months or years until it is rediscovered at four A.M. by a patient in the act of looking for something for an acid stomach. To others, a businessman, a new mother, a high school principal, a cop, people under pressure, "T#3" is something they know will take the edge off that nagging back pain. Something that will help get them to the end of the day, daily, in fact. Something that's there when it's needed, not really a "crutch" but . . . well . . . helpful.

Then there are the small-time addicts, people who, for whatever reason, have gotten themselves hooked on codeine and now troll the medical field looking for a drug source. They come into the ER all the time. They usually have a story, a transparent story if you know what to look for. You could even profile these guys— like airplane hijackers or drug smugglers. Glance down the chart and alarm bells go off.

One typical story goes like this. The patient is from out of town, no access to a regular, or, as you like to call them "real" (as opposed to ER) doctor. He has a history of chronic low-back pain that requires a mountain of Percodan—at least—to take the edge off. And usually a shot of Demerol as well. He's allergic to a lot of different medicines: coincidentally these happen all to be mild drugs useful in treating chronic pain.

Tonight the pain is terrible, terrible, the worst it's ever been. "Please, Doc, you got to give me something for the pain."

Some ER doctors just give them the shot and the prescription. How can you tell the pain is or isn't real? they say. But you've always thought that was part of the job, making that assessment. And giving a prescription-drug addict more drug is not going to do him or her any good.

You stand in the room, gazing at the patient, arms folded. He or she could be anyone, but tonight he's a forty-five-year-old man, well dressed; a handsome leather briefcase sits on the floor beside him. A reminder: addiction transcends social classes.

He says he has excruciating back pain, but he makes all the wrong moves. He sits up in a way people with real back pain don't. He grimaces every time he moves his leg, a kind of hokey facial expression, almost a parody of someone in pain. When you touch his back, he bunches up his face horribly and beats on the bed railing. "That hurts; it hurts, Doc," he tells me, rubbing his right leg. "And it's weak, I tell you, weak."

He's flunked the sitting straight-leg-raising test, and now you are going to try the Hoover test. Both of these tests are used to differentiate "organic" (i.e., "real") from "functional" pathology. They help answer an important question often raised in the ER. Is this true disease or drug-seeking behavior?

The Hoover is a simple test. You have the patient lie down, then you place your hand under his left heel. You ask him to raise his right, his weak, leg. Normally, if someone has true weakness, he or she will attempt to lift the affected leg by placing pressure on the contralateral, stronger leg. People who are faking weakness usually don't brace with their other heel. When they don't, you have a positive Hoover. While this test is not 100 percent accurate, in this case it definitely confirms what you suspected.

"I'm going to recommend . . . Tylenol," you say.

"Doc, you gotta be kidding."

"I'm not kidding."

"I need something stronger. I need a *prescription*."

"The answer is no."

"Why not?"

Because of the nature of your addiction, you say to yourself. This thought is translated as: "Because you'll only be back tomorrow for twice as much."

"No, I won't, Doc. I swear I won't."

"The answer is no."

"Doc. No, wait."

I leave the room and walk back down the hallway. All the time I can hear the echo and reecho, "Doc, please. Please. Please, Doc."

That echo is what addicts always sound like. A constant plea: I need . . . I need . . . I need . . .

Then there are the dealers in prescription drugs, always looking for a way to score something interesting. For them T#3s are small potatoes; codeine really doesn't have much of a high, and acetaminophen toxicity precludes using the drug in high doses at any one time. Still, T#3s do have a street value. After all, they can take the edge off a really bad narcotic withdrawal or blunt that inevitable postcocaine letdown. If a dealer could get a scrip from some ER doctor for, say, fifty pills, he'd gladly take it. No problem.

Then, lastly, there are the doctors who use. After all, what potential addict has such delectable access? The addicted doctor has to be careful, though. That little DEA number that seems the key to paradise may come back to haunt him. It's bad form (also illegal in most states) for a doctor to write a prescription for himself. How to avoid this? Well, one way is to write a prescription for an accomplice and split the outcome (called "splitting scrips," very illegal). Another way is to go into a profession where prescriptions aren't needed and access is no problem. Something like anesthesiology, a job with phenomenal drug temptations (and the highest addiction rate in the business). Anesthesiologists routinely handle drugs of transcendence—nirvana beyond any ordinary user's imagination. And it's relatively easy to hide the use, early on at least. You just mark down two bottles of, say, Sufenta: one for the patient and one for you. The only thing that makes it difficult is the nature of the addiction itself. Always, always, after a while, one vial is not enough.

And so the addiction comes full circle, the doctor is now the addict.

You sigh and put your pen down, not really sure how you got on this train of thought. The prescription is finished: "Tylenol #3, #30, sig: ii po, qid, prn pain." You hand it over to your patient. He smiles. "This should do it," he says. He leaves happy and you remain behind, rubbing your eyes. There is, you think, one more role a physician can assume when writing a prescription, one not obvious at first glance. That is the doctor as enabler, the guy who will write a prescription for pretty much anything the patient wants, even if it is unreasonable. Or even worse: the doctor as drug pusher.

Every city has one: the guy who will prescribe diet pills to anorexics, downers to alcoholics, rainbow-colored pills to patients with chronic fatigue syndrome and Demerol to anyone who doesn't look like an undercover agent for the Feds. He treats "soft diseases," diseases which are hard to quite pin down. Chronic low-back pain, whiplash, fibromyalgia, work-related disabilities of questionable pedigree. A good pill-pushing doctor can jack the patient up on an array of heavy-duty narcotics or stimulants, all the while extracting a small fortune in insurance claims and patient billing. These patients become addicts of the worst sort to treat. They have the perfect excuse to take drugs: my doctor told me to take these.

But you're not an enabler. The idea is horrifying, you think, and as you do you casually flip through this patient's chart. It's now that you realize this is the fourth prescription for T#3s you've given this patient this year. But he's got that arthritis, you think, shaking your head, while at the same time you wonder: "Is he seeing other doctors for the same thing?" That's when you notice you've given him two refills on a sleeping medication you don't remember ever writing for him to begin with.

An innocent prescription, you think. What harm could that do? You shrug as you close the chart. Then you stop. You see a man standing before you, a tall, distinguished-looking man, very Marcus Welby, wearing a white lab coat and a stethoscope draped around his neck. The most despicable doctor who ever lived.

Dr. Daiquiri.

8

DR. DAIQUIRI

I WASN'T ON DUTY THAT DAY. Mary, the unit clerk, told me
the story. It was a Sunday afternoon, a beautiful day outside. The
ER was quiet, at least for everyone in the back. But when Mary
went out to registration, she saw that up front, in the ER waiting room, the place was packed with people sitting, sweating in
the still air. Weird. She went back to her desk in the ER, where
she had a good view through the glass door leading into the triage
office. There she could see Phil, the triage nurse for the afternoon, sagging in his chair, reading a magazine. The whole day
had become so torpid and Sunday-like that you could hear the
flies buzzing in the window, accompanied by the ghosts of old-
fashioned ceiling fans.

Someone came into triage and sat down. Phil busied himself
with taking the vital signs and generating a chart. Mary, bored,
returned to the crossword puzzle before her. After a few minutes
Phil came out of triage carrying his duffel bag back to the nurses'
lounge, apparently to put it in his locker. A few minutes later he
returned. Mary watched him come and go; it was that kind of
day.

A few minutes later another patient came into triage. Mary
was idly watching as the man, a big guy, sat in the triage chair
and offered his arm to Phil. Phil was wrapping the blue blood
pressure cuff around the man's arm when it happened. The thing

we dread most in the ER. The patient went berserk. He stood up, grabbed Phil by the shoulders, stood him up, turned him around, slammed his face up against the wall and held him there with his forearm against Phil's neck.

Mary hit the panic button, a little red knob under her desk that immediately signaled security. "Jesus Christ, no," was all she had time to say. The patient had leaned up against Phil, right arm still trapping him against the wall while his left traveled up and down Phil's back.

Security, actually Larry and Curley ("All they are missing is Moe," Mary once told me), ran into the triage room. As they did, the patient—still leaning against Phil, trapping him against the wall—raised his hand, stiff-armed, holding up something, not a gun; that's all Mary could see. Larry and Curley looked at whatever it was and scrambled out of the room. As they were scrambling to get out, all the men who had been sitting in the waiting room now crowded into the triage area. Some of them had guns.

"Hit the floor," Mary shouted. "We got a situation in triage."

Almost everyone in the ER had lived through a shooting the year before. They knew what to do.

There was a moment of silence or, rather, just the sound of voices coming from triage. No gunfire. After a long pause, Larry opened the door that led back to the ER. "Hey, guys," he said, looking around. He lowered his gaze. "Why are you on the floor?"

Mary raised her head and pointed. "Triage."

Larry pawed the air. "Oh, they're just FBI."

More heads popped up.

"It's a drug bust, guys," Larry said. "It's an arrest."

Mary lumbered up, dusting off her scrubs. "Who the hell are they arresting?"

Larry shrugged as if it should be obvious. "Phil," was all he said.

This is the story: apparently, unbeknownst to all of us, Phil, a nurse for ten years, also had dealt drugs for a living. At some point he figured out that one of the safest times to do a drug drop was when he worked as the triage nurse in the Emergency Department. The dealer/drug delivery man could then come in as just another patient. They would swap identical bags, and the dealer would get his blood pressure checked and drift back out, never making it even to registration: LWBS (left without being seen). Perfect. Just one time, though, this time, some wiseguy must have tipped off the Feds. The waiting room in fact had been filled by undercover agents dressed in jeans and baseball caps, bullet-proof vests under their sweatshirts.

Phil had put a bag filled with $250,000 worth of cocaine in his back locker. Everyone watched as this modest fortune in a duffel bag was hauled out by a federal agent wearing a Cleveland Indians T-shirt.

Mary called the nursing supervisor. "You're going to have to get us some more help down here," she told her. "We've just lost our triage nurse."

"What happened?"

"You really just don't want to know."

Drugs. Drugs in the ER: everything, every variety, every color, shape, chemical state, every degree of licit- or illicitness. All the uppers, downers, laughers, screamers, you could possibly imagine: marijuana, angel dust, crank, cocaine (powder, freebase, crack, rock, crystal). Wet, blunt, acid (orange sunshine, purple blotter, windowpane), black beauties, white bennies. T's and Blues, speed-balls. Strychnine, lidocaine, mannitol and other filler. Then there is the legal stuff: Thunderbird, Everclear, MD 20/20, Sterno, paint propellant, cooking sherry, nitrous oxide (occupational hazard of dentists), Sufenta (occupational hazard of anesthesiologists), methylphenidate (Ritalin) and Robitussin. Rush, Buzz and other carpet cleaners. Rohypnol (date rape drug). Also: Mexican Quaaludes, GHB, youngana (Figian), grappa, Ecstasy, *ma huang*, airplane glue and nail polish remover. White Out, anabolic steroids, "Vitamin K" (ketamine), kif, magic mushrooms, smoking while wearing a nicotine patch.

In the ER we see every imaginable end-stage addict, from the vole-faced punk scarfing the evidence during an arrest to the strung-out hooker who has run out of veins, to the young kid, just seventeen, his creosote hair still slicked back perfectly in place while we frantically try to defibrillate his dead heart; no go, nothing left.

Then there is the other side of the drug problem: addiction. As a doctor I stand in awe of all addiction. We as physicians are schooled in the furthest reaches of human understanding, yet we are so powerless here. Does any other disease have a prognosis so dismal? Response to therapy—what, 17 percent? And the best we can do for therapy now is to invoke the gods.

The doctor whom I am to replace for the afternoon shift is writing out discharge instructions for the patient in room four. On the pink form he prints in big block letters: CUT DOWN ON YOUR DRINKING OR YOU WILL DIE.

My first patient continues the theme. He is an old man, gnarled and bald, stick thin and very drunk. I look at him and think of him as a child of the Great Depression. I know his life; he stays in the fleabag Burnside Hotel, rooms let by the week, sink by the window, toilet down the hall. Television in the lobby. Lives on social security, drinks when he can.

"Wassamatter?" I ask him. He gazes off over my shoulder for a while, then finally says, "Cough." And he does so, producing the moist, musical explosion of a terminal smoker. "And chills," he adds.

"You ever have TB?" I ask him.

"Not me, but my dad did," he tells me. I shudder. This story has been engraved in my heart. What is the differential diagnosis: a sorry soul at the end of the line, a dead-end drunk with terminal bronchitis?

"You gotta quit smoking," I tell him.

"Yeah, doc, I know. But I need something for the cough."

"I can write you for some tablets . . ."

But he has an agenda. "Doc," he says, "what I really need is some cough syrup, some of that codeine stuff."

"I can write you for something better."

"No, Doc. I'd rather just have cough syrup."

I sigh. It's not worth the trouble to say no. And there it is. The doctor as enabler. Is that where this case is going, I wonder, or will it, as always in the ER, be about something else, something completely unexpected?

Eight A.M. Monday morning, one week after Phil was arrested and two days after a pleasant thirty-two-year-old male with a sore throat turned into a psychotic werewolf before my horrified eyes. Please, nothing unexpected today, I grumbled to myself as I picked up the first chart. Chief complaint: "weak and dizzy." I shrugged. If addiction is the *bête noire* of emergency medicine, then its bread and butter is the weak and the dizzy. We see a half dozen, at least, on any busy day. Usually nothing is really wrong. You just slog through a workup, coming away after a few hours and thousands dollars of tests with very little to show for it. That morning as I paged through the patient's chart, noting the vital signs (normal) and her insurance status (Blue Cross) I felt the heavy hand of weariness rest on my shoulder.

Another weak and dizzy.

I leaned into the acute room and glanced at the patient. She was a well-dressed, middle-aged woman. From the distance of the doorway, she looked the part of a respectable citizen with a vague complaint. Blond, pretty, *lots* of makeup. But as I walked up to the bed, I could see that the makeup had been pretty haphazardly applied; lipstick didn't exactly follow the lip line, the mascara was smudged and the eyeliner had wandered shakily. (I was being very careful about makeup around then. The week before, I had treated a perfectly delightful woman of ninety-four for a wrist fracture only to discover *he* was, perhaps, the world's oldest living drag queen.)

Alisa, the charge nurse, was standing beside the woman trying to fill out her chart. "Medication?" she asked the patient.

The patient had a tentative air. "I don't know," she answered, looking around as if she had no idea where she was or how she got here. It took her a moment to focus on my face when I stood beside her and then even longer to register that I was the doctor.

" 'Lo," she slurred to me.

Alisa continued. "Marilyn, do you have any allergies?"

"Let me see," Marilyn said. She gazed off, eyes blank, one hand fumbling with a tissue. "Do I . . . do I . . ." She turned back to Alisa. "Do I what?"

"Have any allergies."

"Oh," she said, lips puckered. She looked down at her hands as if she didn't recognize them as hers. "I don't know . . ." She looked up at me and there was an expression of real fright in her eyes. "I'm sorta . . . I just don't know."

What was the matter with this woman? I asked myself. I moved to swap places with Alisa but was distracted by the patient's handbag on the Mayo stand. It was the kind you see in fashion magazine ads: calfskin, soft as butter and the color of wet sand. A couple of prescription pill bottles had spilled out. I tipped the bag toward me and glanced inside. More pill bottles, a dozen maybe.

"Can I look at these?" I asked.

Marilyn made a feeble gesture of embarrassment. "I can't remember exactly what . . . I'm on. I'm on so many . . ." She trailed off.

I started pulling the bottles out of the bag while Alisa wrote them down.

"Zoloft," I said. An antidepressant. "Ventolin syrup." That's for asthma, but usually given only to children. "Klonopin," a tranquilizer in the same class as Valium. "Tylenol #3," pain medicine; "Vicodin," more pain medication; "Ativan," that's like Klonopin except shorter-acting; "Fluphenazine," a diet pill that probably shouldn't be taken with Prozac; "Halcion," another Valium-like drug; "BuSpar," an antianxiety drug; "Darvocet," more pain medicine; "SOMA," a muscle relaxant; "Tylenol #4"—maybe in case Tylenol #3 wasn't strong enough. And at the very bottom, a large bottle of plain aspirin. Almost empty.

"I took all those . . ." Marilyn said, gesturing toward me.

"All these," I said surveying the mountain of pill bottles.

"No," she said and gestured again. "Well, no, but yes. Those." She pointed at the aspirin bottle.

"How many?" Alisa asked.

Marilyn turned a little, shifting her gaze to Alisa. She looked very surprised to see her there. "I don't know."

I dumped the few remaining aspirin pills out into my hand. "You mean the aspirin? You took all this aspirin?"

Marilyn looked at me blankly. "I don't know," she said. "I think I did last night or maybe this morning but I'm not sure." She gazed at me with an expression of absolute bewilderment. "I think I wanted to kill myself."

"Last night?"

"I think so. No, it was today." She grabbed my arm. "Don't tell my husband."

"Where's your husband?"

"He's at work." She looked away. "He doesn't know."

"About the aspirin?"

Marilyn stared at the wall for a moment and then back at me. "What about the aspirin?"

"She's taken more than just aspirin," Alisa said.

"Ma'am," I said to her, "do you take all these pills?"

She looked at the pile of medicine. "I just take them like I'm 'spose to."

"All of them?" I asked. I knew the answer. I even recognized the name of the doctor who had prescribed them.

My patient nodded, a good girl. "Just like Dr. Daiquiri says."

Dr. Daiquiri. Good old Dr. Daiquiri, AKA Dr. Feelgood, the "Physician with a Prescription," a prescription for any problem you might have. I saw Dr. Daiquiri's patients almost every day.

They were migraine patients or chronic back-pain patients or professional insomniacs. Dr. Daiquiri would send them to the ER for a pain shot when their pain had become so severe that the thousands of pills he prescribed weren't enough. The trouble was that many had been coming in once or twice a week for years. They had received so many intramuscular injections their buttocks had scarred to wood. In between shots they took pills that Dr. Daiquiri would prescribe. Pain pills, diet pills, antianxiety pills. Not to discount cases of very real pain and anxiety, but after so many years of this kind of treatment most of these patients had acquired a new problem to go with their pain. They had become addicts—addicted to prescription drugs. And like any other kind of addict, they had become consumed by their addiction.

So here we were, "weak and dizzy." My patient with her purse full of Dr. Daiquiri pills had turned out to be an overdose. I stood staring at the aspirin bottle. Aspirin overdoses are a bitch to treat. This "harmless" little pill can have deadly effects. Aspirin disrupts the body's acid-base balance; whole organs, kidneys, liver and brain can just shut down forever, depending on the amount ingested. Patients can seize, develop heart arrhythmias; in essence crash and burn at the blink of an eye.

I held up the bottle. "How many of these did you take?"

She tried to focus on the bottle but, after squinting for a moment, gave up and closed her eyes. "Ten or twelve, I think."

I was relieved. This may not be as bad as I thought.

"How long ago did you take them?"

"I think two days ago." She still had her eyes closed. "No, I mean two hours ago . . ."

Great, I thought. That's a lot of help.

An acute ingestion, a suicide attempt. Alisa looked at me and said, "The usual?"

I pursed my lips and nodded. "Honey, we're going to have to put a big tube down your nose and suck those aspirins out."

Pumping someone's stomach, a traditional ER chore. It's usually associated with the "suicide gesture," the "cry for help" that people make when their life goes wrong. Often this can be a very manipulative call for help. ER people look upon these suicide gestures so cynically that nurses frequently threaten to hold classes entitled "Suicide, How to Do It Right."

I stopped myself at the foot of her bed and asked, "What's going on? Why did you do this?"

Marilyn glanced up at me. "I . . ." she stuttered. "I don't know. I don't know anything." She put her face in her hands and started sobbing. "I don't even recognize myself in the mirror."

I was trying to get a blood gas when Alisa put her head in and crooked her finger at me. "Husband's outside," she told me.

"What does he have to say?" I asked.

"Oh, he's not talking to *just a nurse*."

As I walked out to the waiting room, I was mentally shaking my head. An aspirin overdose, strung out on prescription medication, presents as "weak and dizzy." Doesn't it figure? In the ER even the unexpected is unpredictable. I paused at the triage desk wondering who could predict from one minute to the next. You start off thinking you know where you are—I looked around the waiting room for the husband—and you end up . . . well . . . here.

The woman's husband looked just as expensive as she did, only nothing about him looked unstrung. He was pacing, and when he saw me he stepped over and examined me with a critical eye. I winced at what I must look like, a sleep-deprived doctor wearing a once white coat, now splattered with blood and Betadine.

"*It's those pills,*" he said fiercely before I could say a word.

I spread my hands. "Has she ever taken an overdose before?"

"Overdose?" he asked sharply.

"Aspirin. I think. I'm not sure; she's really not making much sense."

"Aspirin," he said in a kind of wonder. "Well, she's taken nearly everything else."

"All prescriptions?"

"Dr. Daiquiri," he said shortly. "She's been seeing him for the last year." He looked away. "She was trying to quit drinking," he said.

I shuddered. A patient and a doctor meant for each other.

"She stopped drinking when she started seeing Dr. Daiquiri— I told her if she didn't, our marriage was finished. *He* put her on all these pills. Things are even worse now than before." The husband looked at me to see if I knew what he meant. "This life is hell," he said shortly. Then, "I would like to see her now." He was not a man to be contradicted.

As we walked back, Alisa, carrying the overdose paraphernalia, stopped me in the hallway and said, "You're not going to believe this . . ."

I grimaced. "What now?"

She pointed with her chin. "Trauma room," she said, "a live one."

In the trauma room Benny and his partner, two city paramedics, were transferring a disheveled-looking young guy in a wet jogging suit from the paramedics' gurney to an ER cart.

"Someone called the police," Benny told us. "He was down in the middle of the road when we found him." Benny cocked his head meaningfully. "He was taking the *occasional* breath; really, really whacked out. We got an IV in him and gave him some Narcan, and"—Benny raised his hands in benediction—"it was a miracle."

Narcan, a drug that reverses the effects of narcotics, works almost instantaneously. An overdose patient can go from no respiration, no breathing at all, to fully alert and awake (and generally pissed off) in less than thirty seconds.

The question here was, what kind of narcotic?

"Track marks?" I asked Benny.

The patient seemed to perk up a bit. He looked around at me and said, "I don't shoot drugs." Speech still slurred, I noted.

"No, no. We know that, tiger," Benny said. He handed me a plastic bag that contained some bottles, prescription bottles. Several. I pulled one out and started laughing. Pathetic, pathetic.

It was a bottle of vicodin. Dispensed: a hundred pills. Doctor: Dr. Daiquiri. Date dispensed: today.

The bottle was empty.

Two Dr. Daiquiri patients in one day, I thought sourly as I stomped back down the hall. And one an aspirin overdose no less. Back in the acute room my overdose lady was lying there in all the glory of an ER washout. She had an enormous lavacuator tube sprouting from her nose and there was charcoal everywhere. Charcoal is given as a sort of generic absorbant: it will bind many toxins and cause them to pass out of the gut harmlessly. It is also black and syrupy and it gets all over everything. Marilyn had already vomited some back up, not unusual for the stuff. It was all down the front of her hospital gown, matted in her hair, on the sheets, on the floor. Beside her sat her immaculate-looking husband. He was leaning back, arms folded, just staring at his wife as if he didn't recognize her, which, considering how she looked, was probably not a bad thing.

I thought she was asleep, but she opened her eyes when I walked up to the bed.

"What's the matter with me?" she asked.

"You take too many pills," I told her.

"But my doctor prescribes them."

"I know," I said. "It doesn't matter."

She started crying, great tears tinted gray with mascara. "I tried to hurt myself," she said sobbing, shoulders shaking. "But I don't want to die. It's not that. It's just that I don't want to be alive."

"Have you thought about a drug treatment program?" I asked her gently.

She looked up at me, too shocked to keep crying. "What do you mean? What are you saying?" she sputtered. "I'm not some kind of," she spit it out, "*drug addict.*"

The husband signaled me for another talk outside the room. He stood in the hallway, arms folded, glaring angrily toward the nurses' station. "All she does anymore is take those pills. I've tried to get her to see a real doctor, a psychiatrist, anybody, but that *quack* has her strung out on so many pills she doesn't have any idea what's she's doing. She lives for those damn pills." He took a deep breath and then asked the obvious. "Why don't they prosecute that man?"

I shook my head. Dr. Daiquiri was one very smart guy. He knew what he could prescribe and how to do it so that he stayed on this side of the law. And he knew how to defend himself. He had threatened several doctors with legal action after they complained to the hospital administrators that he was prescribing too many narcotics. He was very slick.

But I was sure that there was more to this story than just Dr. Daiquiri.

"And you?" I said, looking at him.

He looked away. "I'm moving out," he said. "I want a divorce." He cleared his throat. "That's why she's doing this." He looked back down at me, frowning deeply. "I can't take this life. I can't take all the pills. She can let them ruin *her* life, but I'm not going to let them ruin mine."

I could see his wife from where we were standing. She was gazing off into the distance, one hand on her chest, clutching at her hospital gown. The hand was twitching, trembling, and then it scraped, claw-like across her chest. Her head was bent back and the twitching extended up her arms and shoulders. It took another heartbeat before I realized what was happening. "She's seizing," I shouted.

I rushed to the head of the bed. My first thought was: Good God, what's next? I looked down at her face and as I did I saw the charcoal bubbling from her mouth. *She's aspirating,* I told myself in horror. She was vomiting up some of the charcoal with the seizure. Now she would breathe it down her trachea, into her lungs. She probably was doing so right now. This was a disaster, perhaps a deadly disaster.

She's aspirated, you fool, I shouted to myself. *Why didn't you see this was coming?* One half of me stood there frozen, hands to my face, horrified. The other half, though, the professional half, smoothly took over. I hit the intercom button. *"I need some help in here and call Respiratory."* Then I broke the plastic lock off the intubation cabinet and grabbed at the equipment there. The laryngoscope came first, a flat metal blade with a light attached to a large handle, and an endotracheal tube—ET tube—which goes down through the larynx into the trachea, so that we can breathe for the patient. You don't always need to intubate seizure patients; it's rare for a seizure to last long enough to cause a significant lack of oxygen. But this woman had a gut full of charcoal. She was only going to aspirate and aspirate more. I had to protect her airway, protect her lungs from more charcoal.

On the outside, my professional half smoothly assembled the intubation equipment. The horrified half hadn't disappeared, though. Inside I was seething, arguing back and forth with myself.

If I had known she was going to aspirate, I should have intubated her before I gave her the charcoal.

Still, how many overdose patients had I seen who were as compromised as Marilyn but had never seized?

Hundreds.

Charcoal-stained mucus bubbled up through Marilyn's nose. "Set up suction," I told the respiratory therapist who had just arrived. The room was beginning to fill with people.

I tried to open the patient's mouth but couldn't. The seizure had clamped it shut tight. We needed to stop the seizure before I could even try to intubate her.

"We need Valium over here," I told Alisa. The respiratory therapist got the Ambu bag ready and was fumbling with the suction. Pam, the other nurse, put the pulse oximeter on the patient's finger. This measures the amount of oxygen in the blood: 96–100 percent is normal. Anything below 90 is not good, below 80 is very bad. Marilyn's reading was 90 percent.

Alisa was back with a syringe and some Valium. She drew up 5 mg, injected it and flushed the line. We all stood watching.

Nothing. Arms and legs jerking. Jaw clamped tight. Marilyn was still seizing. Charcoal still bubbled through her nose.

Her pulse oxymetry reading: 87 percent.

"More Valium," I told Alisa, who drew up the other 5 mg from the vial.

She injected it. We all stared down at the patient. She had stopped being Marilyn. She was now the enemy: the patient gone bad.

Nothing. Still seizing. Jaw clamped shut.

85 percent.

"What now?" Alisa asked. Clearly Valium was not going to stop the seizure.

84 percent. 83 percent.

I had a choice. I could try to go through the nose with the tube, pass it down into the larynx blindly and see if I could get the tube into the trachea (not easy). Or I could paralyze her, and when she stopped seizing do the somewhat easier standard intubation.

Which one? Either or. Decide now.

83 percent. 82.

"Get the sux," I told Alisa. "Sux" is short for succinylcholine, a drug that blocks all muscular activity. It produces total paralysis, making it easier to intubate, that is, get the tube down into the trachea. However, if I couldn't get her intubated, she wouldn't be able to breathe on her own. I would be stuck, or rather Marilyn would be stuck. Paralyzed, without an airway, about to die.

82 percent . . . 82 and holding.

When you run a code, everyone moves as if they are running through water. Time dilates and what only takes a minute seems like hours. All that time. Alisa finally returned bearing the bottle of sux aloft.

"A hundred milligrams," I told her. The problem with sux is that it causes the stomach muscles to contract. More aspiration. There were ways to prevent this, but they all took time.

81 . . . 80.

The patient was still seizing, head thrown back, face contorted, arms jerking. Charcoal was everywhere.

Sux in. Pulse ox 80 percent, an oxygen level low enough to cause brain damage.

80 percent and holding.

Slowly, slowly, slowly, the jerking became more pronounced but less frequent. Finally, after one last spasm, Marilyn lay still.

Her jaw moved easily in my hand.

Now I had to get the tube through the larynx, past the voice box and through to the trachea. To do this, I used the blade of the laryngoscope to lift the tongue and part of the voice box out of the way to see the narrow tube, the trachea, and, within it, the twin shutters of the vocal cords.

"I need suction," I said. The respiratory therapist handed me the Yankhauer. I tried to vacuum up the charcoal as best I could, but even so, as I pulled the tongue out of the way with the laryngoscope, I still couldn't see the larynx. I readjusted the blade. Nothing. No vocal cords. The only thing to do was to poke the ET tube in the general direction of the larynx, and hope for the best. I did this. Again. Nothing. The ET tube was hanging up somewhere. I couldn't get it in.

76 . . . 75.

I threw the tube on the floor. "Get me a smaller one," I shouted.

Somebody scrambled for one. We bagged the patient as best we could, but the pulse ox stayed at 75 percent. She was not going to last long here.

I looked again. More charcoal. Please, dear God, I prayed. Just this once. (I know I always say, Just this once.) Someone handed me a narrower tube. I flexed it, inserted the long wire stylet and bent over once again to pass the tube into the dim, charcoal-coated reaches of Marilyn's pharynx.

"You in?" Alisa asked breathlessly as I straightened up.

"I don't know." I pulled out the stylet and attached the Ambu bag. The respiratory therapist gave her a breath. Her stomach rose and fell, not her chest. I was in the esophagus. No good. I pulled the tube out. "No," I said.

I looked down her throat again with the laryngoscope. I could see only the tip of the epiglottis—the sentinel of the larynx. I made another pass, roughly where I had passed it before.

Once again I pulled out the stylet. We reattached the Ambu bag. One breath, two. The chest rose and fell this time, a good sign. I managed to find my stethoscope to listen for breath sounds as the respiratory therapist bagged madly.

Breath sounds. Good breath sounds. We were in.

As I straightened up, I realized that my back was killing me. I clasped my hands together; they were trembling.

We all looked down at the patient, at Marilyn. The respiratory therapist was in the process of wrapping tape around the endotracheal tube to hold it in place. What next? I thought wearily, looking around the room. What fresh disaster awaited me now?

Marilyn's fate was sealed anyway. Destination: ICU. Diagnosis: overdose, seizure, aspiration. I called the medicine service down. Two internal medicine residents arrived, glanced at the patient and then huddled for twenty minutes with the lab reports. Great, I thought, they get to take hours to go over a decision I had to make in seconds.

The senior resident came over to me.

"You know," he said, trying to look casual, "you probably should have intubated her before you gave her the charcoal."

"I know that *now*," I said. "But there was no way to predict when she came in that she was going to seize. I can't intubate every overdose I see. Most aspirin overdoses do okay." *You idiot*, I thought.

The resident shrugged and gave me a look that said, *if he* had been here . . .

I turned my back on him, wondering. Should I have known? Did I miss some clue, something somebody else would have easily seen? I wasn't sure, and the uncertainty made me feel sick inside.

An hour later Marilyn finally went up to the ICU. Afterward I stood in the empty room for a moment bathing in a transient sense of relief. She was now someone else's problem. I looked around the acute room. It was a disaster. Charcoal everywhere, blood on the floor, ET tubes, plastic stuffing, packaging material scattered all over, a garbage bin turned on its side. I stooped down, uprighted the garbage bin and began stuffing trash into it. I didn't think I could handle a task more complicated.

I could hear the recrimination already: the Monday morning quarterbacks, doctors whose specialty is second-guessing any decision involving a patient that goes sour. It's an occupational hazard of the emergency room doctor. This case was particularly bad. After all, I had been one of the doctors who complained about Dr. Daiquiri's prescribing habits. He had already complained to the ER director about me. He was gunning for me in a major way, and I had just handed him a whole boxload of bullets.

But nobody ever said a word to me. Perhaps it was the nature of the case, or that long list of medications on the face sheet of the chart. Other ER shifts intervened and I went on to fresh disasters. Marilyn's and my brief therapeutic relationship was over— or so I thought.

Not quite. My life touched Marilyn one more time and that, surprisingly enough, was in the Medical Records Department. Well, perhaps not so surprisingly. The ghosts that haunt doctors are all housed in medical records. They haunt us because every day minions from Medical Records comb through these charts looking for "incompletes." Signatures not entered, procure notes absent, discharge summaries never dictated. All these missing pieces are tagged for doctors to complete, to sign or dictate—which, of course, the doctor never wants to do because the only thing more boring than signing charts is dictating them. Some doctors will be in arrears with over a hundred charts at any one time. You find scores of them in the Medical Records Department, a heart-stopping pile of records in front of them. They are only there signing charts now because the hospital has suspended their admitting privileges.

It's as if some kind of giant medical mom has told her kids they are grounded.

One night, though, I sat alone in the department. I was working my way through a stack of charts when I found myself opening Marilyn's. It had been six months since everything happened, and I had entirely forgotten her. Now, though, I felt that old rush of nausea. *The charcoal, the charcoal*, I thought again. *Should I have known she was going to aspirate?* Then the nausea subsided and I grew curious about what had happened to her. I started paging slowly through the chart.

She arrived in the ICU and immediately went into ARDS—adult respiratory distress syndrome, a toxic reaction involving the lungs. Then she became septic—bigtime septic—the medicine service thought so, anyway. She was started on three different antibiotics but kept spiking fevers through them. Nobody knew why. Then one of the antibiotics damaged her kidneys so much they almost completely shut down. She was on renal dialysis for weeks.

It occurred to me, as I paged through this chart, that Marilyn had come perilously close to getting what she wanted. She didn't want to die, she had told us, but she didn't want to be alive either.

At last things evened out. Her kidney function returned. Her lungs cleared up. The team transferred her out of the ICU to the floor six weeks after she was admitted. There was another setback, though, a small stroke. She ended up in the hospital rehabilitation unit and had been discharged only a few days ago. Hence her chart was here for my signature.

The weird thing, though, was that after my initial ER dictation, nowhere in the chart did anyone say anything about Marilyn's drug problem. The suicide attempt was taken care of by having a psychiatrist visit her once for twenty minutes. His consult note said she was no longer suicidal; she was depressed secondary to problems in her marriage and would benefit from marital counseling. Nothing about all the drugs. Nothing about the massive amount of painkillers and sedatives Marilyn required during her stay. The doctors had saved Marilyn's lungs, her kidneys, her guts and her brain, but they ignored her addiction, the problem that had brought her here to begin with.

The last progress note in the chart stated that Marilyn was now off dialysis, tolerating an advanced diet and able to ambulate without assistance. Vital signs stable.

Patient discharged in good condition. Referred back to her primary doctor.

Patient to follow up with: Dr. Daiquiri.

9
_____

How to Burn Out

YOU NEVER KNOW you're burned out. When the stress of the job starts destroying mental software, the capacity for personal insight is the first to go. At the onset of *your* great burnout season, the scorched-earth years of *your* life, the only thing you really notice is that just about anything that happens gets on your nerves. The other symptoms: the hair-trigger temper and ferocious mood swings, the trembling hands and the uninterrupted string of hangovers; none of that really registers. You just go on as you always have, pushing through too many shifts, too many patients, too many sleepless nights and harrowing days. Meanwhile, your marriage goes to pot, your kids get screwed up and that nagging back pain gets so bad you start prescribing yourself painkillers for it. A few T#3s can take the edge off any bad day. Face it, though, how can you complain? What are your little tragedies compared to the carnage of bad luck you see at work every day?

Finally, though, one day, you see that you are falling, falling— but you have no idea why. Even now, after you have moved to a sleepier life, there are still moments when, say, some particular song comes on the radio. Or a smell, or the distant sound of an ambulance siren, lonesome as a train whistle. Then, suddenly, there you are again: *Icarus*.

Why should this ever come as a surprise? On the first day of your internship, the surgeon who ran the Trauma Department told you and your fellow interns that by the time you all finished your residency, "The divorce rate in your class will be a hundred and fifty percent. That's because some of you will get divorced, remarry and get divorced again." The surgeon was proud of that. And from that first day on, you went to work in terra incognita. A land unlike any place you had ever seen.

During the worst years it was like getting up in the morning and going into war. Things happened in that small clutch of examining rooms that no one else had ever seen. And if you tried to talk about it, to your spouse or your few friends who did not work in ER, you would get the fisheye—a look of suspicion and disbelief. They didn't really want to know; they certainly didn't want to believe and you couldn't blame them. Even if they were interested, they didn't have the right mind-set to understand what all of you working in the pit relearned every shift. The dead end of rage, the sordid stupidity of drunks and addicts; the awesome destructive power of bad luck. Everyone in that other world, the "real" world, lived in a cocoon of safety. You didn't want to be the one to tell them how much of an illusion that cocoon is.

Only cops seem to know these things. There is a secret fraternal order of people on the front lines. Members include the ambulance drivers who scrape up pedestrian victims smeared across a roadway by hit-and-run drivers; orderlies who wheel the dead bodies down to the morgue late at night; strung-out, exhausted nurses; the even more strung-out ER doctors on the tenth shift in a row. Only insiders could take for granted the casual lunacy of, for example, the patient you saw last night. He was a seventeen-year-old kid—acutely, horribly psychotic—but no drugs, no alcohol—just out there on his own personal pathway to destruction. The police took him into custody after he had set the garage on fire and then tried to stab his little sister. This loopy kid was brought to your Bedlam and, amidst all the other chaos, everyone had to stop what they were doing to get him tied down. As you did, the kid fought back like mad, and all the while he *barked*— barked like a dog. Not just random barking, either. He was barking, of all things, "*Frère Jacques*." Bark, bark, *bark*, bark, bark, bark, *bark*, bark. Nothing would shut him up. You tried sedating him, then you stuck him in a side room with the lights turned out. Nothing worked. He just kept barking, barking, barking, until, finally, the boys from the state psychiatric institute arrived to cart him away. By then you were ready to go with them.

Or that case last month when a sixteen-year-old driver struck another car that was driven by a woman who was eight months pregnant. It was just a fender bender, neither of them more than just shaken up. When the police arrived a few minutes later, the kid told them, "It was my fault, *my fault*." Ambulance 19 brought the woman into your ER, where you watched her for a couple of hours and then released her. The kid refused ambulance transport, went home, shot himself in the head and came in, just as the woman was leaving, as a traumatic arrest. He had left a suicide note that you found pinned with a safety pin to his plaid flannel shirt. The note read in its entirety: "Brain dead."

There was the thirty-four-year-old mother of three whose mild right-hand weakness on admission evolved into a massive stroke that left her completely paralyzed, but—and this was the saddest part—still alive. You were in the grieving room for what seemed like years that day, sitting across from the husband, watching him sob helplessly, while next to him the three kids, the oldest only eight, watched him and cried as well, although they didn't know why . . .

There was the beaten baby, dying as you tried desperately to get an IV in somewhere, anywhere . . .

And there was that mother of a gunshot victim, a kid shot by the police in a drug raid. You went out to talk to her, and she stood there in the middle of the ER waiting room, screaming right up in your face that she would kill you, you motherfucker, she'd kill you if anything happened to her son. And you were *pissed*. . . . "For Christ's sake," you screamed back at her, "why are you yelling at *me*? *I* didn't shoot him. I'm just trying to save his fucking life. . . . "

Then comes the day of the industrial accident, the day you almost get killed.

It started at a freeway overpass, a city construction project that city hall is trying to get done on off hours so the traffic doesn't get backed up. One of the crew, who is up on a ladder, leaned out too far trying to disentangle a piece of rebar and fell twenty feet onto a cement truck. He came in a total train wreck. It took an hour just to sort all the injuries out. Bilateral ankle fractures, a femur fracture, a pelvic fracture, a distended, tender abdomen and a depressed skull fracture. Your job now is to try to patch this guy back together enough so that the surgeons can take him to the OR. It is a routine couple of hours of adrenaline-fueled chaos. Fluids, intubation, x-rays, calls to the orthopedic surgeon, the thoracic surgeon and the neurosurgeon. You are working frantically—running back and forth from the patient to the CT scanner, to the x-ray view box, and then back to the patient—when at one point your way is blocked by a patient in a wheelchair, one leg rest hoisted up, who has wheeled himself out into the hallway. He grabs at your coat as you pass. "When am I going to be seen?" he growls.

You take him in with a glance: sport coat, tie, leather briefcase at his side, clearly an entitled asshole with an ankle sprain.

"Sir," you say, "we had a bad trauma case. We're all tied up with that. I'll see you as soon as I can."

"I have been *waiting* for over an *hour*."

You are not in the mood to humor idiots today. "You're going to be waiting a little longer. I've got a sick guy in here and he comes first."

"Well, get me another doctor."

"I'm the only ER doctor here," you say grimly and stomp back to your critical patient, muttering darkly to yourself. By now the orthopedic surgeon has arrived. He stands tsk-tsking over the x-ray images at the view box. You pause behind him and both of you stand there marveling at how badly bones can break. "Humpty-Dumpty," is all the orthopod says.

The neurosurgeon shows up shortly after. He is in a pissy mood. You are not sure why; after all, this is the first patient with insurance you've had him see all summer. But the neurosurgeon barely looks at the patient; he just stands mooning over the CT-scan images. Apparently he sees a small subdural hematoma, a crescent of blood clot located just under the skull fracture. You missed it when you hastily reviewed the scans.

The neurosurgeon is livid. "If I'd known *this* . . ." he tells you pointedly, jabbing the scans with a finger that looks too wide and stubby to belong to someone whose job it is to tinker within the brain. You stand scratching your head; you can't think how it will change the management all that much. The patient needs to go to the OR and have the depressed skull fracture fragments lifted back into a seminormal position. So the neurosurgeon has to vacuum out a little blood clot as well? What's the big deal?

"Why didn't you tell me this guy was a total fucking disaster?" the neurosurgeon whines on. You shrug. You thought you made that pretty clear. "And what about his heart? If I'm going to take this guy to the OR, I would like to know more about his cardiac status. Did anyone even *think* of calling in cardiology?"

You pedal back across the hallway to ask Mary to page the cardiologist on call. By this time, also by the desk, the man with the ankle sprain is standing squarely on both feet, yelling at Mary, "*I need a doctor now.*" Then, when he sees you, he shouts out, "I can't walk!" You hadn't noticed he was crazy before, but now you see that the suit coat is shabby polyester, several sizes too large, and that the tie is a weird bloody-maroon color that no businessman would wear.

"Well, you are doing a great job of standing," you tell him irritably as you pass by. Beyond him, a police officer leans up against the desk beside a hunched-over man in handcuffs. Even from behind you can see, by the way he has his head ducked down, that the man in handcuffs is sick.

"What's going on?" you ask the cop. You know this cop. Mike

something. Everyone calls him Mikey. You treated him for an ear infection the week before.

"Heroin withdrawal," Mikey tells you.

The man turns toward you. His face is that putty color you usually see only on the freshly dead.

You had forgotten that this is Sunday, heroin withdrawal day. It's a police thing. They like to bust heroin addicts late Friday afternoon, just after the courts close. Then an addict can't get bonded out until Monday morning, when the courts and the bail bondsmen open back up for business. An addict will be stuck in jail with no hope for dope all weekend. Friday night, Saturday morning, noon and night. Withdrawal time. By Sunday at noon— after thirty-six hours off the stuff—a hardened career criminal who wouldn't tell a cop the time of day if he thought the cop wanted to know, was now clinging to the officer's leg, ratting out his own grandmother, anybody, everybody, just to get out and get another fix. That's when the cops would start asking serious questions.

So this was just another Sunday morning heroin withdrawal patient.

You pat Mikey's back. "You should be in church," you say.

"Mea culpa," Mikey responds. You pause for an instant to glance at the patient.

Usually you have a less than compelling clinical interest in these patients, but today there is something that touches you about this man. It's always hard to guess an addict's age, but he looks over fifty—an old man for a smackhead. A survivor. But survivor or no, you can tell he is at the end of the line. You pause beside him for a moment, wondering how often lately you've felt exactly that way—the way he looks now, the sorry bastard—and, as you think this, you feel a weird sideways beat of your heart accompanied by a murmur of melancholy. Well, you think, at least you can do something for this burned-out dude, since there seems to be nothing you can do for yourself . . .

It isn't that it happens so fast that you almost don't see it, it's that it happens so *casually*, almost as if the man with the ankle sprain is reaching into his own pocket instead of over to the officer's holster, where he fumbles for a moment before coming up with a gun, the officer's gun. The other hand pats at the maroon tie as the man steps back out of Mikey's reach. With the gun wobbling in front of him, the man begins looking beyond the heroin addict next to him and then beyond Mikey. He lifts the gun, which seems to wobble drunkenly in your direction. It takes a moment for you to understand he is trying to aim that gun at you.

You stand there, frozen. Someone else shouts, although it seems to come from your throat, "Look out! A gun!" That's when the ankle-sprain patient, trying to control the trembling gun, lifts his arm, still aiming right at you. There is a hollow noise, like fake gunfire on late-night TV. *Move*, you scream to yourself, and finally you unfreeze and go down to the floor, rolling around to the other side of the desk.

There is shouting from everywhere and echoes of the gunshot that recede immediately. All sound suddenly vanishes, evaporates. Then the patient screams, "*I—want—my—x-ray—now!*"

You huddle against a file cabinet, not sure if you have been shot. There is blood on your hand and you wipe it on your shirt, wondering if this means you are going to die soon. Then it seems as if a moment dilates, doubles and triples, because you find the time, really no more than a single soft heartbeat, to think, No, no, no. I'm alive. It's okay. I can't be hurt, I can't die, I'm immortal. Then with another heartbeat you wonder how many people go down, all the way down to their death, with that thought in their mind.

Then you think: Mikey! Did *he* actually get shot? Was the gun really pointed at him and not at you? Where is he? And just as you think this, you realize that Mikey is right beside you, down on his knees looking away from you. That's also when you realize that you can't see where the man with the ankle sprain is. He looked straight at you as he shot. Now you know he is searching for you. As you sit there, back against the file drawers, you realize that the patient with the gun is going to come around the corner any second and here you are, the sitting duck.

You turn to get on your hands and knees, then you creep to the edge of the desk and peer around. On the other side of the hallway, behind the crash cart, two of the nurses, Nancy and Jesse, lie, heads flat on the ground. Are they shot? Are they dead? Beyond them, issuing from the acute room, is the only sound—the magnified electronic bleat of the monitor pacing off the heartbeats of the industrial-accident patient.

Just as you recognize that sound, you hear another, a crack, which you realize is not the sound of another shot but the sound, resonating through the suddenly noiseless ER, of someone out in the triage area stepping onto the rubber floor mat to trigger the electronic door to open. Didn't they hear the gunfire? you wonder. What idiot was trying to get *in* here when everyone else is desperate to get *out*?

The door swings slowly open with a buzz you had always heard but never really noticed. You know that when the door opens all the way, whoever is standing there will be completely exposed to the patient with the gun. You also know that if you shout something, try to distract that patient, whoever is at the doorway might have a chance to get away. But then the patient would be doubly sure where you are. The small shout that you muster dies in your throat. You can only put your hand out, and as you do, you see the door swing wide open. A woman in a blue suit, no—a police officer—a woman police officer, Mikey's partner, is now standing in the open doorway. She must have been out in the waiting room. She has her hands up, clasped before her, pointing a gun into the room. There are three sharp booms. Glass breaks; then there is a loud cascade of thumps as something weighty strikes the desk, tumbles and then hits the floor.

The officer lets the gun drop a few inches and then fires again, twice more. Then she stands there in the doorway, the gun still pointing out in front of her into the ER. You stay frozen, too, a hand to your heart.

A shadow forms behind the officer. It is Mary Ellen, the triage nurse of the day.

"It's okay," she tells the officer. "It's okay now, it's okay." She put a hand out and brings the woman's arm down. The only other sound is the echo and reecho of the gunfire in your ears.

You and Nancy are the first ones up, both of you scrambling out to the front of the desk. The ankle-sprain patient lies crumpled, face forward, on the linoleum tile. He has one arm flung out; the gun is just beyond his fingertips. You go for the gun first, and as you heft it, you realize it is just as dangerous in your hands as in the patient's; the weight alone feels lethal. Beside you, Nancy has put her hands down around the patient's neck, an intimate gesture, as if she was gently choking him. Then you realize she is checking for a pulse. You look up at her.

She shakes her head. "I'm not getting anything."

"Get a gurney," you tell Mary Ellen.

It is more of a brawl than a resuscitation. By the time you get him up on the gurney, the guy is cyanotic, purple-hued and gasping like a fish. His shirt blooms with red blood, exactly the color of his tie. You tear open his shirt and find a bullet hole on the right side of his chest between the sixth and seventh ribs. You grope around and find the exit wound just under the armpit. Through and through; nailed him in the lung.

"Get a chest tube set up," you yell at Jesse.

You could be a Keystone Kop. Every piece of equipment slips out of your hands; you can't find the landmarks; your hands shake as you heft the scalpel. But you get the chest tube in and when you do, the blood pours like a mighty tidal wave from that sucker's chest. Miracle: you get a pulse back and then a blood pressure. You've saved his life, for the moment anyway.

The bullet must have hit a major blood vessel in the lung, though, because blood just keeps pouring out of the chest tube, almost as fast as you pour type O blood in. This patient's pressures hang in the 80s, systolic. He's confused and combative, fighting off everything and everyone while you frantically try to find a surgeon willing to come in and take him to the OR. The thoracic surgeon on call is still up with the industrial medicine patient—removing his spleen, it turns out, and every other surgeon on staff is either in the OR or otherwise conveniently unavailable. Nobody wants this guy. Who can blame them? You are asking a surgeon to cancel an afternoon of paying patients in order to take some madman to the OR. One of the surgeons tells you bluntly: "It's not *my* problem. I'm not on call." Meanwhile, back in the trauma room, security is strapping the patient down while Donna shouts, "Sir, could you lie there and be quiet so we can save your fucking life?"

Finally Dr. Love, who wears his cowboy boots even into the OR, cancels the rest of his appointments for the day and waltzes in, a hero of the first water.

The only other injury in the whole disaster is to you. You aren't sure when it happened, but you now sport a bloody streak on the left side of your neck. Either you brushed against something sharp or a bullet brushed against you. You retreat into the bathroom to check it out and find the police officer on her knees on the floor, vomiting into the toilet bowl.

"I'm all right, I'm all right," she keeps saying, trying to wave you away.

By now the place is acrawl with cops and plainclothes detectives. Everyone wants statements, but all you can remember is a trembling gun pointed like a nightmare right in your direction. His gun, her gun. You can't be sure.

You and Donna, the charge nurse, sit for hours working on the incident report, the standard method of reporting any hospital problem. Donna's bitching; the cops are all bitching as well. "I'm going to be filing reports for the next fifty years," the district officer tells you bitterly. This is what terror devolves to: paperwork.

Then it's over. And yet it's never over. Your hands shake on the drive home, but after a stiff drink, you fall into a sleep that is deeper than any you have had in years. You have this dream that you still have every once in a while. This first time you have it, it doesn't even feel like a nightmare. You wake up fine—at least that's what you tell everyone. "Not to worry." And everyone seems to believe you, though they probably don't believe you as much as you believe yourself. This job can't get to me, you think, not me.

The truth is, though, that it already has.

Six months later comes the day you blow up, the day of the great temper tantrum. In one way what happens has nothing to do with the day the man with the sprained ankle tried to kill you. In another the two events seem ineluctably welded together. A line connects one day to the other, a line that points straight down.

It is another busy Sunday, so busy you can't possibly keep up. Patients are pouring in—no one sick—just the walking wounded. But there are so many . . . And nothing is going right. The labs are taking forever; the x-ray tech disappears and is finally found sleeping in the break room. Because of two call-offs, you are two nurses short; three if you count the fact that you are working with Louis, the world's most incompetent ER nurse. The first patient of the day is a full arrest, an elderly woman with multiple medical problems. Her death shouldn't have come as a surprise. But the family goes bananas, screaming, wailing, carrying on out in the waiting room. "It's your fault she's dead," her daughter screams at you. "I'm going to sue this hospital for everything it's got." Then the blood gas machine breaks down. And through it all you keep getting ambulance call after ambulance call. "This is seventeen, we're coming to you with a forty-four-year-old woman with a headache. . . . This is twenty-four . . . ninety-year-old female, first-time seizure . . . nursing home patient . . . DNR. . . . Ambulance eight . . . John Doe found down . . . bystanders were doing CPR but it looks like this guy is just dead drunk."

You stand for a moment and watch the paramedics unload a

drunk old man who looks like he doesn't have many binges left in him. Maybe, you think idly, maybe you can develop a yardstick to measure that sorry-assed, end-of-the-line look, that look of loneliness and late-night sorrow. If you could, you would have a new vital sign, a clinical tool that could tell you how close someone was to life's dead end. You could use it on all heroin addicts, on the would-be suicides and burned-out cocaine addicts, the hookers, the police officers, the late-night truckers, the other night dwellers. Above all you could use it on yourself.

About one o'clock you pick up a new patient's chart. It's a woman whose boyfriend has "the drip." That means another pelvic exam, and you have already done three today. You wade back to the "pelvic" room and find a sullen woman with an even more sullen boyfriend crouched in the corner. "You have to leave," you tell the boyfriend, who rolls his eyes and takes his time ambling out the door. He is wearing a T-shirt that reads NUMBER ONE COP KILLER on the back along with a splash of fake red blood.

You already know how cops get there: that point where everyone, even the innocent, seems to bristle with provocation. You've known about that place theoretically, but you've never been there yourself. Not until today. The fact is, you want to tear that shirt off the guy's back and cram it down his throat.

You look over at the woman, who weighs in somewhere around three hundred pounds. You dread the parting of her massive thighs, and of all those future thighs waiting for you. You grumble a few questions at her and then get ready to do the pelvic exam. That's when you discover that there is . . . no stool.

You always use a certain stool during pelvic exams. There is only one in the ER like it; it has wheels on it. You had sat on it all morning, but now—and you look all over the room for it— it's gone.

You stalk out of the room into the hallway. There Carol, the charge nurse for the day, is stocking the IV cart.

"Where's my stool?" you shout at her.

"What stool?" she says, not even looking up.

"My *pelvic* stool."

"Your *pelvic* stool?"

"Yes," you shout and something in the tenor in your voice finally makes her look up. "For *pelvic exams*, for Christ's sake. What do you think?"

Carol points. "Why don't you use the chair?"

You cannot believe how stupid she is. "That chair has no *wheels*." You look around, irritated beyond belief. "*I need my stool*."

Carol stands there a moment, hands on her hips. She just looks at you. "*Doctor*," she says finally, "get a *grip*."

Carol, whom you have known for a million years, has just called you *Doctor*, a clear early-warning sign that you are being inappropriate. But you can't see that, of course. All you see is a hallway lit with white, hot light, no shadows anywhere, just the brilliant fire of your anger. You turn and storm into the nurses' station. You kick a chair violently out of your way and announce to your startled co-workers, "Goddamn it, I'm not going to do one more pelvic exam until somebody finds my goddamn stool."

Nobody says anything. The room is silent, so you go on.

"*This is ridiculous. I shouldn't have to put up with this.*" As you say this, actually shout this, you dimly realize you are gasping for breath. At this point you lift the clipboard you hold in your hand and fling it across the room, where it strikes the wall. When it hits, you hear again that sonic boom of gunfire and you start shaking, just like on the day six months ago when that man pointed a gun at you. In retrospect you realize that things can really happen that way: you get shot at one day and six months later, out of seeming nowhere, you realize that you, too, are as mortal as any of your patients.

After that, it's all over. Everything that happens after this, none of it good, you could have seen reflected in the eyes of the people in the nurses' station that day. All of them knew that—nothing personal—you were losing it. They knew you couldn't take it anymore. They had from where they were sitting a perfect view of your future, the steady road downhill. The only one who couldn't see it at all was you.

You still have that recurrent dream, the one you had the night that patient went wild. There really isn't any action in it; it's mostly a feeling, this terrible feeling of foreboding and of darkness. With the feeling is the image of an old man, *that* old man, the heroin addict who stood next to the cop that morning. He is just standing there, looking at you. He has one hand raised up toward you. . . .

That's basically it, that's the dream. . . . The hand is raised before you, palm flat, as if motioning you to stop. There is actually a visual paradox in this dream; you know that the hand is dead and rotted away, but you can see it is also intact in front of you. Associated with this somehow is something about a room that's all white, and sometimes in the background of the dream there is someone singing a few bars of music. It sounds like the chorus of a pop tune with a single phrase sung again and again. The phrase is "Get over it." When you hear this, you awake to the sound of sobbing. It always takes a minute, maybe more, before you realize that the person who is sobbing is you.

10

MURRAY

IT HAPPENED SO LONG AGO, I have only a skeleton memory of the story. (I was a young doctor when it happened and was still transfixed by trauma's drama.) To be told, the story has to pick up bits and pieces from other, more recent catastrophes, ones that happened yesterday, for instance. I've had to people it with doctors and nurses I know now, since the only person I remember for sure from the place where this happened was Sheila, the knitting nurse. I remember her only because, unlike the rest of us, who worked off job-related stress by smoking, drinking coffee and picking at our sores, Sheila knitted afghans.

And I remember Murray, the doctor on for the day.

Murray was an attending that year, the last year of my residency. I was in training at "the Mecca," an elite institution—specializing in liver transplants and functional bowel syndrome—improbably located in the midst of one of the biggest ghettos in America. Upstairs from the ER, great Nobel Prize–winning research was carried out and complex, extremely expensive surgery was performed. Downstairs in the ER, though, we practiced medicine in a war zone.

That summer the streets were on fire in the inner city; the police nominally patrolled the streets during daylight, the gangs ruled the night. This meant that, in addition to the usual domestic type of violence you have in any ER, we saw terrible things:

machete slashings, butcher-knife dismemberings, Uzi slayings, cop-versus-bad-guy shootouts, four- or five-year-old kids riddled with bullets and clearly too dead to even think about trying to resuscitate. Bosnia had nothing on this swath of ghetto except maybe a few more land mines and a few less Uzis.

That summer we saw the first wave of the crack epidemic coming through, watched the early stages of destruction of a generation from our unique vantage point. Sometimes we saw crack addicts with acute symptoms: a myocardial infarction in an otherwise healthy thirty-four-year-old man; exacerbation of psychotic symptoms in a schizophrenic. Mostly, though, we saw the crackheads when they were at the end of the line—badly addicted, broke, strung out. They would come crawling into the ER desperate, begging—please, please, please, help me. And we could give them a sandwich and a couple of telephone numbers to call in the morning.

But far worse than any crackhead were the guys on PCP—phencyclidine—an animal tranquilizer. We would not see these guys later, when they'd hit bottom. We would see them when they were still high. The police would bring someone in, usually chained down because the patient had gone on a rampage. A man high on PCP knows no fear, feels no pain, has the strength of ten and the sensibility of a raging elephant. He can upend a hospital gurney, break out of five-point leather restraints, overcome a herd of large security guys and escape into the night with the kind of grace otherwise only seen in the majorly psychotic. Someone with a bad PCP high *is* psychotic, hallucinating madly, in a state of aggressive terror. One guy, very high, saw a large dog attacking his mother, so he killed the dog. Only there was no large dog. He had been hallucinating. But his mother was there—he had killed *her*. The police brought him in, under arrest, of course, because he had a cut on his hand. He kept telling the officers: "Call my mother. She'll bail me out. Call my mother." One of the officers kept saying in return, "We can't call your mother. You *killed* your mother."

"Come on," the guy would say in reply. "That's not funny."

*   *   *

There were, back then, the Latin Kings, the Vice Lords, the Disciples, the Spanish Cobras and of course, the legendary El Rukins, among many others. These were the gangs that ruled the Chicago streets. Each gang had a gesture, a symbol. Two fists raised up with forearms crossed, that was the Popes. Their colors were blue and black. Two fingers outstretched and the hand held in a let's-pretend-gun position, that was the Villa Lobos. Their colors: green and black. Colors were always a big thing, a way to mark out territory. That year, though, the cops were cracking down; things had to be really low key. Gangbangers, who used to wear in-your-face bright blue or green jackets, now wore regular T-shirts (Snoop Doggy Dog and his "Doggy Style" tour was a favorite imprint) along with their regulation low-slung jeans. Colors would be there unobtrusively, visible only to a special kind of eye: a wrist band, a sweatshirt hood, shoelaces. My very first night in the ER we got three shooting victims (two died) from a drive-by shooting at a local takeout place—Popeyes. Each victim was wearing green shoelaces on his right sneaker only. They were the Insane Deuces taken out by the even more insane El Rukins.

Murray was on the night a sixteen-year-old kid came in all shot up, two bullets in his belly and two in each leg. Just as everyone began to work on him, starting IVs, attaching the monitor leads, the El Rukin who shot the kid to begin with came into the trauma room, shot the boy twice in the head and then disappeared into the night. The police never found him. The kid died, of course, and everyone else was pretty shaken. None more than Murray, though. He talked obsessively about it, reliving every second, over and over and over. The man with the gun, the boy on the table, the expressions on the nurses' faces. All in all, those two minutes just pushed Murray that much farther over the edge.

If that ER was a pressure cooker, then the pressure had gotten to Murray. He was a tall, thin and very nervous man, perpetually possessed by the largest number of facial tics, twitches, verbal mannerisms and idiosyncratic gestures I have ever seen in one person. These were endlessly repeated; he was like an autistic adult. Murray never said no. He said "No, no, no, no, no. Absolutely not, no, never. I mean it, no. You can tell him no, no, no. That's my last word, no." Or, "I'm just going to tell you once, I only want to say this once, once, do you understand me? Just *one time*." He would go in to see a patient and half the time come back out, head down, muttering, "This is senseless, senseless. I'm right here thinking about this and I can't believe how senseless it is." He would turn to anyone standing near him, a resident, a unit clerk, another patient. "Senseless," he would tell them. And he would be right; sometimes it was senseless in the extreme: babies with colds for a week brought in by belligerent grandmothers at three in the morning; tanked-to-the-gills, smashed-into-pieces drunk drivers; maced police suspects; I'm-here-for-a-pregnancy-test patients; my-doctor-told-me-to-come-in-right-away-and-that-you-should-give-me-some-Demerol patients; grown men whimpering like babies over sore throats; patients who said, just as you were leaving the room, "Oh, by the way, Doc—I had sex with a hooker last night and so I need an HIV test." (Bonus points if you could guess the name of the hooker.) After a while most of the rest of us had gotten used to just how senseless it could be, but Murray never did. He remained terminally amazed.

Murray's first chore of the morning was to go to each of the phones he might use during the day and wipe off the receiver with alcohol swabs. He would then wash down his desk area with a special kind of super disinfectant. (This was *his* desk area. No one else could sit there for the duration of the shift.) Then he would take out a new pen—he always had a fresh one at the start of the shift. During the course of the next few hours, he would proceed to destroy this pen. He would gnaw on the cap until it was frayed into plastic bits, and if he was upset about something, he would bend the pen back and forth in his hands so that, when he went to write with it, the end of it would veer off at a crazy angle.

Murray washed his hands all the time—all the time. If he was not on the phone, seeing a patient or destroying his pen, he would stand at the sink in the nurses' station with the water running over his hands. He could stand like that for half an hour or more; you just had to get used to the sound of splashing water when you presented a case. When he was not otherwise engaged, I know he was counting the number of hand swipes. He would move his left hand over his right, washing, for a certain number of strokes (I'm not sure how many, I think it varied with the circumstances) then he would reverse, right hand over left. He would stop and dry his hands on a paper towel, still listening to you. After a moment he would look back down at his hands, seem to notice a little speck of dirt and go back to washing again. At the end of each hand-washing session, he would carefully wipe out the sink with paper towels, wiping down the faucet and stainless-steel bowl. After this he would stand there for a minute, gazing down reverently into what must have been the only spot of cleanliness and order in that great chaotic sea of an ER. Only then would he, reluctantly, finally turn away.

Murray had been at "the Mecca" for six or seven years. "He used to be a really great guy," everyone would say. No one could exactly pinpoint when the stress had finally gotten to him. But how could it not? Who else could come into a place like this, day after day, week after week, for all these years and not be in some way fundamentally fried? But stressed out or not, Murray did have something that was bad for any ER doctor—a volatile temper. Murray was a terror when angry. He could work himself up into a frothy rage about little things, someone spilling coffee, or not flagging an order properly. His face would become beet red, his eyes would bulge out, and after a while he would look as if his head might explode. He would yell. Rant. Weird things would set him off. For example, baby pacifiers used to enrage him. He would rip a pacifier from a little kid's mouth, and as the mother looked on horror-stricken, he would fling it into the trash can, shouting, "Never, never, never, never. Do you know—never— what those things do?" (I worked with Murray for years and never found out just what it was that pacifiers do. He never said and everyone else was too afraid to ask.) Or fevers and mothers who didn't give their child enough Tylenol. "Stupid, stupid, stupid, stupid, stupid, stupid. Do you understand me? Stupid." He would tower over some poor woman in his best hectoring stance, a finger just millimeters from her nose. The look in his eyes would be one of transcendent, almost psychotic exasperation.

Everyone, of course, worried about Murray's sanity. But it wasn't just Murray; the sanity issue was germane to us all. We were all more or less in a perpetual state of shell shock. The pressure was everywhere—unrelenting. It crept into every facet, crack and crevice of a person's psyche. It rotted the woodwork, scarred the metal joists and broke down, without pity, the fragile scaffolding almost all of us use to hold ourselves together. Murray wasn't the only casualty. He was just the loudest.

I wasn't on the day this happened. I was doing research that involved, at the time, going through paramedic run sheets. I was sitting at the radio console. The radio went off—everyone else was busy—so I answered it. It was a bad transmission, lots of static.

"This is [inaudible] fourteen, [inaudible] do you read me?"

"Not very well but go ahead."

Static . . . static . . . "gunshot" . . . static . . . static.

"Please repeat."

"Twenty-two-year [inaudible] shot . . ." static . . . static . . . "head" . . . static.

"The patient is shot in the head?"

"That's an affirmative. . . ." Static . . .

"He or she is twenty-two? You're breaking up."

Static . . . static . . . "months . . ." static.

"Please repeat."

"We had a pulse but [inaudible] repeat" . . . static . . . "months . . . now."

The radio transmitter clicked off.

I stuck my head out the doorway. "Hey, guys," I announced. "You're getting a gunshot wound."

Everyone looked around at me.

"To the head."

Everyone groaned. Murray, who had a chart attached to a clipboard, slammed it down and said, "This is ridiculous, yes, it's ridiculous. What a ridiculous way to start the day. Ridiculous."

The clerk hit the trauma button, and in a moment the page came though overhead on the hospital paging system.

"Dr. T., emergency room. Dr. T., emergency room." (This was the loudspeaker euphemism used to call a trauma code—sometimes a source of confusion. One morning during rounds a patient remarked to me, "I don't know who Dr. Tea is, but I tell you he sure was busy last night.")

Everyone began to migrate to the trauma room. I sat alone at the radio console for a few minutes and then shrugged, what the hell, and got up to follow them, to look over their shoulder. I was young and a trauma was still exciting, the "real reason" I went into emergency medicine.

Who else walked back there that summer evening? There was Sheila, of course, the knitter of afghans, otherwise so unobtrusive as to exist as a redheaded blur in my memory. There was Sudesh, one of my fellow residents. Sudesh wanted to move to Florida after his residency and specialize in emergencies of the rich and famous. There was manic Ted, a nurse who would teach students how to place a nasogastric tube by putting it down himself. And of course there was Donna, trauma nurse queen, wit tart as lemons. It was Donna who had commented to me and to Murray's back after he had said something inexplicable, turned, and walked away, "Do you think that if I go home and put a metal colander on my head I could communicate with the planet that man is coming from?"

"What else did they tell you?" Sudesh asked me.

"I couldn't get any information. They were breaking up so bad."

"Great," Murray said. He was walking in front of us, looking like he always did, head down, slope-shouldered, sack-butted. "Absolutely—I can't believe it—great. Great, great, *great*."

By now the "Dr. T." call was echoing throughout the hospital. The trauma team would have heard it. They were probably busy doing nothing, maybe watching TV in the surgical lounge since it had been quiet so far today. The "scout" medical student would be on his way down to see if this was a "real" trauma. Anesthesia was, as always, busy being busy. (If they were doing a case, they didn't have to come down and they were always doing a case.) The on-call pharmacist was also to come down to help mix drugs and such. The pharmacist at this hospital was always the most reliable about getting to the code. He or she actually ran down the hallways and would even take the stairway if it was faster. But when he or she got there it was—so what? What was a pharmacist to do about a sucking chest wound? Public relations also weighed in very early, just checking to see if whoever the paramedics dragged through the door was in some way newsworthy (small child? high school athlete? interesting story? somebody white?).

For the people in the ER though, the first responders, this was "heads up" time. It starts the moment after an ambulance calls in a trauma and it extends until the doors slide open and the patient is revealed. No matter what the paramedics told you on the radio or, in this case, tried to tell you, you never really know what is going to roll through your door until it actually does. That's when the victim of a gunshot wound to the chest turns out to be someone who was shot with a twenty-two and the bullet bounced off his clothing. Or a simple facial burn from a mishap with the oven turns out to be someone whose face has melted down to a third-degree burn so severe it exposed cartilage. It might take twenty minutes for the paramedics to cut a drunk driver out of his crashed and burned motor vehicle, but he turns out to be fine, ready for discharge in no time, while the person he hit, someone in a Volvo, no less, who is up and walking at the scene, turns out to have a dissecting aortic aneurysm and dies on the operating table. There is just no telling.

I stood to the side that day, not a player. Murray could be very peculiar about who participated in *his* code. I knew all the moves, though. Sudesh stood at the head of the bed checking the intubation equipment: the plastic endotracheal tube, a syringe, a wire stylet, a little lubricant; the stuff that saves lives. After this, he turned on the suction, and when it wouldn't work started poking at the plastic tubing, looking puzzled. Murray stood off to the side, arms folded, head bent, chin resting on his chest. He was mumbling; I couldn't hear what he was saying, and it was probably just as well.

That was when, apropos of nothing that I could see, Sudesh turned to Donna and said, "You know, this is not a real life."

"You're right," she replied. "This is not a real life. This is a test. If this had been a real life, you would have been instructed where to go and what to do."

Sudesh turned away, shaking his head wearily. Ted laughed. (This was his third double shift in a row.) Sheila rolled her eyes. I can remember everyone in the room that day, or were they at another resuscitation? Was Sudesh on the night before and Sheila on day shift and had she already left? And Donna? Why do I remember Donna when I didn't work with her until years later? As I think back, what I remember, more than anyone I knew or anything that happened, is the pervasive sense of exhaustion, of being up for hours and hours, days and days, weeks, months. Exhaustion was like dust, settling over everything. You felt as if you had to swim through the day; the drag coefficient of even the littlest gesture made you ponderously slow. You even thought slowly. The whole world seemed darker than you ever remembered it—and the memory of the real light had almost vanished. And with the exhaustion came the phantoms of emotions, monstrous feelings, panic, terror, paranoia. Sudesh, standing by the bed, looked punch drunk, bedazzled by the suction equipment. This was his eighth twelve-hour shift in a row.

"Tune in tomorrow, whiny guys," Ted said, "for another episode of *Days of Our Lives*."

Murray turned on everyone. "*Would you all be quiet!*" he shouted. Then he glared at me, but he said nothing.

From outside in the ambulance bay we could hear the backup buzzer. The paramedics would be rolling in any second.

"All right, all right, *all right*. Let's go, let's go, *let's go*," Murray shouted at everyone, even though there was really nothing anyone could do.

Four paramedics swept in, one doing chest compressions, one holding an IV aloft, another bagging the patient and the last wheeling the cart. They all looked terrified. The victim's head was swathed in bloody Kerlix. Blue sweat pants, T-shirt. Man? Woman? The belly was massively distended.

"Twenty-two-year-old shot in the head, we think times two. She had a pulse when we got there, but we lost it. It was a big-time bloody mess in the field."

"Breathing?" Sudesh asked.

"Agonal, at best. I'm not sure."

"Wait a minute, wait a minute." It was Murray. He had moved over and now stood in front of the hospital gurney, blocking the paramedics' way. He raised his hand. "*What's this?*" he shouted, pointing at the swollen belly. He glared down at the lead paramedic as if whatever it could be was all his fault.

The paramedic took a deep breath. "She's pregnant."

"*Pregnant!*" Murray shouted. "*Pregnant! What do you mean pregnant!*" He stood nose to nose with the paramedic, waving his hands.

One of the other paramedics, the one holding the IV bag, leaned forward and said directly to Murray, enunciating each word carefully, "She's—going—to—have—a—baby— In two weeks. She's term. And she doesn't have a pulse."

Murray turned back and shouted, "*Would you all be quiet!*" again. He turned to Donna, "We need anesthesia down here; we need OB; we need pediatrics—neonatal, we need . . ." He stopped, apparently having run out of things to need. He turned back to the patient and stood for a moment staring at the abdomen. Everyone stood silently watching as Murray leaned forward and put his hands on the belly. He looked as if he needed to touch it to believe it. Only then did he step aside so that the paramedics could get through.

"*Come on, come on, come on. What the hell, what the hell are you waiting for?*"

The paramedics looked wrung out. Sweat was dripping from the forehead of the paramedic doing chest compressions. "She's lost a bunch of blood. We've got two IVs in her, but we can't keep up, she's still bleeding like stink. We tried tubing her but the scene wasn't secure; nobody knew what was going on, just who had the gun or what. The family was making a big scene, so we had to just run with what we had."

"Did you get a blood pressure at all?" Sudesh asked.

"Nada. But that's not to say . . ."

Everyone shifted around to help move the patient off the gurney. All I could really see now was her sweat pants and cheap white sneakers covered in blood. Sheila leaned over and started attacking the sweat pants with her trauma scissors before they had even moved the patient off the cart.

"Hold CPR. Hold CPR," Murray shouted. "Hold CPR. We need to roll . . . She needs . . . Side, side. She needs a side. . . . We need to turn . . ." In a panic nobody knew what he meant. (It's a simple thing; you want to position a pregnant woman so that the fetus and uterus don't cut off the blood supply to the lower body.) Finally Drew, another resident (didn't I know him from some other time and other place?), pulled the patient's arm, rolling her to the side of the cart. But with this it became almost impossible to do CPR. There was a clumsy minute while everyone tried to figure out what to do. Imagine the chaos of desperation, a room full of people all scrambling to try to save a life but having to contend with reality: not enough room, not quite sure where to stand, a falling IV pole, IV lines everywhere, monitor leads, head bleeding (and you are aware, as you fumble, that each drop of blood on the floor is bringing the patient just that much closer to the end of the line). There seemed to be no way to brace the patient properly. Finally someone wedged a few towels under the backboard and the medical student was told to crawl up there and get started with chest compressions. He did so, his face white as a sheet. The woman's Kerlix-bound head lolled to the side; blood was everywhere.

"What did you have on the monitor?" Murray demanded of the paramedics. He wasn't quite shouting now.

"Mostly idioventricular, I think. She didn't flat-line on us."

"Who shot her?" someone asked—a rotating intern who didn't know any better.

"Shut up," Murray said, his face right up next to hers. "Who the fuck cares who shot her? We're not here to play detective." He turned and addressed the room at large. "Somebody set up for a central line."

Donna leaned over the head. "Oh, jeez," she said. "Guys, I think I see brains here."

"Let's get her moved. Let's move it. Move, move, move."

Everyone did the best they could.

"One . . .

"Two . . .

"Three. Let's go, let's go, let's go." Murray paced back and forth in front of the bed. He looked like a coach on the sidelines fuming at a referee's bad call. "Drugs!" He was shouting again. He leaned over the paramedic who was trying to catch the IV bag on one of the overhead hooks. Murray pointed, his finger a hairbreadth from the paramedic's chest. "Drugs?"

"Epi. That's all we've given her."

"Do we have a pulse?" Murray shouted. "*Do we have a pulse?*"

Drew came forward saying, "Hold CPR." When the medical student paused, he palpated the neck of the patient. "Nothing," he said.

"This *woman* has no *pulse*," Murray said through clenched

teeth. "We've got to get that baby out. Where's OB? Page OB overhead."

"Keep your shirt on," Donna told him.

Sudesh moved up to control the airway. He stood, ET tube and laryngoscope poised, ready to intubate, except that the paramedic managing the Ambu bag couldn't move out of the way; he was trapped in a snare of monitor leads and IV lines. Murray paced back and forth in front of the cart, talking to himself, his nervous tic animating his face. He put on the characteristic Murray posture, head down, arms wrapped around his chest and hands buried under his armpits. This was Murray's style. He could stand brooding or pace back and forth like this throughout an entire code, listening to everyone and following the code more with his ears than with his eyes. Even so, all the while he paced he looked more like any one of the schizophrenic walkers we had patrolling the psychiatry ward. More than that, he looked like a caged animal. He even growled as he walked.

Donna and Ted started doing the routine stuff: hooking up the monitor wires, strapping on the blood pressure cuff (not that, at the moment, there was any blood pressure to measure). Defibrillator, drug box. Eileen checked the IVs and got set to start another, a large-bore one for the blood we would need if the patient showed the least signs of life.

This was it, the golden hour. In emergency medicine this may be the only chance you get to save a life. Sixty golden minutes, each is an opportunity won or lost, each weighs in with the question Live or die? Live or die? Questions synchronized to the ticking of the clock. Can't get an IV in? The patient will die. Can't get the patient intubated? Dead, dead, dead. Can't find the cause of the hypotension? Don't make the diagnosis of a ruptured aortic aneurysm? Get the central line in too late? Drop a lung? Don't recognize within the slobbering, comatose drunk before you the massive intracranial bleed? More than one of these? Then the patient dies. And the pressure is on you, big time. It's because of you that the game gets won or lost. But the question is, how long can you play the game with stakes like these.

Murray stopped pacing. "Where's trauma surgery?" he shouted. "Where? where?"

"Here," an intern said as he walked in through the sliding glass door. "What's the problem?"

Murray bore down on him.

"*Where's the rest of your team?*"

The intern looked around uncomfortably. "They're on their way," he said. "I think."

Murray pointed. "Well, she's got a bullet in her head. It would sure be nice if trauma could *make a guest appearance*."

The OB-GYN intern followed the surgery resident in. I knew him. He was a sweet guy but easily baffled. He also looked like he had not made it through puberty. This did not help matters.

"What's going on?" he asked me in a don't-have-a-clue voice.

"She's shot in the head," I told him.

He looked around at me. "And you called OB?"

"She's pregnant," I said.

"How pregnant?"

"Real pregnant. And she's a full arrest."

"Oh," he said. "Jesus." He took a sharp breath in and exhaled slowly.

Murray was still pacing. "Where's OB?" he demanded of no one in particular.

The intern visibly shrank back. "I'm here," he said.

"Well." Murray bore down on him. "*Where's pediatrics?*"

The intern shrank back further. "I don't know."

Murray pointed. "There is a woman here and we don't have a pulse and we are doing CPR and she is pregnant. She's going to have a baby and she's not pumping any blood to that baby. You've got to get that baby *out*." He leaned over the intern, prodding him with a finger. "Call your senior down now."

Ted had connected the patient up to the hospital monitor.

The surgery intern raised his hands. "Hold CPR, please. Checking for a rhythm here."

Everyone paused and stared at the monitor screen, waiting for the artifact to settle out. And there it *was*, a rhythm of sorts, slow and broad-based. Her heart was at least going through the motions.

"Do we have a pulse?"

Sudesh was still fumbling with the intubation gear. He reached out and massaged the woman's neck again, looking for a carotid pulse. "Nothing," he said.

"Epinephrine," Murray shouted. "Come on, come on." He wheeled around, looking for the OB intern. "Where's your chief? Where *is* your chief?"

The intern was on the telephone. He raised the receiver so Murray could see.

"We need fluids," Murray shouted, again to no one in particular. "We need a central line in her."

The surgery intern nodded. "I'll do it," he said. Then he looked at the patient. "Where?"

"Where, what?" Murray said.

"Where do I put the line in?" He motioned toward the patient. He was right to be puzzled. The head of the bed was packed with people. It would be hard to find room enough to get to her neck or shoulder.

"I don't care where you put it," Murray said. "Just put it in somewhere."

The OB resident called out from where he stood by the phone. "My senior wants to know if she has had any prenatal care."

"*I don't know*," Murray shouted. "*She's been shot in the head. She can't talk.*"

The intern's mouth O'd. The enormity of the situation had finally gotten through.

"C-section . . ." he breathed into the phone. "Crash C-section." He turned to all of us. "We need a c-section tray."

From somewhere next door in the storage room Sheila shouted back, "I'm looking for it."

At the head of the bed Sudesh had succeeded in intubating the woman. He and the respiratory therapist were trying to tape the tube into place. He motioned for me to come over and help bag. (Or did he? Do I remember this right?) I must have put some gloves on (or was this before we all took the HIV stuff seriously?) and grabbed at the Ambu bag. This was my first close-up view of the woman's head. A matted collection of blood-soaked dressings were plastered over her forehead and held in place by layers of Kerlix.

"Let's see what we have here," Sudesh said.

"I found the tray," Eileen shouted.

Sudesh slipped off the bandage as if it were a hat. Beneath was the forehead with a bullet hole. A clean shot. A hole the size of a dime that was oozing blood.

This is the dead end of violence, unstylized and unshorn. An argument, a flash of gunmetal and its result is a hole in someone's forehead. I thought of all the gunshots casually exchanged between the hero and the villain on a television show. That was the fantasy; this was the reality of a stray shot or two.

Blood and edema had already swelled the area around the wound.

"See any brains?" Donna said, leaning over.

"No," Sudesh said. "Not yet." Then, "The paramedics said they heard two shots . . ."

The patient's right eye was swollen, puffy. "Two shots," Sudesh said again. He touched the hole in the woman's forehead. "Shot number one." Then he palpated the right eyebrow with his gloved thumb and lifted the lid. The globe of the eye was gone; there was nothing there but an oozing pool of blood and egg white–like tissue.

"Bingo," he said. "Shot number two." He called out to Donna, who was recording. "Two gunshot wounds involving the face," he said. "One midline on the forehead; the other into the orbit. The forehead one's an entrance wound, I think." He palpated the rest of the scalp. "I've got another bullet hole here, guys. Back of the skull, occiput. Maybe an exit wound. It's big, really big." He pulled what was left of the bandage out, lifted the woman's head as best he could, and bent down, peering at the back of the skull. "Guys, I think we are talking brain matter here."

"*Hold CPR,*" Murray shouted. We all looked up at the monitor, waiting for the artifact to fall away. And there it was, a narrow complex rhythm, a sinus rhythm. Rate: 120.

"Do we have a pulse?" Murray thundered.

Sudesh massaged the patient's neck again. "Maybe," he said. "Thready. Someone get the Doppler."

"Should I hold CPR?" the medical student said, pausing on an upstroke.

Murray turned to him and shouted, "*God damn, you don't hold CPR until I tell you to hold CPR and I'm not telling you to hold CPR until this woman has a certified blood pressure.*"

The medical student, looking stricken, resumed CPR.

Murray pointed to me. "We need two units of O-neg blood, right now."

I surrendered the Ambu bag and went over to the phone to call the blood bank. Another medical student was standing close by looking somewhat sick to her stomach.

"Blood bank," I said, pointing. This is the medical tradition: scut flows downhill. "*Now.*"

She dashed out past two police officers who now stood in the ambulance bay doorway looking on with a sort of noncommittal curiosity. I went over to them.

"What happened?" I said, or rather, whispered, so Murray wouldn't get upset. "How'd she get shot?"

The first officer shrugged. "Gang stuff. Somebody had a beef with her brother."

I looked at them both expectantly.

"Boom, boom," the other cop said. "That's all we know."

"Where'd she get hit?" the first officer asked me.

I touched my forehead and then my eye.

"She gonna make it?" the other asked.

"Not a prayer," I told them. "You may as well go ahead and notify your homicide detectives."

"Yeah?" the cop said skeptically. He looked up at the monitor. "But she's still got a heartbeat . . ."

I shrugged. "You're right; she does have a heartbeat."

"Well, then she's not dead yet. We're not supposed to call homicide until they are officially dead."

The medical student doing CPR was flagging, I could see. He was sweating like the paramedics had been. His glasses kept sliding to the bridge of his nose and he'd try to nudge them back into place with his shoulder so he wouldn't break his CPR rhythm. Nobody made a move to replace him. Nobody but me even noticed.

The OB intern came back from the phone. "My senior is in the OR," he said. "He'll be down as soon as he can."

Murray pointed at the patient. "*Now!* I want that baby out *now.*" He grabbed the intern's right wrist and he stuck something—I think it was a pair of trauma scissors—into the intern's hand. Then he dragged, literally dragged, the intern over to the foot of the gurney and pointed with his other hand.

"*You are OB. This is your responsibility. I want that baby out and I want it out now.*"

The moment of truth. The intern peered up at Murray, then at the patient, then back at Murray, as if trying to calculate which was the most frightening. The answer was clear: Murray.

The intern's lips moved but he said nothing. Perhaps he was praying.

"Come on," Sudesh said, *sotto voce.* "You can't know less than me."

Meanwhile Murray turned and surveyed us all. "Where's neonatal? I told you to stat page neonatal. Where the hell is the team? Hell, team, hell, team, team. Where?"

As if on cue, the doors to the main ER opened. The medical student who had gone to fetch the blood now came back in carrying two units.

"Where's neonatal?" Murray demanded of her.

The medical student looked around, bewildered.

"Never mind," Murray said. "At least you got the blood."

Sudesh opened up the OB pack. I edged over; I had never seen an emergency C-section before (or since). I had only the vaguest idea of what needed to be done—but then, obviously, so did the OB intern. The trauma intern, now joined by his resident, peered over from where they were suturing in a femoral line. They looked equally baffled.

"I'd open with a ten-blade," the trauma resident told the OB intern.

Sudesh left the head of the bed and was now standing next to the OB intern trying to help. He sorted through the equipment in the C-section tray, poking at the retractors, Kelly clamps and forceps.

Eileen had dumped a great brown pool of Betadine on the woman's belly. This was the only gesture toward sterility. We all knew it didn't matter. The mother had been lost from the very beginning; the problem now was to save the child.

"Go," Murray shouted. "Go, go, go, go, go."

I looked over at the OB intern, who was standing with a scalpel in his raised right hand, staring down at the woman's belly like a high diver staring all the way down to the water so far below.

"Do it," Murray shouted. He was standing at the intern's shoulder.

The intern cut a curved incision along the lower boundary of the woman's belly, exposing a deep layer of fat. Immediately this fat herniated through the incision as a result of the pressure transmitted from the chest by CPR. It was eerie-looking, almost as if the belly was breathing in and out.

"Okay," the intern said. "Okay, okay." He parted the fat with the scalpel, then followed behind it with his fingers, feeling for the muscle wall of the abdomen.

"Watch out," Sudesh said.

The intern felt along the abdominal wall. "Rectus," he hissed, "rectus, obliques."

"Where are you going to cut?" Sudesh asked.

"There, there," the resident said. Murray stood over him, breathing fire but saying nothing.

The intern's hands were shaking as he cut. We all leaned over, trying to see as best we could.

"Deeper," Sudesh said. "Go deeper. We've got to see better."

"Where's the bladder?" the intern wanted to know. "I need to go just above the bladder."

"Is that it?" Sudesh asked.

"We need some retractors," the intern said. "I can't see anything this way."

Sudesh grabbed up two small shovel-like devices and attempted to wedge them into the open surgical wound.

The intern's right hand disappeared into the woman's belly. He looked like he was rummaging around in a sack, groping blindly as he searched for the uterus. Then he made another cut, it seemed, and then cut again. He must have opened up the uterus now with a little incision. "Bandage scissors," he said, waving a bloody hand at Eileen.

She fumbled through the tray looking for them.

"Those," he said, "those." She handed them over. He maneuvered them into the wound and started sawing away at the uterine wall. "Shit," he said at one point. He cut some more and then, "I've got the head. I've got the head."

Sudesh repositioned the retractors, trying to get a better exposure of the uterus. "But can you get it out?" he said.

The intern buried his other hand deep within the patient's belly and stood for a moment, tugging like mad.

"You're not going to get it out that way," Sudesh said. "You've got to make a bigger incision."

The intern's face was red and his forehead glistened with sweat. He struggled, both wrists and forearms buried deep within the woman's belly.

"It wouldn't be so bad," Murray shouted over the intern's shoulder, apropos of nothing I could see. His face was purple with rage. "It wouldn't be so bad if she wasn't so . . . *damn* . . ."—he spit the word—"*fat*. This woman is *fat*."

He looked up at me standing a couple of feet away from him. "Move back, move back," he told me. "Give them some room."

I retired to the doorway. As I paused there, the two pediatric residents walked in and stood beside me, both looking sleepy. One had a Mickey Mouse tie on, the other had a pliable Goofy figure wrapped around his stethoscope. They peered around the room and visibly paled.

"What?" one of them asked me. "What happened?"

"Gunshot wound to the head."

They looked over at the adult-sized figure on the gurney and said, "So why are we here?"

"Crash C-section. She's pregnant. If they can deliver the baby and there's anything there, you guys are on."

"*You've got to get that baby out,*" Murray screamed again. "*Out, out, out.*"

"Oh my God," the resident with the pliable Goofy doll said. They both stood there, apparently transfixed.

"The Isolette is over there," I told them, nudging the one closest to me.

"We've still got to make the incision bigger," Sudesh was saying. He took the scalpel away from the OB resident and extended the cut, first in the skin of the abdominal wall and then deep within the abdomen, up into the body of the uterus. He started groping around as well, elbow-deep in the woman's belly. After a moment there was a river of blood, and the OB intern suddenly hoisted up, from deep within the woman, a very dead-looking baby.

"*Cut the cord, cut the cord,*" Murray shouted.

Sudesh and the OB intern struggled to clamp the umbilical cord. Finally they succeeded. Sudesh cut between the clamps. The baby was free now, ready to live or die on its own. Her own. It was a girl.

"Give it here, give it here," the pediatrician with the Goofy doll shouted.

"*Suction, suction, suction,*" Murray kept shouting over him.

I became aware of someone else standing beside me. A tall man in an immaculate white lab coat. I knew him but I couldn't place him.

"What's going on?" he demanded of me.

"Woman shot in the head," I said. "They just did a crash C-section." I recognized him then: Dr. Cobb, chief of OB-GYN. He was one of the big guns. Big guns don't usually cover the ER. He must have heard something was going on.

At that moment Murray hoisted the baby into the air and stepped forward to the Isolette. "Get out of the way," he shouted.

"Holy Moses," Dr. Cobb said. He waded into the crowd packed around the bed. As he pushed his way toward the gurney, people looked behind at him and fell away when they saw who it was.

"Gloves!" he demanded of Donna, the surgeon barking orders to the lowly nurse.

"They're over there," she said, pointing.

One of the medical students handed him a pair of sterile gloves.

Dr. Cobb stood for a moment, contemplating the abdomen. Finally, "Who opened this belly?" he demanded.

"I did," the OB intern said.

"What the hell do you think you were doing?" he said, pointing down into the depth of the woman's abdomen.

The room became quiet. The only person talking was Murray barking orders to the people clustered around the Isolette. The intern looked down at his gloved hands and at the scalpel he had there. He then looked deep into the belly, trying, it seemed, to figure out what Dr. Cobb was gesturing at. He didn't seem to have much more of an idea than I had, watching as I was from across the room.

"Who opened this uterus?" Dr. Cobb thundered again.

The intern shrank back.

"What do you call this? The 'Jack the Ripper' approach? While you were at it, why didn't you just take out the spleen as well?"

"Sir," Sudesh said. "I extended the incision. We had to get the baby out."

"You had to get the baby out! Well, what about the mother? How are you going to put her uterus back together?"

(Murray, over by the Isolette, was handed a 3-5 ET tube and threw it across the room. "*That's way too big*," he shouted.)

Sudesh peered up at the chief. "Well . . . ," he began.

"This woman is a setup for uterine rupture. Her next pregnancy is going to be a disaster. She's be lucky if she goes to term."

"Sir," Sudesh said in a small voice. "She's been shot in the head."

"That's no excuse for poor technique!"

Murray heard this somehow and turned around. "What the hell are you talking about?" he shouted.

"Are you the attending here?" Dr. Cobb shouted back. "Because this is inexcusable."

Murray came back over to the gurney, people scrambling to get out of the way.

"*What the hell are you talking about?*" he roared again.

"This woman's uterus is a disaster."

Murray said nothing. He just stood there, eyes wide, face twitching, his nose not more than three or four inches from Cobb's. He was trembling with anger. I thought of all the times before when I watched Murray lose it, and I realized this time was different. All those other times Murray had lost his temper over little things, minor irritants. This time was something new, something I had never seen in Murray before. This was rage clearly justified. And it seemed to me as I watched Murray standing there, wild-eyed, stretched to the breaking point, that this was the definitive time, this was the end of the line. The slipping was over. Murray was now in free fall. At the time I'm not sure what I thought he was going to do, but looking back I always see Murray standing there in that crowd of onlookers, one hand raised, clenched, held up close to his face. Cobb stood before him, gazing first at the fist and then at Murray's face. The two of them just stood there for a moment, eye to eye. Cobb blinked first. He stepped back and looked around, nodding to himself. Murray then leaned over the cart and pointed emphatically toward the woman's head. "This woman was shot *in the head*. She is *brain dead*. We are trying to save the baby."

Dr. Cobb opened his mouth, then closed it, looked around and opened it again. "Oh," he said.

Murray bore down on him. "If this woman had another baby it would be a *medical miracle*."

Dr. Cobb stepped away from the bed and looked around. I could see him realize that he was in a strange land here. This was not some sterile operating room, all order and control. This was a place where lunacy prevailed.

I will give Dr. Cobb credit. As he stood there, I could see it dawn on him what was going on. He looked first around at all of us and then into the belly of the patient. Finally he looked up at the intern and said quietly, "What are you closing with?"

"0' chromic," the resident said.

"Here," Dr. Cobb told him. "Get me a needle driver and more chromic and I'll help."

Murray brought the kid back. By the time the baby left the resuscitation room, she had a good pulse and was breathing a little on her own. It was as bad a thrash as the delivery had been. Murray did it all, though, intubated the baby in an instant, got all the lines in, treated her acidosis. The two pediatric residents stood to the side throughout, looking awestruck. They never said a word.

After it all, Murray stood in the middle of the trauma room in typical Murray mode, arms crossed, growling, as he watched them wheel the Isolette upstairs. He should have looked triumphant, but he merely looked like Murray. He was tic-ing like mad, chin up, right eye twitching as he shouted, "*Move, move, people, you gotta move, here*," as if anybody was going to do anything else.

The mother made a comeback as well, such as it was. As soon as the baby was out, she rebounded. The first measured systolic blood pressure was over 200. But by now Murray had lost interest in what was left of her; he scarcely glanced at the patient's vital signs and shrugged when the trauma resident told him it would be an hour or more before they got the woman up to the ICU. He did stop at the door, though, on his way out, and looked back at us. "I don't want that woman to die down here, guys," he said. "I want her to die in the ICU, where she belongs. So move it, move it." Then he left.

I helped wheel the woman, accompanied by monitors, IV poles, ventilator, over to CT. This was the stone age of CT times. A simple CT took fifteen to twenty minutes to perform, developing the film another ten minutes. (Now it is practically a finger snap.) Finally the radiology tech hung the processed film up for us to peruse. There we all gathered in the obligatory attitude of prayer, gazing up at the lighted x-ray box, eager to see the injuries in black and white.

The first bullet went through the frontal sinus, tumbling as it went, creating a shower of bone chips. It then cavitated a swath of tissue running from the frontal sinus back through the frontal and parietal lobes before it exited though the occiput, the back side of the skull. The second bullet entered through the orbit and passed obliquely down into the brain stem. It ended its brief flight just above the medulla. There it now rested, a great metallic mass, no longer bullet-shaped, ringed by a shadow of radiographic artifact.

It wasn't necessary, really, to understand the bullets' paths. One only needed to take one look at the scan to see that the brain had been blenderized. Ours was an academic concern only.

We all stood for a moment, Monday-morning quarterbacks, arguing over the path of the bullets as they entered the patient's skull. Finally someone voiced the obvious question: "Is she brain dead?"

"Are you serious?" the trauma intern asked.

"We're gonna have to document it in some way," the trauma resident said, nodding. "Why don't you give Neuro a call?"

And so the Neurology team came down. Three residents, all wearing immaculate white lab coats. They hemmed and hawed over the patient and examined the CT at length. Finally they all declared that she was probably brain dead *but* . . .

"We want to do calorics," the lead neurologist told the team.

Caloric testing involves the vestibular system, a primitive and very fundamental component of the working brain. To stimulate the vestibular system, you inject cold (or warm) water into the ear canal. The presence of the water cools the inner ear. In normal people this will produce nystagmus, a rapid twitching of the eye. An abnormal response would be deviation of the eyes without the twitching.

This woman had nothing.

The neurologists talked about this for a long time.

"I think we should do an EEG," the senior resident told us. "You never can really tell. Her heart is still going strong."

Donna shook her head. "Give it up, guys," she told them. "Isn't it obvious that the wheel may be spinning but the hamster is gone?"

It was late. I had done nothing on my research project; I had spent the whole afternoon rubbernecking a code. I needed to go home and get something to eat that wasn't junk food and get some sleep in a supine position.

On the way out I stopped at the plate-glass door just beyond Security's desk and looked out at the view of the parking lot and the big steel oxygen generator that was, apart from a rhomboid of sky, all we could see from the ER. It was the dusky end of a moody, thundercloudy sort of day. The sky was a flat expanse of gunmetal gray, now nearly black. As I stood there, Murray walked up beside me and he stopped as well, not to talk to me, apparently, but to look outside, at the world out there. I could see his reflection floating in the glass. He looked totally worn out, frayed, wasted, spent. I caught a glimpse of it that day, but now I know that look cold. It's the look of someone who has spent years in a room filled with all the losers of the world, and who has become, through all this, just another loser as well, another crazy guy stalking the hallways, an addict at the end of the line, a would-be suicide more pathetic than tragic. There Murray stood, face twitching like mad, silent as the grave. I saw that face as my face in ten years, fifteen, my face superimposed on his. But would I recognize that look if I was wearing it?

I have seen Murray's face again here and there over the years. The last time was a year or so ago when we had a hanging victim in from jail. This man had hanged himself in his jail cell using his pants somehow as a rope. He was very dead by the time he got to us, but still, I was transfixed by the expression on his face. His face was rage red, just like Murray's always was when Murray was angry, and somehow it looked as if it had frozen in the midst of a Murray-like tic.

One of the officers stood not far from him, looking down at the prisoner's face as well, shaking his head. "I can't understand it," he said. "The guy was going to be bonded out tomorrow."

"Jesus," I said. "What did he do to get arrested?"

The officer shrugged and kept shaking his head. "Unpaid traffic tickets," was all he said.

When I was in training, we staffed the helicopter medical transport service. The helicopter pad was on the eighth floor; you had a pretty good view of the city just standing up there, looking out across the campus. When you lifted off on a run in the helicopter, though, peeling away from the helipad with the helicopter canting at some impossible angle, you could see it all, the whole South Side of the city. Block after block of empty brown brick buildings, boarded up and tumbling down. Vacant lots, tattered billboards, derelict trucks, stalled cars, burned-out wood-frame houses. Everything looked either lost or abandoned. And there you were, going out on a mission to save lives, looking down on the whole cityscape from the hull of this vibrating monster. And after a while, after months and months of playing doctor, with too little sleep, too much violence, too many bad nights over broken bodies—in short, after a year or three of residency—all this near-celestial panorama began to look more and more like the ninth circle of hell.

11

How to Vaccinate Children in a War Zone

I WORKED AS A PHYSICIAN in Bosnia during the war, mostly in a hospital in Zenica, a town in Muslim-held territory. This gave me a worm's-eye view of the war. Like most of my colleagues there, I didn't see much further than my next patient. Broad political implications were lost on us. All we saw were the humdrum human byproducts of war: land-mine injuries, grenade injuries, shrapnel wounds, along with a not surprising number of suicide attempts.

The hospital was the largest in the region, and daily we would see, in addition to war victims, typical medical things: severe high blood pressure, heart attacks, strokes. We had very little to work with, of course. There were, in the entire hospital, two Bosnian-controlled stethoscopes, a single ventilator, and a vintage 1948 ECG monitor we used to get electrocardiograms (not that we could do much with the information). The hospital had exactly three ampules of morphine, enough to treat fifteen minutes' worth of pain, no high-blood-pressure medication, and frequently no electricity or heat. In the "intensive care unit" the nurses would borrow my watch in order to take a patient's pulse.

It was freezing cold. The sky stayed a uniform gray bank of clouds; only occasionally would we have a couple of hours of gelid sunshine. I soon fell into a routine. I woke up to my little short wave radio alarm, scrounged breakfast (wearing gloves and using a lantern), then plodded my sleepy way down the hill to replace the night doctor in the Zenica Hospital Emergency Department. There I would get ready for the first flush of land-mine injuries produced from the morning reconnaissance missions and the shrapnel wounds from the night before.

One day, though, the routine changed. The public health doctor was sick, so I was asked to go with a nurse to vaccinate a group of refugee children now housed with their parents up in the hills outside Old Vetiz.

"How many do you think will be there?" I asked Jason, the director of the relief agency I was working for.

He squinted. "Twenty," he said, "maybe forty."

We were sitting in a cafe in Zenica, drinking a morning cup of Turkish coffee and watching the passersby already out to shop in the market. Across from us was a shopping square where a Serbian shell had landed not long before, killing eleven people. At night you could sometimes hear the shelling, just thick, dull thuds, and sometimes you saw small, mysterious-looking fires up in the hills.

There is this weird domestic side to war. In the market that morning, even though there could be shelling any minute, everyone seemed to be going about their business as if there were no war, as if this were any other time except now; as if this Monday were any Monday in January. It did help that there was chicken and flour for sale now, unlike last year, when everyone starved. There were also raw coffee beans and cigarettes, if you had the right connections. The city was dreary but habitable, except for the shelling. Jason and I could have been sitting in a cafe in any down-on-your-luck town in any Eastern European country. Middle-aged women were nicely dressed, bundled in heavy coats and carrying big quadrangular purses held close to their bodies. The girls, mostly Muslim, wore long dresses and demure scarves to cover their hair, but they still managed, somehow, to be flirtatious. There were boys on bicycles and some old men sitting on the wooden bench in front of the mosque across from us, sunning their faces, talking, talking. And here I was about to vaccinate children. How more everyday could any medical chore be?

I walked down to the offices and found my driver, Amir. The first thing he had me do was put on a flak jacket. We were going to Travnik to the local hospital to pick up the vaccines we were to use—nothing fancy: measles, mumps, rubella, tetanus, diphtheria. The route was largely secure, I was told, or at least it was the week before. Then it was on to Old Vetiz, where a group of Muslim refugees was expecting us. Amir, the driver, was a big, beetlebrowed Bosnian, slow-moving and serious. He and I loaded up vehicle 778, a venerable Land Cruiser, with ice chests and powdered milk and headed south out of town, past the refugee market where Jason and I had drunk coffee, past the dead steel mill, past the horse-drawn wagons and the stream of pedestrians, both local and refugee, heading into town.

We also passed the occasional UNPROFOR tank: lone, white monsters with "UN" stenciled on the doors and hoods. Each tank had a soldier sitting upright in the turret. I would wave as we went past and the soldier would wave back. Tanks or no, they looked like sitting ducks.

Amir drove like a madman, just like all the other Bosnian drivers I had ridden with. There was the usual Central European pedestrian-be-damned attitude, but Bosnians here had one-upped this to anything-smaller-than-a-deuce-and-a-half-be-damned attitude. Passing was performed under heart-stopping circumstances: around blind corners, on one-lane bridges, in the midst of some townlet where children were playing. No one's horn, lights or brakes really worked. In Bosnia it was probably much safer to be shelled than to be driving.

We were traveling through what was the frontier between Bosnia and Croatia when they were at war. The land was now entirely desolate. Large houses stood vacant, with roofs missing or whole front walls gone, allowing you to see, doll house–like, into what was once someone's life. Barns were flattened. There was no livestock anywhere. No telephone lines; no roadway signs. The road itself was cratered from shelling. We detoured up hillsides and down into river beds to get around the worst of it—of course without ever slowing down.

Amir pointed out the bullet/grenade/shell blasts in the stucco of the houses and the frames of the eyeless windows. He told me that this area had been shelled for weeks and everyone who lived here had died. First the Croats took the territory and killed all the Muslims, then the Muslims retook the territory and killed all the Croats.

"Stupid," Amir muttered more to himself than to me. "Stupid, stupid." He sped up to pass a small pickup truck with several large panes of glass loaded in the back. This was the first civilian vehicle we had seen since we left Zenica. *Glass,* I thought. Well, at least someone was optimistic about the future.

The hospital in Travnik was smaller than in Zenica but just as bustling, perhaps more so. The corridors were crowded with Muslim women and children, one-legged men on crutches, tired-looking nurses. We made our way to a large freight elevator, possibly the only working elevator in Bosnia. The doors opened in slow motion and closed with the stolid finality of a tomb. We inched our way up, the wires twittering above us. A man—a double amputee—had wheeled his wooden wheelchair in at the last minute, and he sat looking around as if still dumbfounded by fate. Amir shook his head.

"This country . . . " he said under his breath.

We got lost and stumbled around until we finally found the pediatric ward. No one there, though, had any idea where the vaccine was stored. A snippy pediatrician told us we had come on the wrong day at the wrong time and of course that was why no one knew where the vaccine was. And she was terribly busy (she didn't look particularly busy) and we should wait until they had time to look, *if* they had time to look. Amir translated this for me in an undertone, punctuating his narrative with Bosnian expletives and a shaking head. We waited until it became clear they had forgotten us. Amir pushed me forward. "Say something," he told me.

"Say what? I can't speak enough Bosnian to say anything."

"No, no. Say something in English."

"She can speak English?"

"Just go ahead, talk."

I found the pediatrician in a back room, smoking. "Excuse me." I cleared my throat. "This is our one chance this month to get the refugees vaccinated." I was lying, of course. I had no idea what the schedule was. "It's imperative we get the vaccine today, now."

"Yes, please," the doctor answered.

Ten minutes later we were given the boxes of vaccine. Amir was muttering menacingly as we rode the elevator back down.

"She speaks English?" I asked Amir.

"She can speak maybe four words of English."

"So why did you have me . . ."

"She was too embarrassed to say she didn't understand you. Besides, you are an American. In front of you she has to pretend that she knows what's going on. It's the way they all are."

"Who all are?"

"Bosnians. My countrymen. They're idiots. They don't know how to organize anything. Everything they do in this country gets fucked up. These people are worse than the Russians."

We got back in the truck and continued on to Old Vetiz, where we would pick up a nurse. On this route fighting had been heavy as well, Amir told me, but many of the houses appeared at least marginally intact and inhabited. Some had windows barricaded with long, stout logs set at an angle. This was the best protection available in case of shelling. Other houses had been surrounded with rolls of barbed wire. There were some jury-rigged fences, a few chickens and some goats here and there. We finally rattled into a damaged but still intact-looking village. This would be Old Vetiz. We turned off at a small road lined with houses and stopped at a house snug up against the road. Amir beeped his horn loud and long. A window banged open and a woman's voice responded. For a moment she and Amir engaged in animated conversation, then the window closed with a bang.

"That is the nurse," Amir said with a sigh. "She'll be here in a moment."

Amir and I got out of the truck and walked down to the corner. We both stood gazing around at the blue, cloudless sky. It finally dawned on me that this was a beautiful day, almost spring. Old Vetiz was Sunday-morning still. We both watched a jet, high and silent, head east. The wind shook the trees a little, and three old men, each with a walking stick, rounded the corner and ambled slowly in our direction.

Amir pointed to a curve in the road. "See there."

He about-faced and pointed down the opposite way. "Five hundred meters," he said. He turned to the left. "Five hundred meters." He looked at me. "Muslims held this—five hundred meters square. Muslims held this and all around them were Croats. Nothing but Croats. It was a siege. No one could get in; no one could get out. The Muslims had some guns, weapons, you know, but not much. The Croats had more weapons but, to be frank, they didn't have that much either." He studied the house where the nurse lived. "That nurse and one paramedic were the only medicine here. For six months." He glared at the old men. "If you were shot in the leg and got blood poisoning, you died. If you were pregnant and couldn't deliver your baby, you died. If you went crazy, you also died . . ."

"And then?"

Amir squinted up toward the hills, thoughtfully, as if he was trying to remember. "And then the BIH army came over the mountains. In the middle of winter they made it through. They chopped trees down to get a truck in. They had food and weapons, and it was the first time these people had eaten something other than potatoes for months. The doctor came with them and he turned a schoolhouse up in the mountains into a hospital. That's where we are going."

"So this town is Muslim now?" I said.

"No, no. There are Croats here, too."

"Still?"

"Well," Amir said, "for now."

The nurse was big, bright and bustling, with hennaed hair, red-buffed fingernails and a suitcase-sized handbag. She lit up a cigarette as soon as she got into the truck and then talked a mile a minute to Amir as he silently drove on. We soon left the river valley and started up into the mountains. The air became alpine crisp, and the mountains surrounding us still cast a morning shadow across the road. We passed from a cratered village road onto a dirt track, ascending all the while. Eventually we turned into an almost impassable trail and climbed still more until we reached a small clearing where a couple of ramshackle buildings sat. There were some children playing on the frozen ground in front.

Amir grunted. "Well, they know we're coming."

When we got out of the truck, the children stopped and stared, as usual, chiefly at me, the obvious outsider, the infidel. The littlest ones stood at the door of the main building, regarding me somberly as they sucked their thumbs. We stepped through a small, rough-timbered door and into the hospital.

It was a four-room schoolhouse. We had entered a sort of anteroom that served as the triage area: a ten-foot-by-ten-foot cubicle with a desk, a sink and a couple of chairs. To the right, through two blankets that served as doors, was the hospital "ward." Amir pulled a blanket aside and I peeked in. There were four beds, neat as pins, two of which were occupied by dozing soldiers with bandaged heads. We walked beyond the anteroom into a larger room, which appeared to be the rest of the hospital. There were two examining tables and off in the corner an oversized ceramic stove. An ancient gentleman with a luxurious, snow-white mustache looked up from where he was stirring the fire. A woman standing by one of the examining tables lifted her arms and enveloped each of us in turn in an enormous embrace that smelled of peppermint. Introductions were made. The peppermint lady proved to be a practical nurse. The man by the stove was called Asur. His sole function seemed to be to feed the stove with firewood. A tall, gawky young man with acne was introduced as the paramedic. He would actually administer the vaccines. I was to perform a quick physical exam.

These were refugee children we would be seeing. Most of them were two to three years or more behind on their vaccinations, if they had received any at all. Already there were rumored to be several cases of German measles in the refugees from Bihac.

But first, of course, was coffee. This was made and served up while the nurse, the paramedic and the old man looked on, kibitzing all the while. It was good dark Turkish coffee but I really didn't want to drink it. There seemed so little here—five small cups and they used a metal medical-instrument tray to serve them on. The sugar bowl was passed from hand to hand, the precise amount titrated on a little spoon before it was slowly stirred in. The sugar bowl was almost empty.

As we all sat drinking silently, I heard a faint hum outside—like the muted noise of traffic or a rushing river. I listened for a moment before I realized it was the sound of children—many children.

"How many kids are we going to see?"

"I don't know. Maybe a hundred."

"Croatians and Muslims both?"

Amir glared at me. "This is a Muslim clinic."

"Why is it so far out of town?"

"Muslims don't go into town. There are Croats in town."

"But town is still a part of Bosnia."

"Muslims don't go to Croat clinic."

"Why is that? Because they can't?"

"No, because they are Muslim."

Suitably unenlightened, I examined one of the vaccination kits while I finished my coffee. It was supplied by the World

Health Organization and was rather ingenious. Needles and syringes were packed in a box, the box doubling as a waste container as the syringes were used. You attached a plastic syringe to the metal needle using a spring-loaded device. After use, the needles were to be inserted into a small plastic cup and the syringes put back into the box container. When the kit was finished, the box, now filled with flammable syringes, could be burned, leaving just some ash. The only medical waste was the small plastic container with the needles, which could then be buried. Even more ingenious was the fact that all the information about how to use the box was relayed using pictures only—no words. A universal medical device.

I tried to imagine a world with a hundred diseases just like AIDS—diseases that could savage a whole generation in a heartbeat or two—in which no one had the power to stop them, nothing worked. That was life before vaccines. Polio, measles, rubella—killers all—and in just one generation we have forgotten them. To many doctors, myself included, many of these diseases are almost theoretical. I, for example, have never seen a case of diphtheria or pertussis. The two cases of tetanus I have seen were both in intravenous drug abusers, the only safe harbor for the disease remaining in the U.S. In one the diagnosis was made not by me but by a Filipino nurse, who said she had seen hundreds of cases back in the Philippines. Here in Bosnia I had already seen several cases of rheumatic fever and a case we thought was miliary tuberculosis, diseases now rare in America. It was sobering to think that the mundane process of vaccinating these children might ultimately save more lives than any UN-brokered peace treaty. At least I told myself that.

Finally the time came to open the side door that led outside. By now the faint roar of children had turned into a tidal wave of sound. When the door opened, the crush outside was so bad that one child fell immediately onto the floor while two others spilled over on top of him.

Our first patient was a frightened tow-headed boy, a little on the thin side but otherwise healthy. I was more worried about his mother, a tubercular-looking woman with a bad cough and a mouth full of rotting teeth. She handed over the child's passport with a nervous flutter of her hands. Vaccination information was kept in passports in Bosnia—otherwise the passports were considered useless. Her shoulders trembled as she tried to hold her son still while I listened to his chest. His lungs were clear, heart okay. I made a notation on his card and sent him on to the anteroom, where the paramedic was waiting to inject the appropriate vaccine. Upon entering the anteroom the child immediately began to scream. I could hear his mother speaking sternly to him in Bosnian and then the sound of a slap, which made the child wail all the more. The next child, whom I had begun to examine, heard the screaming, rolled his eyes and looked at me. I could see myself momentarily as he saw me, the embodiment of all the evil in the world, a monster in a white coat. He let out a scream, and since his mother was holding his hands down, tried to fight me off with his feet. He, too, was physically in pretty good shape.

Next.

A little girl and her younger sister, both thumb suckers; one clung to an elderly rag doll. Next, a set of twins, mirror images, who both were somehow sporting matching Bart Simpson sweaters. Another little boy showed us where he had cut his finger. The nurse kissed it and then I kissed it too. At that point he burst into tears.

Obviously, despite the war, babies were still being made, children were growing. The next generation of Muslims was there already and growing, a generation that so far had known only war. The children were for the most part surprisingly healthy. I wondered how much food and clothing the parents had forgone to keep them this way. They were also well scrubbed and dressed neatly. But there were some disasters here. A little girl with a heart murmur that sounded like a sewing machine, classic for ventricular septal defect—a hole in the heart. In the States this could be repaired; here she would die young. Another with a cleft lip and palate, a serious-looking little boy led in by his five-year-old sister, who asked me to fix his lip. A child with a hand laceration, unattended and now festering. A child severely underweight and with a cough. Tuberculosis? Parasites?

All was chaos, but in a good-natured way. I had Amir teach me Bosnian for "beautiful baby," *krasno bebe*. "*Krasno bebe!*" I would exclaim to the mothers. "Beautiful child!" There were teething problems, problems with cradle cap and ringworm. As the morning wore on, women brought in tiny babies, one a month old and another only six or seven days. New mothers handled the children as if they were fine porcelain. Experienced mothers, the ones with three or four kids in tow, handled the babies as if they were a sack of potatoes. They'd fling them over their arms while they delivered a swat to the other kids.

One father, in uniform, brought his daughter in. He squatted down to comfort her, a beautiful little girl with hair so blond it was really white. She stood safely in his shadow as he pulled her to his chest and patted her back to reassure her. "It's all right," he kept saying. "It's all right; it's all right."

I compared these children in my mind with the kids I knew from the city of Zenica itself. There the kids were street scamps, tough kids, mean. Those kids acted like miniature gangsters; they played real war. One would follow you with the barrel of his Y-shaped stick-cum-machine gun, or bomb you with acorns from the branches of a tall tree. Some would shadow you wherever you walked and rush you every so often to make sure you hadn't changed your mind about giving out some spare change. Not all the children were like this. There was, for example, the little girl in a pink pinafore with pink ribbons in her hair (a triumph in these circumstances) holding her mother's hand as they went to market. There were neatly dressed children going quietly to the Orthodox church or to their mosque. Also, on the outskirts of town, there were children working: carrying water, hauling stacks of firewood, minding the occasional goat. They seemed mute and solemn and like little old men.

In town the children who begged were mostly Gypsy children, I was told. They certainly begged like professionals. They created a diversionary scene in front of you, with at least twenty ten-year-old boys chanting, "Deutsche marks, deutsche marks, deutsche marks," while the twenty-first went after your wallet from behind. By then there was no Bosnian currency; all transactions were in German marks. If you tried to give the children Bosnian coins, they just gave them back with a look of total disgust. However, if you gave a single pfennig to one of them, you would have the entire pack stuck to you like glue wherever you walked. Crying, wailing, hands lifted, and, if that didn't work, getting down on their knees, pleading. These kids can spot a foreigner a block away—just like the old days under communism when any American in an Eastern bloc country stood out like scarlet. Those kids had flawless eyes.

On my first night in Zenica, after I had locked up and gone to my room, I heard a bang, bang, bang downstairs. Someone was pounding on the door. I found my flashlight and went back down the stairs. The bottom half of the door was textured glass and I could see through it the moon shadow of a child.

"What?" I asked.

More pounding on the door.

"What do you want?"

There was a plaintive, tinny whisper on the other side of the door. "Deutsche marks," the child moaned.

"Go away."

He continued to bang on the door. "Deutsche marks, deutsche marks . . ."

"Go away."

The banging stopped, then started again. I switched off the light and stumbled back upstairs. Behind me, I could hear the voice, disembodied, there probably long after the child has gone, that tinny, whispering voice: "Deutsche marks, deutsche marks, deutsche marks."

*   *   *

At noon the nurse locked the doors and restirred the fire for coffee. I went out to the Land Cruiser and brought in a box of biscuits I had managed to find in Zenica. The paramedic came back in accompanied by a tall man of about thirty-five wearing a baggy sweater. Disheveled hair.

"Dr. Pamela. This is Dr. Yassar."

As I stood up to shake his hand, someone called him back out to the ward. When I sat down again, Amir whispered in my ear, "That man is a hero to these people."

I looked at Amir. "How come?"

"He was with the men that came up over the pass, the men who broke the siege of Old Vetiz. He built this hospital here and was the surgeon—the only doctor—these people had. He did everything. Everything. He is a good man."

"Where did he do his surgery?" I had an image of amputations done with a buzz saw by a campfire.

"Right in there." Amir pointed. "Go look."

There was a door on the north side of the room. I opened it and peeked inside. It was a small room that obviously was used as a full-service operating room. In the center was a wooden table, something like an old kitchen table with an extension at one end. There was a tall, modern surgical light pulled over against the side wall. In one corner there was an old bookcase that served as storage for medical supplies—gloves, instrument kits. Against the other wall was the oldest anesthesia machine I had ever seen, a big metal box surrounded by a hodgepodge of rubber tubing and copper and glass containers. Next to it on the floor was a suction machine with a foot pump to drive it.

I tried to imagine bringing that anesthesia machine, with its glass containers, that suction pump, those instruments, over a mountain pass in the dead of winter. But it was very simple. I couldn't.

At four the parade was stopped again, and everyone gathered in the anteroom for more coffee. The practical nurse brought in an enormous cheese pie for all of us. Forks were laid out. We ate directly from the tray because, Amir whispered to me, there were no plates.

The surgeon came back in from the ward room. I asked about his anesthesia. "Do you use much ketamine?"

"Yes, all the time. Very good drug. I use it for all my amputations."

Ketamine is an odd drug. It is an excellent "field anesthetic" for use in war zones. But it does have one major drawback . . .

"Do you find that people hallucinate as they wake up?"

"Oh," he said, waving a fork. "Always. And it can really be terrible. We need four or five people to hold some raving soldiers down."

I wanted to ask the surgeon more but Amir said no. "Not now. He has to see patients. We'll finish with the children and go for coffee afterward."

In the afternoon we vaccinated even more children. By midafternoon we had seen over three hundred. I had to stop examining any but the sickest. They all began to blur into one another. At last, though, the door was closed. The stragglers were sent away with "Come back next time." I went out to the anteroom, where I found the used contents of the WHO vaccine kit scattered everywhere—syringes on the windowsills, needles on the floor, the box upended and empty. The instructions were wadded up by the sink. So much for the WHO kit.

We closed up shop, the paramedic, Amir and I. The doctor met us out by the truck. "We're going for beers," Amir told me as we piled into the car. I tried to figure out where in the hinterlands of Bosnia we would find beer.

The doctor and I, with Amir translating, talked medical shop. Have you had much experience with these new drugs, cephalosporins? Do you use staples for skin closures? What is your specialty?

He couldn't really understand me when I told him I specialized in emergency medicine. "You only take care of accidents? How can you only take care of accidents?" He was a humorous-looking guy, tall, long-faced, with a three-day growth of beard. He had the air of being a happy man, with overtones of thoughtfulness. He seemed like a man who, even in the most difficult of times, was satisfied with life.

We drove for about twenty minutes—bouncing along a little rutted gravel road. Unexpectedly the gravel turned into pavement, badly scarred but recognizable. We rounded a corner and there was a parking lot—with not a single bomb crater. A *parking* lot. Over a little bridge at the far end of the lot was a low-built, rough-timbered rambling building looking out over the stream and beyond a small pond.

"What the hell is that?"

"It's a hotel," Amir told me.

"A hotel?"

"From before the war."

"Here?"

"Oh, yes. People come up here to fish. Used to come up."

"And now?"

"Oh," Amir said, pointing. "The soldiers stay here to relax, you know, after bad times on the front."

The paramedic looked around. "They bombarded everything around here. Everything. But for some reason most of this place survived."

We went inside. There was a large lobby that clearly had once had furniture. The front desk was to the right and empty; the whole place seemed empty until we walked into the large dining room. There three or four tables still stood, and at one a couple of military officers sat idly. They were being served by a lanky waiter dressed in a tuxedo jacket and shirt but no tie. He beckoned us toward a table that overlooked a pond.

"Nice job he has," the surgeon commented.

We ordered a round of beer and talk turned immediately to the war.

"What was the siege of Old Vetiz like?"

"Well," the paramedic said, warming up, "the Croats attacked us at Vetiz, but we held the line and the Croats couldn't get through. We used everything we had as a weapon. Everything. Like fire extinguishers, for example. You take a fire extinguisher and fill it up with explosives and then you put it in a metal tube with a little gunpowder—and you point it at the Croatians and—well, it works pretty good. After that the Croats were losing ground, so they bring in a special unit with helicopter and special soldiers. And we Bosnians ask ourselves: if we don't have real weapons, how shall we make them think we have real weapons? So we got a submachine gun and we mounted it on top of this big metal drum so it would have a bigger noise. When we fired it, it sounded like—like an antiaircraft gun. That kept the helicopter away; we scared the pilot. So the Croats brought in the Croat special forces. They were going to have a surprise attack. But the Bosnians knew that the special forces were there, so the Bosnians let them creep up. We let the Croat special forces move closer in, closer, closer. We held our fire until the Croats got so close, you know, that they were really on Bosnian territory, then the Bosnian soldiers crept around behind them and boom-boom. No more Croatian special forces."

The paramedic looked up at the rafters. "Sixty Bosnian people died in four months."

"How?"

He shrugged. "The usual way. Snipers mostly."

The waiter returned with beers and bowed over the surgeon as he poured his beer into a glass. The surgeon sat gazing at it thoughtfully and then looked up at me, a glint in his eyes. "I think everyone in America has this idea that all Muslims of Bosnia are fanatical extremists—all the women are in purdah and all men want to die in a jihad. But we are not like that at all."

I thought of a poll I had seen before I left: only 40 percent of Americans could identify the Serbs as the ethnic group that was fighting against the Bosnian government.

"What was the fighting like here?" I asked him in return.

The paramedic slapped the surgeon on his back and said, "Go ahead, tell her."

The surgeon came over the mountain with the Bosnian army. Their mission was to break through to Old Vetiz, to provide relief and advance the front. They built a makeshift road through the forest and made it to a small valley, this valley, about three kilometers from Old Vetiz. The surgeon set up a hospital in the old four-room school house. He used that ancient ventilator for anesthesia (and plenty of ketamine). Rudimentary supplies were provided by the army—medication, suture material, surgical equipment, all brought over the pass. "You know what we saw most of?" he asked. "Head injury—we couldn't do much for those sorry bastards—penetrating wounds to the neck, chest and abdomen. I had three cases of hemothorax in the chest, and I hadn't enough new blood to transfuse so I used the blood from the chest, what do you call that? Yes, auto-transfusion. Well, I didn't explore them, I couldn't because we were being shelled. And all three survived. Three patients! I could probably publish it as a case report, don't you think?"

The paramedic leaned toward me. "This surgeon did all this five hundred meters from the front. Constant bombardment and sniper fire."

"I saw things I would never forget," the surgeon continued. "Never, never."

"Like . . ." I said. I immediately felt ashamed for asking. But I didn't stop him.

"Like an old man up on that ridge right there. He took his grandson—the Croats usually just ignored the kids that were underfoot—so the grandfather wrapped up explosive around his grandson and set the detonator and sent him down to play where the Croats were in the valley. Then, BOOM. Dead five soldiers and one grandchild."

"How could anyone . . ."

"We have to stop them some way," he said to me, suddenly fierce. "You see, we have no weapons, the Serbs and the Croats have all the weapons. We have no helicopters, no missiles, nothing but what we can scrape together ourselves. But we must fight them or they will kill all the Muslims. Believe me. They will line us up before our own graves and shoot every one of us. They'll destroy even the *memory* of us. They will murder us all."

We drove back home in silence, Amir and I, through the blighted landscape. At the offices we counted through the forms. We had vaccinated nearly five hundred children. Still I knew there were many more.

I was late for my evening shift in the ER. It was quiet when I got there, no major traumas all day. My first patient was a woman with a sprained ankle, another everyday event in the midst of war. I sent her over for an x-ray. The radiology tech sent her back, telling her, "We don't waste radiology film on ankle sprains."

An old woman, gnarled and worn, had an infected wound on her arm. She had fled with her family over the hills a few weeks before. She was the only one of the family to survive and she still seemed completely bewildered. She wanted to tell me her story. Maybe if she told a doctor her story it would make more sense. But she didn't have a chance; there was another patient.

The patient was a slender, very nervous-appearing young man dressed in blue jeans meant for someone twice his size. He was complaining of headache, a swollen neck, chest pressure, problems with his kidneys and weight loss.

Through Yasha, my translator, I asked the obvious question. "Are you in the army?"

Yasha and the patient talked for several minutes until Yasha raised his hand to stop him and said to me, "He's in the Black Swan battalion."

"What's that?"

"It's a very, very . . . tense group. They are the advanced troops, always on the front line, always in bad places. In America I think you call them the Green Berets."

The young man in front of me did not look like suitable material for the Green Berets. But where to start? This man was complaining of everything. "Has he ever seen a doctor for these complaints?"

"Yes."

"What did the doctor say?"

"He said he was mad."

"Mad?"

"Yes," Yasha said. "Like crazy."

"Crazy how?"

Eventually we got the full story. The patient had been very close to a grenade that exploded about six months before. Most of his platoon was killed. Since then he had been terrified of the war, of dying. One night in his barracks he thought his platoon mates were trying to murder him. He leaped out of bed, grabbed his gun and began firing at random. Fortunately no one was hurt.

He was then placed in jail where he was told he was mad—crazy—but not crazy enough to be discharged from the army. He was on leave now but was supposed to report back tomorrow morning.

I checked him over. Other than the weight loss—which I believed because of his baggy pants—there was nothing abnormal on his exam.

"We can check his urine . . . We can check . . ."

Yasha explained this to him and then turned back to me. "He doesn't want any tests."

"He doesn't want tests?"

"No."

"Does he want medication, is that why he's here?"

More animated conversation. Then: "He doesn't want medication."

"Then what the hell does he want?"

This time Yasha and the soldier talked for a long time. Finally, Yasha turned to me and said, "He wants a statement that says he's too sick to be in the army and then he wants a visa to leave the country."

I closed my eyes and pressed them shut to ease the headache. When I opened them again I found Yasha gazing out the window to where a lonely light bobbed in the distance. Yasha had been a medical student before the war. He, too, was desperate to get out.

"Tell him," I said, "that there is nothing I can do for him. Tell him we don't give out visas in the Emergency Department." It's just a fact of life.

"He wants to know if we can write him something that would say he was too sick to fight."

I looked down at this fellow, shivering on the gurney. He looked as fragile as a young girl. He just didn't want to die. What was the matter with that? As a doctor I should understand that. There should never be war.

I put one hand on his shoulder and reached out for his other hand. "I'm sorry," I said. "He has to go to a military doctor for that. Maybe they can help him. I can't do it."

There was, ultimately, so little I could do. I stood there asking myself, Am I really making a difference?

Then, I thought, well, vaccination.

Earlier in the afternoon, up in the mountains above Old Vetiz, back when I thought I was making a major contribution to the war effort (these things can turn on a dime), I had gone outside to take a break and sit in the sunshine. I sat on the steps of the schoolhouse and looked around. A dozen men stood talking in the yard, a few in uniform, or as much of a uniform as men wore in Bosnia. The others were dressed for farming. One young soldier flirted with a young girl with long hair. The women stood off near a fence chatting happily. The scene was utterly bucolic. It was then that I realized that these were the former Muslim inhabitants of Old Vetiz—the ones who held the siege as long as they could. They must have finally retreated to the surrounding mountains. I knew this was going on elsewhere. Territory was fought for and then finally abandoned when the townspeople melted into the mountains. This was a short-term solution only. It was only a matter of time before the Serbs or the Croats claimed this land as well.

Amir joined me and we walked up the hill. There was a field in front of us, and then above us stood what looked like an old barracks or stable. And there was some kind of statue, human sized, arms raised in a sort of benediction. "What is that?" I asked Amir.

He looked up. "It's a monument. To the war."

I looked around at him. "The war?"

"Not this war, the other war. World War Two."

We walked up the hill through the brush, stepping over mounds of dirty snow.

"That barracks there," he said pointing, "that was used by the Ustasha during World War Two. A concentration camp. A death camp." Amir stopped, reached down and plucked a stalk of grass. He chewed its end thoughtfully.

"This is where they killed—what is the word in English—you know, people who fight for freedom?"

"Partisans."

"Yes, partisans. This is where they killed the partisans and tortured them. It used to be a slaughterhouse, a regular cow slaughterhouse. Then it became a human slaughterhouse. My uncle died here, I think. We don't know for sure."

We arrived at the top of the hillock. There was a small memorial: a statue of a woman gazing at the ground sorrowfully, arms outstretched. Underneath her on the pedestal "1945" was etched in the granite. There was a coda in Bosnian carved underneath. I didn't ask Amir to translate it. I was afraid that somewhere it would contain that classic memorial phrase, beloved of survivors and those who remember, the ever hopeful

"Never again."

12

HOW TO TREAT TETANUS

Also a sign for them is that we bear their progeny on the
  laden ship.
If we will, we drown them,
and there is no helper for them
nor are they saved, unless as a mercy from us . . .

—The Koran

IN NIGERIA WITH *MÉDECINS SANS FRONTIÈRES*, I, the lone
American, drove the French crazy in many ways, but one way in
particular was by taking photographs. "You are here as a doctor,"
Pierre told me as he watched me rack down my camera lens on
a child covered with necrotic purpura, "not a tourist."

"I am also here to bear witness," I told him, zeroing in with
my camera now at a different angle, "to witness what I've seen."

He had no response to this. But I did. Photographing made
me queasy. I felt like a predator, even though, every time I would
ask permission (not with words, of course, not with my ten words,
max, of Hausa). I would touch the camera with an index finger
and then gesture to my potential subjects. They would always nod,
yes, but how could they do otherwise? We, who came with everything that saves lives, how could they refuse us? Worse was that
after the first day in this land of infectious atrocities, I pho-

tographed only the worst of the worst, some terrible confluence of tragedies: the woman dead with cholera found one morning at the edge of the camp—she couldn't make it the last one hundred feet to the clinic; the boy who had lost half his face to meningococcal purpura; the old man dying alone and covered with flies; the baby already dead. There I was, checking different angles, trying to get the correct exposure. "I want others to witness this," I told my medical colleagues, but my justification was something of a sham and I knew it. I was right, too. Most people back in the States would look through the first few images only, in my book of photographs, and then they would put them aside. Or I would show a couple at a medical lecture, to illustrate a clinical problem. The room would always go very quiet, and there would follow a collective sigh and a few amplified coughs. "Wow," someone would say. Then we would move on. This was not for them. Nothing they had ever seen could be like this. Ultimately, the only one I really bore witness to was myself. I pasted the photos that meant the most to me into a scrapbook, and I would leaf through the book sometimes, late at night, after a bad shift in the ER, just to remember. There was the kid with purpura that had necrosed his entire right foot. There was *that* woman (me standing beside her wearing a ridiculous grin and a Hemingwayesque safari jacket the clinic staff told me only an American would ever wear) we brought back from the dead, who was now *yaworeke*, cured. Then there was the strangest picture of all, the backseat of a car—a little sedan—where a black man lay, pietà-like, over the laps of two other frightened-looking men, their black faces burned white in the false light of the camera flash. One of the men is holding up a glass bottle of saline, the other grasps at the IV site. The figure on their lap is rigid, stiff, as if he were badly painted, or rather, if you thought of him as a sort of Christ, as I thought of him, he was an immobile Christ of a twelfth century-triptych, no later.

This man had tetanus.

* * *

I was rounding one afternoon, out in the fly-infested "intensive care verandah," when I stopped at a patient who had been puzzling me for days. He was a young man who, someone told me, was a policeman in a small village some distance from Kano. His three brothers were caring for him. He had been here on the verandah for three or four days. "Meningitis, fairly classic case," I had told myself initially. (Of course, my workup consisted of lifting the man's head up to see whether his neck was stiff—it was.) I had treated him with oily chloramphenicol and when that didn't work, ampicillin. He was one of the few patients who didn't either die or get better; he just slowly, slowly kept looking worse and worse. Was this a weird case of meningitis, I asked myself, or was it something else? Occasionally we would find, after a day or two of symptoms that suggested meningitis, that in fact we had a cholera case in our midst. We would have to drag the patient off to the cholera camp and dowse the ground where he or she had lain with chlorine bleach. But this wasn't cholera. Sometimes I would wonder—malaria? Cerebral malaria? I had no way to tell other than empiric therapy, so I went ahead and gave IV chloroquine. Sometimes when I did this, the patient would make a stunning recovery—but not very often. I tried chloroquine on this patient, but he only seemed to look a little worse, just as before.

That day I just squatted there, looking at him. The man was conscious but extremely weak, a strange type of weakness. He could gesture a little with his hands, but he had trouble speaking, or even swallowing. His brothers would try to feed him a little soup, but it was clear that for this man even opening his mouth was extremely difficult, almost painful. That morning the patient lay back stiffly, his head in the lap of one of his brothers. As I watched him, his hands made the pill-rolling gesture common to Parkinson's patients, while across his naked belly there were ripples of abdominal muscle contractions, a wave of fasciculations— tiny, chaotic muscle spasms. Whatever this was, it didn't look like any meningitis—meningococcal, malarial or otherwise—that I had ever seen.

I picked up his hand. It immediately assumed a claw shape. I tried stroking it gently, but this only seemed to make the hand spasm worse. I checked his temperature, using the only thermometer I had, my hand on his bare chest. Maybe a low-grade fever. As I hunched over, looking at him, the medical director of the mission, Jean-Paul, a Zairian political refugee with a lifetime of experience in tropical disease, walked by and paused. He must have been puzzled by the sight of one of his doctors kneeling by a patient as if in prayer. He looked down at me, an eyebrow raised in question.

"*What is this?*" I asked him.

At this he looked even more puzzled. Thinking back, I realized that the expression on his face was incredulity. He couldn't believe I didn't know what this patient had.

"This man has tetanus," he said, nodding his head at me, and then walked on.

I sat back on my heels and looked down at the man. "Tetanus," I said in wonder. "Lockjaw!" To an American doctor this was a disease as mythical as the plague. There are, maybe, a handful of cases a year in America.

I jumped up and ran after the director, catching up to him out on the barren brown yard in front of the hospital. "Tetanus," I said. "But what do I do?"

He looked at me as if I were daft. "Why, you send him to a tetanus hospital." He moved on, shaking his head again.

I walked back to where the man was and gazed down at him lying there on the dirty floor. A tetanus hospital, I thought. For a moment I imagined a real hospital with real beds and real sheets and floors not covered with contaminated needles. Screens on the windows. No flies. I thought of my hospital back in the States. I saw before me, like a mirage of precious water, our supply room. The room was crammed with everything you could ever want to take care of a sick patient, shelves and bins filled with endotracheal tubes and Foley catheters, syringes, sterile needles, bottles of Pedialyte, triple-lumen central lines, Betadine, hydrogen peroxide, We Care hand lotion, suture kits: everything disposable, use once and throw away.

I found Simon, my nursing assistant. "Jean-Paul says we must send this man to a tetanus hospital," I told him, "wherever that is."

Simon gestured vaguely to the east. "By the old city," he said.

"Do they have a way to get there?"

Simon shrugged. "I will find out."

It turned out that they did. The brothers had a friend with a truck, an ancient Ford pickup, which showed up just at sunset. The three men loaded the patient into the flatbed and fastened the tailgate closed with bailing wire. The whole truck seemed to be held together by rust, baling wire and the Nigerian equivalent of duct tape. I could see it rumbling down the potholed, washboarded Kano dirt roads, shaking each bump into this man's bones. At least he would make it to a tetanus hospital, I thought, where people knew what to do much better than I. I hadn't thought about tetanus, other than to give the vaccine, since medical school.

Out of curiosity, when I went home that night, I stopped at the MSF offices to search our medical library. The library consisted of four books, three medical texts and one medical novel. (Called *The City and the Covenant*, it opened inauspiciously with the sentence: "The uterus of the woman on the bed contracted according to its cellular intelligence.") The most recent book of the four was a textbook of internal medicine—published in 1964. I had to blow the dust off the top, just like in the movies, and when I cracked the book open there was that tropical smell of something ripely rotten. Someone had visited this chapter before me. I found a bookmark there, a clipping from a newspaper that crumbled when I touched it. I glanced through the text. The first thing that caught my eye was the phrase "horse serum"—the book was that old. In the middle of the page was a drawing of a "spore forming bacillus" shaped like a squashed cigar. *Clostridium tetani.* The tetanus bacillus.

"The bacterium surrounds itself with a protective shell," the caption read, "that makes it resistant to heat, cold, floods and desiccation. Tetanus spores are everywhere, in the soil, on animals, in humans . . . *blah, blah, blah* . . . facultative anaerobes." That meant *Clostridia* lived without oxygen.

"The disease is more common in the tropics than in temperate zones. In third world countries tetanus is a disease of the newborn; *Tetanus neonatorum*. Typically the infection occurs because the bacillus invades the umbilical stump at the time of birth, particularly if, as is common in underdeveloped countries, the midwife uses a dirty knife or a contaminated piece of glass to cut the umbilical cord. In some countries the infant mortality rate from tetanus approaches 50 percent."

I paused considering the sentence. "Approaches," what a delicately euphemistic term. But what that coy sentence meant was that in underdeveloped countries one half of *all* babies born died of tetanus. I knew this fact after reading through an MSF report on health care in Nigeria. Things were no better now than they were in 1964. Worse probably.

"The tetanus syndrome," the book continued, "is not caused by the bacillus *per se* but by an exotoxin." I looked up from the page. I remembered this from medical school (the memory accompanied by the faint perfume of formaldehyde). An exotoxin is a poison that bacilli, under the right conditions, manufacture and export to the body of the host. In some lungless part of the body—say a necrotic wound or a cut—the conditions become just right for the *Clostridium* to flourish, multiply and manufacture exotoxin. The exotoxin makes its way to the circulation and is disseminated throughout the body. The toxin is called *tetanospasmin*—one of the strongest poisons known to man.

Tetanospasmin mimics the neurotransmitters that govern our muscle system, causing muscle cells to fire. The bacterium itself doesn't do this; only the toxin does. When the body is awash with tetanospasmin, the muscles depolarize—contract—chaotically.

This produces the tonic-clonic movements and the muscle seizures that are the hallmark of the disease.

I went back to the text. "The first signs of tetanus are small muscle spasms that involve the muscles of the neck and the jaw. Patients become unable to swallow normally or even open their mouth. Hence *lockjaw*, as the common name for the disease."

This was the stage my patient was in now.

"*Treatment*." The essential part. I lingered here because I knew tetanus was treatable, quite treatable, even in 1964 and even in Nigeria. Not much magic here. Just penicillin, Valium and "horse serum," (now replaced with cloned tetanus antitoxin). Penicillin kills the tetanus bacillus, Valium reduces the muscle spasms, and the tetanus antiserum deactivates the toxin. One, two, three. This is the regimen they would use in the tetanus hospital.

I went back to my room and looked through my own library. Somehow I had lost my book of W. H. Auden's poems. This reduced my library from four volumes to three, one of which was a textbook of tropical disease. This book had pages and pages about traveler's diarrhea but nothing in it about tetanus. My other two books were the *Lonely Planet Guide to Africa on a Shoestring*, and *The Complete Poems of John Berryman*.

John Berryman did seem more relevant to Nigeria than Auden—in his claustrophobic, paranoiac, boozy sort of way. His mood matched more the political situation here. Throughout the week, there had been riots in Lagos and in some of the up-river towns. There was no gasoline; this despite Nigeria's position as one of the top oil exporters in the world. In Kano people stood for hours in line waiting for a liter or two. The cholera epidemic in Bauchi was even worse than the one we had here; we had no resources to do anything about it, and nobody else seemed to care. Meanwhile, the newspapers featured headlines such as "Abacha Honored by the Federation of Trolley Conductors."

And so I turned to my Berryman. I sat up that night, reading him by flashlight:

> I am, outside. Incredible panic rules.
> People are blowing and beating each other without
> mercy.
> Drinks are boiling. Iced
> drinks are boiling. The worse anyone feels, the
> worse treated he is.
> Fools elect fools.

Nigeria pinned down on paper.

The morning after I sent the patient to the tetanus hospital, I started rounds and found him in his usual spot, still surrounded by his three brothers. They looked as if they had never left.

"What happened?" I asked the brothers.

"The hospital had no beds."

"No beds? Did they give him anything?"

The brothers shook their heads.

"Did they say when they would have beds?"

The brothers shook their heads.

"He's much worse," the brothers told me. One of them showed me how badly the patient's muscles spasmed by attempting to flex and extend his right arm. The arm was stiff as a board.

I squatted down next to the patient and momentarily put my face in my hands. "*Iced drinks are boiling.*" When I looked, up I saw Simon, the brothers, even the patient, gazing back at me expectantly. I was the doctor; I must do something. I reached out and patted the man's shoulders. This set off a ripple of spasms that spread across his chest onto his neck and belly. His arms rocked stiffly, his legs extended, quivering, tensed. His whole body shook, and you could see under the skin his twitching muscles: fasciculations. His arms twitched as well. His belly was as tense as a drum. This could have marched right out of the textbook I had read last night.

I sat there, momentarily a scientist, watching the fasciculations with interest. The millions of tiny muscle cells, contracting chaotically, produced muscle spasms. The effect was such that the entire muscle leaped to tense life. I could see on the patient, as if he were a weight lifter, the well-demarcated rectus and oblique muscles of the belly; the sternocleidomastoid on either side of his jaw was tensed, straining to bring his head down. Then I looked up at the man's face. It was in full spasm now as well. His eyes were open wide; they seemed to stare, like some cartoon character, right out of his head. His lips drew back in a hideous grin so that all his teeth showed. *Risus sardonicus*. The broad grimace of tetanus—also seen in strychnine poisoning. Contracture of the masseter and other muscles of the jaw and mouth caused the lips to draw back in a "sarcastic smile"—really more like the hideous grin of a naked skull. How could they have refused him at the tetanus hospital?

Oh, God, what to do. I thought back to the book last night. Treatment: Valium, penicillin, "horse serum." Well, I knew we had the Valium—we used it to treat the seizures commonly seen in the meningitis patients. We also had a small supply of penicillin (differing slightly in chemical makeup from the ampicillin we used to treat the critical meningitis patients). The last drug I was not so sure of—rather I was sure we didn't have it in our supplies. The question was: could I get it elsewhere?

There was a pharmacy nearby. I had never visited it, but patients would sometimes show me packages of medicine they had bought there: Cephazolin, neomycin cream, ibuprofen.

I peeled the label from a liter of normal saline and wrote on it, "tetanus immune globulin." Underlined.

"Here," I told one of the brothers, handing him the label. "Pharmacy."

The man stared down at the label in his hand, looked up at me, then got to his feet and fled.

I started an IV in the patient's arm and taped over it with my usual sign:

TOUCH THIS IV
AND YOU DIE
—DR. GRIM

Simon went to chase the Valium down while I rummaged around in my portable supply box. There was a little bit of everything in there: angiocaths, IV tubing we used as tourniquets, vials of ampicillin and oily chloramphenicol. I found a syringe and plucked it out, cradling it in my hand. There was something comfortable in the feel of this plastic; handling it has been my life's work. The smooth cylindrical 10 cc syringe, as simple as water, the plunger working like a piston in my hands. I returned to my box, groping around, and fished out several 20-gauge needles in their little shrouds, half plastic, half paper. Comforting to touch.

Simon returned with the glass ampule of Valium: 10 mg in 2 cc of saline. I broke the neck, dipped the needle in and inverted the bottle as I withdrew the plunger to fill the syringe. This must be how an addict feels when he gets his little kit out, I thought. The feel of the spoon, the warmth of the match. That knowledge of "I'm in control now; I know what needs to be done."

The patient's brother returned with an ampule labeled "Tetanus Immune Globulin." There was some murky-looking liquid inside. Who knew what it was? I broke this ampule open and sucked up the contents with another syringe. Needles, syringes, ampules of drugs. I was in my element now. Even these few things were enough to make me think: technology. I was in a great mood. We were going to fix this guy.

I injected 5 cc of Valium and then sat back to watch. It was like watching a choppy sea become calm. The muscle tremors and wavelets subsided, and a moment later the patient sank back with a sigh. His shoulders unclenched, and his head dropped to one side. How many days had he been tied up in muscular knots like this and I hadn't even noticed? Slowly the patient turned his head to look upward. After a moment he raised his left arm up and reached, stretched. There was no spasm. He looked up at me and reached out his hand as if to show me that his arm worked; he could control it. Then very carefully, as if he were afraid something would break, he smiled.

The next step, I thought, was to find out where the *Clostridium* was hiding. In most people infected with tetanus, the portal of entry was a cut in the skin that had become infected. I asked his brothers. "Has he injured himself recently? A wound of some kind?"

"No, no," the brothers said.

"Was he usually a healthy man?"

"Yes, yes. Very healthy."

I did a quick physical—nothing was obviously abnormal, no hitherto-missed festering wounds. I squatted there for a while, musing; while I did, the brothers told me a little more about the patient.

They were all men of the Hausa tribe, the largest tribe in this area. The patient served as a local sheriff in a town about twenty miles away. (Apparently, although he was a government employee and therefore on the national payroll, he didn't receive enough salary to go to a private hospital for treatment.) A week ago he had become very sick. His brothers had heard that they might find a hospital here that treated sick patients for free. In order to get to the hospital, the brothers managed to get a ride part way and then they walked the rest of it, another four or five miles, carrying their brother.

The patient had a wife and two sons. Three other children had died last year.

Cholera.

At noon I stopped and sat at the old wooden table we wrote charts on, to eat one of my oranges. Simon sat down next to me, and together we went through the numbers: sixty-two patients in house today. Nineteen patients admitted in the last twenty-four hours, ten discharged and eleven dead since last night. Our mortality rate was averaging about 20 percent. Not great.

Why was I here? I asked myself for the tenth time that day. Sure, we could give these people antibiotics and all, but look at how many still died. All these deaths preventable with just a vaccination. What this country really needed was a workable public health system. Everything we were doing now was just a temporary bandage, not a solution.

I sat there glumly peeling my orange and when I finished, I split it open. Nigeria, hell for people, is a paradise for oranges. When you open one, there is an immediate citrus smell so rich as to seem distilled. Never had I eaten oranges like those sold at every crossroads in Kano. Pyramids of beaten-looking, overripe fruit attended by girls of eleven or twelve, this their last year before the everlasting banishment to womanhood, house arrest and the Muslim veil. Sitting there, eating that orange and looking around, I had the momentary thought that we were doing better, or at least it seemed that way. Last week deaths were running closer to 30 percent of all patients admitted.

Maybe we *were* accomplishing something here.

There was a rustling in the bushes. I looked up. This was usually when a little girl I knew would come to beg at the camp. She would sneak onto the hospital grounds by climbing between the slats of the fence and then through the bushes. Once inside, people left her alone. She was the only beggar whose presence on the hospital grounds was tolerated.

It was her, coming to beg. From a distance she seemed to be just a normal little girl dressed in rags, but as she came closer, you could see that something was wrong with her face. She had normal eyes but a protuberant muzzle-like nose and enormous malformed lips that gave her face a dog-like aspect, as if it were half human, half basset hound. This was because the girl had leishmaniasis.

Leishmaniasis—in this case cutaneous leishmaniasis—is a scarifying disease caused by a protozoan, *L. tropica*. The protozoa in her case affected a localized area of the lower face. Her face was normal from the forehead down to the cheeks and the superior part of the nose, but the disease had eaten through everything beyond this. The tip of the nose had become tubercular and looked snout-like. Her upper lip had become huge, elephantine. It was purplish, and encrusted with oozing sores. Her lower lip had partly rotted off and what remained was necrotic, avascular, black. Her jaw dangled open; she had lost the ability to close it. Drool seeped perpetually out of one side of her mouth. I don't know how she ate.

Yet her forehead and eyes were those of a very pretty young girl.

She was a feral thing. Once, one of the other doctors had tried to examine her. The moment he put his arms around her she kicked, bit, screamed, until he let her go. Personally I couldn't even imagine touching her without gloves and a mask, her face was so obscene.

She lives in a world, I thought, where almost everyone feels that way. No one could imagine touching her. And she can't be more than ten.

I had long ago given her my last American dollar, so today, when she showed up, I fished out some Naira and held it out to her. She grasped at the notes greedily. Besides the Naira, I also tossed her an orange. She came forward to grab it and then leaped back out of my reach, squatting on the hard ground, turning it over and over, monkey-like, in her hands.

I went back to writing on a chart but found, after a few minutes, that the girl had crawled under the table and was playing with my shoelaces. She whispered up at me unintelligibly. Simon bent near her and said something rapidly in Hausa to her. She scurried away.

"What did you say?" I asked Simon.

"It's an Islamic prayer of good riddance. She must stop begging now."

Sixty patients to round on; the day broken only by the few minutes I spent with my oranges and the *Kano Times*. There was really no escaping the weight of the days. It pressed down on me like a heavy stone on my chest. I would get short of breath sometimes thinking about how many dead I had seen and how many there were in the future. Probably there were people dying right now, and if I got up and walked over to the acute tent I might even save a few. I knew Jean-Paul was up to his ears in the cholera camp. But still I lingered on, trying to garner some strength. I was tired; I could see it in myself. I could feel that I was cutting into my personal reserves.

Someday those reserves would be gone.

At the end of afternoon rounds I went back to see my tetanus patient. He had stiffened up somewhat since the first dose of Valium, so I gave him another. I wondered how long it would be until the penicillin would do the trick. His third dose was due at 8 P.M. The nursing students would administer it. The brothers were going to try to feed him now. I checked again before I left. He was resting more comfortably.

I went home that night thinking, Tetanus patient: Treatment Day 1.

In the morning the man looked a little better. He sat up, braced in the lap of one brother while his other brother spoon-fed him some soup. The man managed a weak smile at me and even lifted one arm a little. I bowed my head over him. Praise God but pass the penicillin.

I looked up from my bow. The two brothers were bowing their heads in return to me.

Tetanus patient: Treatment Day 2. Pt doing well, eating soup. Plan: continue penicillin and Valium.

Sometimes the deputy minister of health came on rounds with us. He always wore a snow-white jubbah that gave him a regal air. He would walk with me making suggestions for better therapy—usually this involved drugs we did not have. One day he stopped in front of my tetanus patient and gazed down on him. I presented the case.

"You know," he said, "metronidazole is currently the preferred antibiotic."

"Where can I get metronidazole?"

"Perhaps MSF has it stocked?"

I shook my head. MSF was here to treat meningitis.

"Then I suppose penicillin will have to do."

He liked doing rounds with the nurses and the medical students. Just like a lot of doctors in the States, he liked showing off what he knew. After an hour or so of this, in which nothing of substance would get done, he would then get back into his chauffeur-driven car and drive off to whatever important meeting deputy ministers of health had to go to in Nigeria.

He's a physician, I thought. Why isn't he here with the rest of us? What the hell was I doing trying to save the lives of people in this country when that man isn't willing to do the same?

I had nightmares about him, about his chauffeur-driven car, about the enormous compounds with walls and guards and security entrances. In my dreams I always wanted to know—why was I here? Nigeria is a wealthy country. It leads the world in oil production. Shell Oil generates millions and millions of dollars in revenues a day. But the Nigerian people, the Hausa and the Ibo and the Origoni tribes, people who have lived atop these fabulous oil reserves for a millennium or more, get nothing, or less than nothing. The rich, the few fabulously wealthy families, live in well-guarded compounds and, when they get sick, go to private hospitals or fly off to the U.S. for their medical care. Everyone else, the other 99.9 percent of Nigerians, lives as vulnerable to meningitis, cholera, tuberculosis, leprosy, as in the nineteenth century.

Sometimes, though, an epidemic catches the attention of the "international community" and various aid organizations. People from these aid organizations go to the Nigerian government and persuade the powers that be that "something should be done." So the outside aid organization rides in to the rescue. We arrived in Nigeria with seven tons of medication and supplies, but seven tons means nothing here. It's hardly even a fraction of what is needed.

But we come anyway. We even save a few lives, but only a fraction of the lives that need to be saved. Soon, we will leave and when we leave there will be nothing to take our place. The meningitis epidemic, cholera, measles, typhoid fever, all preventable diseases, will return and continue as before. The only solution is a political solution, national public health programs, responsible corporations who reap only as much as they sow. Shell Oil with a conscience. Nigeria doesn't need us. What we do here is less than nothing. We take the pressure off the powers that be, making it easier for those who plunder to keep on plundering. This is the humanitarian aid paradox.

Tetanus patient, Treatment Day 3: Patient looking much better. Eating soup but still can not feed self.

Treatment Day 4: About the same. Requiring more Valium.

Treatment Day 5: About the same.

Treatment Day 6: Spasms well controlled but requires Valium every four hours.

That was what I wrote down. What I said was considerably more upbeat. Every morning I would tell the man's brothers, "He's getting better. Look! He's getting better," and they would smile and bow their heads. By Thursday, though, I had to admit that he looked worse, not better. If I laid my hand on his shoulder, it would produce an earthquake-like spasm just as it did when I first saw him.

I went back to the 1964 textbook of internal medicine, looking for more advice. I thumbed through the parts of the chapter on tetanus I had skipped the first time around, back when I was sure that all the man needed was a little penicillin. There on page 872 was a list of the dead-end part of the disease: myocarditis, inflammation of the muscles of the heart, which leads to heart failure; respiratory embarrassment from spasms so fierce the patient cannot breathe. Pneumonia, thromboembolism. Bad things, all.

"Environmental stimuli must be minimized. The patient should be placed in a dark, quiet room. Adequate analgesia must be maintained, as the muscular spasms are extremely painful."

Extremely painful.

I ran my finger down the page and stopped it at a sentence I had missed when I read this before. "Survival rate is about 50 percent."

Fifty percent! I thought. It can't be that low. Then I thought, well, that was in 1964. The survival rate must be higher now that we have better medical technology. I paused at the thought. Not that I had any access to medical technology. Monitors, scanners, surgical procedures. Where was I going to find those in Nigeria?

I went to bed that night and lay awake thinking about the humanitarian aid paradox. I must have fallen asleep, because I awoke suddenly with the confused noise of a hundred voices, talking, talking, talking, all about medicine. The voices disappeared in an instant, almost before I heard them. I lay there sweating in the darkness, wide awake now, and I knew why I was awake. I knew what those voices were; no translation was called for. They were the sounds of my own self, the darkest part of me babbling like mad, as I grimly wrestled with my conscience.

The next morning I reexamined the patient as best I could, but just palpating his abdomen set off fit after fit of muscle spasms. Noise, too, set him off and the noise level on the verandah was terrible; children were screaming, women shouting, patients moaning, nurses calling to each other across the ward. Dark and quiet, the textbook had said. There was enough noise to keep this man shuddering and shaking almost constantly.

I sat back on my haunches and looked down at the patient as he looked up at me. He tried to smile at me, but instead he triggered off a set of spasms. His lips drew back in a rictus of pain. There it was again, *risus sardonicus*.

The spasms are extremely painful . . .

What is the furthest extreme of suffering? I wondered. Where is the endpoint of agony? Is there a place where, if you are in severe enough pain, greater pain doesn't register? Is that point far away? Does anyone return from there? Can they ever tell us what they have felt? Is there a language for it? Would we, under any circumstance, ever want to know? And why the suffering? Why this man? Why this dead end here, a mat on the floor of a tent. *The paroxysms are associated with excruciating pain.* I looked at him, shaking my head. Christ only suffered as all men suffer. There was nothing new on the plains of Calvary.

I searched out Jean-Paul again. Today he was supervising the outpatient clinic. This was part of the old hospital, which had real rooms with real beds. Unfortunately the real beds were really just bed frames and rusty coiled metal springs, the floors were filthy, there were no screens on the windows, and generally the place had such an air of haunted filth that most of my tent patients refused to transfer over once a "bed" became available.

I found Jean-Paul on the back steps of the intake office, examining a measly child.

I told him everything. I told him about the constant spasms, the failure of the penicillin, the excruciating pain that we could assuage for only a little while. Jean-Paul listened and as he did so he passed a large handkerchief over his broad face, nodding his head.

"He's not getting better," I said. "He's getting worse, I think. I don't know. Are you sure this is tetanus?"

"The source," he said.

"The source?"

"Does he have a wound anywhere?"

I shook my head. "The brother says he didn't cut himself anywhere as far as they knew. I looked him over and I couldn't find anything."

"Well, the *Clostridium* is hiding somewhere. Gall bladder, gut. I don't know."

"What should I do?"

He shook his head, not really listening. "The noise, too. Very bad for him."

"Then what should I do?"

"Send him to the tetanus hospital."

"But they had no beds."

"Maybe they do now. You go with them. They can run tests."

Tests. I walked back up to the tents shaking my head. Jean-Paul was right. I couldn't even get an x-ray here. We were lucky to have IV catheters. I had no business treating this man under these conditions. Clearly the patient needed to go back to the tetanus hospital.

I found Simon and told him that the brothers needed to take the patient back to the tetanus hospital. Simon went off to find them and then quickly returned.

"They tell me they have no way to get there."

"What happened to the friend with the truck?"

"He died a few days ago. Malaria."

Jesus, I thought. That's Nigeria. The rich get rich and the poor get malaria, cholera, leishmaniasis, meningitis.

There was a shadow; Avi, the driver, had been trailing me. "Jean-Paul says to use the car if we can find nothing else."

"The car" was Jean-Paul's personal vehicle, a motheaten microsized two-door sedan. Doctors without Borders did not go for expensive transportation.

"How the hell are we going to get him into that car?"

Avi shrugged. "Is here a choice?"

I shook my head. If this man went into horrible spasms at the touch of my hand, think what it would be like to cram him into the back of a two-door car. But despite what I thought, I said: "Maybe. Maybe we can, if we take enough Valium . . ."

The logistics were this. Simon and Umar, who was another nurse, would ride over with Avi and me to the hospital. The brothers would follow by grabbing one of the overcrowded pickup trucks that served as buses in Nigeria. The patient would ride in the backseat with Simon and Umar. We gave him 10 mg of Valium. The brothers carried him to the car and laid him by the door. He wasn't doing well; despite the 10 mg of Valium, he had stiffened just from being moved. I gave him another 5 mg of Valium, then we all grabbed on to whatever we could grip to hoist him up. We had to put him into the backseat by cramming him past the front passenger seat. It was like trying to fold up a spring-loaded manikin. Every time we would try to bend the patient's arms, the legs would extend. Every time we folded the legs, the arms would fly up. It would have been funny if it wasn't so horrible. Every touch made the man shudder; every movement brought another wave of fasciculations and muscle spasms.

Simon stopped and held his hand against my arm.

"This is not working," he said.

"More Valium," I told him. "And for God's sake, we can't lose this IV."

We injected the man with another 5 mg and then 5 mg more. Twenty-five mg of Valium IV. This would knock anyone out.

While Simon and Umar stood talking strategy with the brothers, I watched the fasciculations subside and the clenched muscles relax. After a moment I reached down and flexed and extended the man's right arm. "Let's try this again," I told them.

Simon got in first and dragged while we pushed the patient into the backseat. The patient was limp for a moment only. The minute Simon tried to set him upright in the seat, the patient's arms and legs sprang to full extension and he rocked to and fro in agony, terror in his eyes. For a moment I turned away. I couldn't stand to look.

Umar clambered into the other side with the patient, hoisting the saline bottle. I got into the front and twisted around, facing them. "Give him another ten milligrams," I told Simon. We were entering a pharmacologic no-man's-land here, as far as I was concerned. I had never given anyone this much Valium IV. The patient's head arched back and he quivered; each muscle was delineated.

Avi started up the engine and we moved cautiously forward. It was no use. As Avi tried to ease over a pothole, the car bucked a little and that was enough to send the patient into more muscle spasms. It was agony just to watch that frightened, dying man quaking at each bump.

"Give him another ten," I told Simon.

"That's forty-five," Simon said doubtfully.

"I know, I know."

The patient sagged back now against Umar. Umar cradled him with one arm as best he could. Simon gave another 10 mg of Valium.

"How long to the hospital?" I asked Avi.

"Ten miles."

"Jesus Christ, ten miles. You've got to be kidding."

We took a right at the sign for Maladrin and sped frantically down the streets, first along the wide row of shops and then, after a right turn, into a part of the city I had never seen before.

The tetanus patient remained wedged between Umar and Simon. Froth had formed on his lips. He looked a little like a rabid dog.

Out of habit I started to go through in my mind what really needed to be done for this patient. He was septic now, I was sure. His infection, once localized, had now run wild, affecting every organ system, the heart, the circulation, the lungs, the kidneys. Septic shock. At home, we would first go for better IV access and control the airway. We would paralyze him, intubate him. Then we would give this guy at least three different antibiotics, none of which had even existed ten years ago. Blood gases, central line, the race upstairs to the ICU to meet "the team." Interns, residents, nurses, the ICU director. The team would give another set of three entirely new antibiotics. Then the serious technology. They would look for the source and use everything available. Head-to-toe CT scan plus MRI of the spinal cord and the brain.

The heart would need an echocardiogram looking for cardiac-wall motion abnormalities to rule out endocarditis. The lungs—chest x-rays, ventilatory support. Also, at home, we would be doing clinical trials—something to help future patients. Maybe we'd enroll this patient in a new ventilator study, one that looked promising enough to raise the dead. (They always start out that way.) Then EEGs, labeled white cell scans. Someone would suggest a Swan-Ganz catheter, someone else would cite recent literature critical of Swan-Ganz catheters. Someone would want an abdominal CT with triple contrast; someone else would argue that, no, an MRI would give more information. The intern would miss the arterial line, the medical student would have trouble with the Foley, and yet, in all this chaos and uncertainty, the right things would somehow get done, and mostly right decisions would be made and the patient's life would somehow be saved.

And the technology, I thought, as I gazed down at my man, now sheened with sweat, his face assuming a permanent horrific smile that twitched more widely with every bump. He had reared back, his spine arched, his legs butting into the front car seat. Umar held his right arm, where the IV still, somehow, hung on. Simon wiped the man's brow with an old rag with one hand and kept the glass liter of saline aloft with the other.

Then the most important thing, I thought. At home we could treat his pain. We could make it tolerable, even transparent. Valium, morphine, Demerol, Fentanyl. If nothing else, this man would never know he was dying. Not like now.

The streets crawled by.

The road was rockier and hot, hot, hot. As always in the afternoon, the air was muddy with pollution, and each passing car brought wave after wave of dust that billowed up from the unpaved streets. The sun echoed from any hint of glass, from the chrome car bumpers, from the bleached white jubbahs. We swam through the dust, past an old gated wall, then climbed a little through winding streets until we reached an open area, a dusty yard flanked by some nondescript once-white stucco buildings.

I turned around in my seat to look back at the patient. He looked as if he would die at any moment. He struggled for each breath, each time like he was climbing a mountain. His jaw muscles were still spasming, despite all that drug. His face was still wrapped in that hideous grin. I didn't dare give him any more Valium.

"This is it," Avi said, skidding to a halt.

We all looked up and as the dust settled we saw a couple of ramshackle buildings flanking the dirt lot where we had parked. A scrawny, scraggly chicken-like bird was the only sign of life.

Avi pointed up at the most ramshackle of the buildings, a two-story "office building," its plaster walls a dirty dun color and its big, black windows encased with bars and sided by shutters that hung askew.

"That is the intake office."

I leaped out of the car and trotted across the potmarked driveway and up the cement stairs into the shadows of an inner courtyard and another stairway. There was no comfort in the shadows. It was as oppressively hot in the courtyard stairway as it was outside in the car. The stairway was black with dirt, and the walls were as crud-encrusted as the stairs. I rounded the corner of the stairway. Here was, it seemed, the intake office, atop another set of stairs. A large room angled off the end of a short hallway. It was empty except for an old wooden desk where two Muslim women, their heads covered with kerchiefs, sat squabbling. Nurses, I assumed.

They looked up at me, half laughing at what they saw—a foreigner, a white woman with her hair uncovered who looked very frightened.

"Yes, yes," I said. "I'm a doctor from *Médecins sans Frontières*. I'm from the meningitis camp. We have a patient I need you to see."

One of the women shook her head. "We are closed now. You need to come back in the morning."

"No," I said. "This is a patient with tetanus. He can't wait. He needs to be admitted to the tetanus hospital or whatever . . ."

"Tetanus ward is full," the other nurse said. "You must come back in the morning."

"You don't understand. This man is dying of tetanus. We cannot take care of him. Someone needs to see him."

The nurses stopped smiling up at the white woman standing before them. They were beginning to get irritated with me. Their faces assumed an implacable mask. (This must have driven the colonialists mad.) "Tetanus intake is only in the morning. We only see tetanus in the morning."

I put my hand to my head. The heat inside the room was suffocating. I felt dizzy, presyncopal. I steadied myself, putting my hand on the table and shaking my head.

"I want to talk to your doctor."

One of the women lifted a finger and got up, disappearing down a dark corridor, and reemerged in a moment accompanied by a young man. He was pulling on a dirty white lab coat over his jubbah. It was the only lab coat I saw in Africa.

He was a young man. His hair was slicked back; his face had a soulful look to it. He looked the part of the handsome young doctor.

"Yes?" he asked.

"I'm a doctor from the meningitis clinic. I have a patient here with tetanus. We have been taking care of him over the last week, but he is not getting any better at all, *at all*. You need to admit him to your tetanus hospital."

The doctor nodded sympathetically. "I understand," he said. "Unfortunately, we only have tetanus intake in the morning."

"You *don't* understand. This man is dying of tetanus. It doesn't matter what time intake hours are."

The doctor nodded his head. "Well, of course, since that's the case, we would try to make an exception but unfortunately there are no beds."

I looked around. "I don't believe you."

The man took a step back, offended. He put his hand over his heart. "We are completely, entirely full."

"Come with me," I said, grabbing his arm. An infidel woman touching a Muslim man. He recoiled in horror but I kept tugging. "You will come and see this man."

"I understand your position," the doctor said, trying to wrest his arm free.

"If you understood my position," I told him, "you would find this man a bed."

"But we are full."

"I want you to *see* him."

I dragged the doctor down the courtyard steps and back out into the sunlight. Simon was there standing by the car. Umar was still inside with the patient.

"Open the door," I yelled at Simon. "Open the door."

The doctor came to a stop a good ten feet from the car. I propelled him toward it as Simon opened the door and pushed the front seat forward, out of the way.

The man lay limply now, glistening with sweat. He was barely breathing. His eyes were open, staring blindly out at us all. There was froth on his lips.

"I see," the doctor said. "An advanced case."

"He's dying," I said.

The doctor looked at me and I saw him for what he was, a smarmy show-off, interested most in looking good and minimizing his own workload.

"For this advanced a case," he said, "we just have absolutely no beds."

"Fine," I said to him. "If that's the way it is. Simon, take the patient out of the car."

Simon looked up at me.

"I said, take him out of the car."

The doctor intervened. "I said, we have no beds."

"I understand that," I told him, my face up close to his. "But this man is dying and there is nothing I can do about it. *I*, personally, am sick of being the one who watches him die. So I'm going to put him out here on the street, and now *you* can watch him die."

I had an audience now. Simon and Avi, the driver, moved around to one side while the nurses from the intake office gathered around behind the doctor. The doctor looked from the patient over to me. "Don't be insane," he said almost under his breath.

"Don't be insane?" I shouted. "Don't be insane? That's what you want me to do?"

He looked at me with a half smile on his face. He had me beaten, he thought, and he knew it. He had me beaten because he didn't care. It didn't matter to him what the patient looked like. He wasn't giving in. His pride was at stake.

At that point, perhaps because the noises of our voices were echoing beyond the yard, a man in a dirty jubbah carrying a machine gun rounded the corner and ambled toward us.

"I've told you . . ." the doctor said again. I knew this technique, just keep repeating the same useless thing over and over again until the irritated foreigner gives up and goes away. Especially effective when backed by artillery.

"I've seen them die," I said. I surprised myself. I had no idea what I would say next. "I've seen children die. Every day I go to work and I see children that are dying because there is no clean water, because they have worms, malaria, cholera, typhus. And what do you do? You close your clinic at eleven in the morning. No patients, no beds."

He stood there now, fully revealed in the floodlight of my rage. He wasn't a doctor, he was a bureaucrat. There was nothing compelling about life to him, except perhaps his own. He was master here. When I left this country, it would be he who took care of the patients I left behind.

"And as for you!" he shouted in return. I had finally gotten him angry, this Nigerian doctor. The smarmy superior expression had given way to cold fierceness. He was in my face now, screaming back at me. "Who are you? Someone who comes here to my country and stays for a while and then goes back home. At home you have everything there is to have. How can you judge me? How can you judge my people?"

I stepped back and looked down at my patient. He was still frothing at the mouth, his eyes were wide but sightless and he was nodding his head rhythmically. The clonus was back. We had given him a total of 45 mg of Valium, and he still had spasms.

"This is what matters," I said, pointing. "I don't care about what I have at home; I don't care about politics or religion or anything. I care about this man. I want this man to live. But I can't do it, so I'm bringing him to you. You tell me you have no beds, and if that is true then he'll have to die out here on the street."

"He's not my responsibility," he shouted back at me. Now he was trying to stare me down. Behind him the man with the submachine gun was watching our faces, back and forth as we talked. Clearly he didn't understand a word we were saying.

"You're right," I shouted in return. "*Nothing* is your responsibility."

"Look," the doctor said. He raised his hands, backing away from me. Now he spread his hands out asking for sympathy. "I've been up since five-thirty this morning . . ."

I came after him. "I don't care when you got up. This man is dying and he's going to do it right here. Simon. Take the man out of the car."

"No!" the doctor said.

We stood nose to nose, the doctor and I. Both of us hated each other, hated everything about this. The doctor stood there to outwait me. He was going to show me and show the nurses behind him who was boss. Except he wasn't sure how much I was bluffing. I wasn't really sure myself. I knew that if I had to physically drag this man myself to whatever they had for beds in the tetanus hospital, if that's what it would take to save his life, then

I would do it. And beyond that. What could I do that was beyond that?

I turned to the man with the machine gun. "You want to shoot me?" I asked. "Go ahead and shoot me. You want to create an international incident out of this, that's fine with me. But I'm going to make sure you take care of this man if it is the last thing I do in this country. And if you want to shoot someone who is trying to save a life, then do it now and get it over with."

The man with the gun had stopped staring at me and was now staring at the patient in the car. I looked as well. Other than a faint hiccup motion every ten seconds or so, he looked as if he was dead. The man with the gun, an old man I now saw, shook his head slowly. He said something quietly in Hausa to the doctor.

The doctor looked at me, then at the man with the gun and then back at me again. His posture suddenly changed; he looked cornered. He turned to the side and looked down, scratched his neck and kicked at something in the dirt. I didn't hear what he said the first time, and I had to ask him to repeat it.

"All right," he said, "all right, all right." He turned to the man with the machine gun (security guard? out-of-uniform soldier? heavily armed passerby?). "Ward C," he said; he turned on his heel and retreated back up the steps.

"Ward C," the nurses echoed.

"Okay," I said. "Where the hell is that?"

It was across the street but the hospital had no stretcher. We carried the tetanus patient by holding on to his clothes. One of the nurses led the way. "What now, what now, what now?" I chanted to myself.

Ward C was Quonset-hut shape, vintage World War II temporary housing. It was one of four or five long, narrow buildings found a hundred yards from the intake office. We crossed the street and hurried up the short walkway littered with trash that led to the entrance of Ward C. The doors were open, letting a rhomboid of sunlight into a long, darkly hot room. Two women sat at desks. There were two rows of beds, maybe fifteen beds on each side of the room. The ward was in no better shape than the intake office. The floors were grimy, windows blankly screenless. No light except for what came through the windows, no curtains on the windows, no curtains between the beds. No mattresses on the beds, just bare bedsprings, and no patients—or rather two patients. One on the right near a desk and the other halfway down the row of beds on the left.

Neither of the women at the desks had moved. They both stared at us as if we were some type of unearthly vision. "Are they nurses?" I asked Simon, who shrugged noncommittally.

"Where is the tetanus ward?" I asked them.

Wordlessly, one of the women pointed to the far end of the room.

We carried the tetanus patient down the row of beds. At the other end of the ward there was a room or, rather, a closet. Inside was wedged a single bed with bare springs. We laid the patient on that bed.

The tetanus ward—this was it. I looked around, thinking of the injunctions: the patient must be in a dark, quiet room. Well, it was dark here and quiet. It was deathly quiet, and only the steel gray threads of cobwebs caught what little light there was.

There was nothing here. Nothing, nothing, nothing.

I knelt down next to the man and put my hand on his shoulder. He was far away now, eyes wide and staring, foam still bubbling from between his lips. His arms hung loosely at his sides, but his thoracic muscles were twitching like mad. I realized then that this man wouldn't get better and there was nothing I was going to do about it. It didn't matter where I brought him or what medicine I gave him. None of this mattered. I could pray all I wanted. I could give him all the medicine I had; this man was dying a terrible death of a preventable disease in a joke of a hospital in a country that floats on oil. And there was nothing I could do about it.

The tetanus hospital, I thought, what a joke, a mirage.

The old feeling, the feeling that I was the only one who could help this man, washed over me again. I cannot let this man die, I thought. I cannot, cannot, cannot. I am all he has. I racked my brains. What had I missed? Where was his wound? Why wouldn't the penicillin work?

But I knew I had lost him. I was all this man had and I was letting him die. What if I had demanded more of that doctor or had known a better hospital? Maybe it would be better to take him back to the meningitis camp, I thought, and then I remembered the ride with the man jammed into the back of that car.

There was no way he would survive the ride back. And even then, what else could we do for him? What else was left?

"Doctor," Simon said. He put his hand on my shoulder. "You must go."

I stood up. I found I was clutching at the medications we had brought, 100 mg of Valium and several ampules of penicillin. Simon took them from me. "I will wait here and give these to the brothers when they come." He bowed his head. "Otherwise the nurses will steal them."

"We'll bring more tomorrow," I told him. "Tell them we'll come back in the morning."

"Yes," Simon said. "Yes, we will."

I understood then what the doctor in the yard was trying to tell me, although for whatever reason, he could not come out and say it: we have nothing for this man. We have no medicines, nowhere for him to rest, no nurses, no doctors, no equipment.

All that I had accomplished after that mad ride was to find a place for this man to die.

The next day Simon went up to the tetanus hospital with more Valium. There he found, miraculously, that the tetanus patient was still alive. The three brothers gathered around him watching him as he lay there rigid, bathed in sweat, struggling to catch each breath. By then his chest wall muscles were constantly clenched; they were slowly smothering him. Simon tried more

Valium, but it seemed to have no effect. The patient died, finally, about the time of afternoon prayers. Without expression, his brothers wrapped him in the blanket that had been with him since the beginning of his illness. They thanked Simon and told him they had no money to pay him. Then they picked their brother up, walked down the road we had driven up so frantically, and disappeared into the city.

A few days after the tetanus patient died, the first of the monsoon rains appeared as a morning shower. Jean-Paul had predicted this would be the end of the epidemic and it was. Whatever climatic conditions had made the meningitis epidemic possible left with the first rain. My tent population of sixty dwindled to thirty, twenty and then ten. There were no corpses waiting for us when we started morning clinic; the people we saw were moderately ill and after a while barely ill at all. It was time to go home.

The night before I left I dreamed that I went home and found my hospital had been closed down. No one was there. The parking lots were empty; all the doors were padlocked shut. I tried them all in succession. I couldn't get in until I walked around to the emergency entrance. The emergency department door swung open magically when I approached. I walked in past an unmanned security office, then a vacant triage desk, and continued down the empty hallway past empty rooms. The place had an air of everyone having left for a moment intending to come right back. Charts were on the desk, the computer screens were lit, doors to the rooms were open, gowns and sheets lay rumpled on the gurneys. All those signs of life, but there was no one there. I realized then that nothing at home would be the same as when I left it; then I awoke in that dank room with the understanding that nothing here would be different when I went home.

I sat up in bed, wide awake now. I felt for a moment as if someone had handed me a pair of special glasses. Suddenly, I could see this epidemic with epic clarity.

In front of me I could see the faces of my patients, all the ones I had gotten to know on my daily rounds—the patients who survived and moved on; the ones who died while we tried to start IVs and get antibiotics into their systems; the patients already dead by the time I saw them. The only answer I had to the humanitarian aid paradox was in the particular. We came here trying to save individual lives: the policeman's son, the bus driver's daughter, the young man with the tribal tattoos, the elderly woman who, while she was sick, nursed her even sicker granddaughter. The blind woman, the old man with the ebony cane. These few people are alive because we were here. We have received their blessings and their thanks for what we have done—although it required a pact with the devil to do it. Though it has really been so little compared to what needed to be done.

What Nigeria needed here was a revolution. Some heroes to smash the gates of Abacha's palace and liberate it for the people. Nationalize Shell Oil. Destroy Lagos. Destroy this city, hotel included. Save themselves. Save their children. Save me if they had a chance.

I was packing late one afternoon with the door open for light. The porter appeared and leaned against the doorstep. Behind him the rain splashed on relentlessly. It had been raining since early that morning.

"You are checking out?" he asked. "Do you want your bags carried?"

"Please."

"Did you enjoy your stay in Nigeria?"

"Yes, very much."

"Was it a pleasant vacation?"

"It was a wonderful vacation."

"You go back to America?"

"Eventually."

The porter clutched at his shirt pocket, then brought something out to show me. It was a ballpoint pen with a blue hub. "This pen," he said with a touch of awe, "was made in America."

"Excellent," I said and then turned my head away so that he could not see me smiling.

He started off with my bags, wheeling my suitcase through the mud. I looked around the room for anything that I had missed. That's when I found a copy of the Koran, covered in dust, in the drawer of the bedside table. I did not disturb it.

13

STATELESS

Stateless: [f. STATE n. + -LESS.] 1. Without a state or political community. Also, destitute of state or ceremonial dignity. [OED]

"Today's ceasefires and armistices are imposed on lesser powers by multilateral agreement—not to avoid great power competition but for essentially disinterested and indeed frivolous motives, such as television audiences' revulsion at harrowing scenes of war."

—Edward N. Luttwak, *Foreign Affairs* magazine, July/August 1999

IN MAY 1999 I CAME TO MACEDONIA with Doctors of the World to work in a camp for Kosovar refugees. There, on a good day—or rather a bad day—and they were all bad—each doctor saw at least one hundred patients during a twelve-hour shift. Most of the patients had minor complaints in the clinic—things that served as a pretext for the real reason they were there: anxiety, depression, despair. After a while I stopped asking questions about the patients' symptoms and just started asking what had happened to the man or woman sitting opposite me. Then I would just sit back and listen to the stories. All these stories. Women giving birth in the woods, old men walking for days over the mountains, diabetics without insulin, children with unattended broken bones. None of the stories were any better or worse than any other—they were each horrible in their own way—but some stories were harder to forget . . . like the story of the deaf girl.

She was about ten years old and had been deaf since she was six months old from a bout of meningitis. Late in April, the Serb paramilitary forces entered her town and broke into her family's house. There they found the family cowering upstairs. One of the paramilitary (they are called just that, no one graces the term with the explanatory "soldiers") lined the father and the mother next to each other up against a wall, the mother holding their six-week-old baby. The Serb then asked the husband, "Who do you want me to kill? You or your wife and child?" As he said this, the deaf girl started screaming, screaming at the top of her lungs. "The loudest scream I have ever heard," the mother told me. The soldier turned around, and at that moment the family could see that the soldier had changed his mind; he was not going to kill any of them. He shouldered his Kalishnikov and as he did, the little girl began laughing, a laugh almost as loud as the scream. It took them several hours before they got her calmed down enough to stop this insane laughter. Ever since then, though, every morning in the camp, the little girl would wake up laughing the very same way. She would laugh and laugh until her mother would shake her and slap her. No one knew what the girl was thinking—or dreaming—that made her wake up with laughter; she couldn't speak at all because of her deafness. Every morning, though, it was the same thing: laughter and slaps, slaps and laughter.

Everyone had a story about what happened to them at the border—where they crossed, what the Serbs did there, what the sheltering country's border guards did. The refugees we saw had fled to Macedonia. Given the dramatic urgency of the situation, it wasn't surprising that the Macedonian method of dealing with refugees was initially ad hoc, at best. But over the course of weeks and hundreds of thousands of displaced persons, there did develop an informal method of "processing" refugees at Blace. This was the main transit point for most of the refugees attempting to enter Macedonia.

Essentially, if the Serbs were in a giving mood, they would allow the refugees to cross through the Serb border onto about a mile-long strip of pavement into no-man's-land. No-man's-land itself ran as a swath of heavily mined territory between Kosovo and Macedonia. This land, while a subject of dispute between the neighboring countries, also served as a buffer zone. In no-man's-land the refugees would wait, sometimes for hours, usually for days, to see if the Macedonian officials would let them through to safety and relative freedom. Those that got across were interned initially at Blace Camp itself, a hellhole land of mud and tarpaulins strung between trees. After this, everyone was bussed by the Macedonian authorities to one of the main refugee camps. Camps like Stankovac I, Stankovac II, Cegrane, had, at times, held over thirty thousand refugees apiece.

On the other hand, if the Macedonians decided to close the border, the refugees were sent back into Kosovo and into the arms of the Serbian military and paramilitary forces. The Serbs would get rid of them by beating them away with sticks.

In the camp clinics we were heartbreakingly busy. We slept, ate, drank, and dreamed about patients and the camp, about the things we saw and the things we heard. In the morning, every relief worker would sit at breakfast and swap dreams. I dreamed that Milosovic had come to our house to dinner and we tried to poison him, but, Rasputin-like, he refused to die. Alan dreamed that our house was bombed by NATO (foreseeable). Paul dreamed that we all went to an Orthodox monastery and found the dining room filled with howitzer-packing Mafia dons. Even awake, though, there was a hallucinatory aspect to the world around us. NATO jets flew overhead nonstop; the sky was pinstriped with jet streams.

At our camp we lived in a sun-bleached world of white tents and white gravel, a well-organized desert. At night, the camp inhabitants moved like shadowy specters in the harsh halogen vapor lights that lit the camp perpetually.

One night I was sleeping, dreaming of demons, then suddenly found myself awake, sitting upright in the backseat of a Land Rover as it bounced from pothole to pothole. "Where are we going?" I asked the back of the driver's head.

He turned his face so that I could see it in profile in the oncoming light of a passing NATO convoy. "Blace," he told me. It was Dini.

"Is the border open?"

"Serbia side, yes. Macedonia, nobody knows. There are refugees in between. They are waiting."

"How many?"

"Many, many."

"Why are we going there?"

"Because you are a doctor."

Bafti, my translator, sat slumped next to me, chin down, arms folded, head nodding with each bump in the road. He was sound asleep. Bafti was sixteen and had learned his nearly flawless English from watching TV. Like most of the people we worked with, he was as much a refugee as the patients we saw. His family had crossed over a month before. "It wasn't too bad," Bafti told me. "The first day of the bombing we were hiding at my grandmothers's house until they started burning the village. Then we ran into the woods. They were shooting at us the whole time, bullets going over our heads, my little sister crying. Then we walked and walked with nothing to eat for three days. But we were okay. Other people did worse."

Bafti had a moon face, open and innocent, that matched his gentle spirit. He translated everything for me, the young woman who might be pregnant, the old man with gangrene of the foot, the KLA soldier tortured by the Serbs, the little girl who saw her mother and father killed. All the stories. The tortured, the maimed, the starved, the dying, all talked to Bafti, who passed them on to me. I only saw him cry once; Bafti had a special knife—a gift from an American friend—and someone stole it.

We went through sleeping Skopje, an ancient town with now a purely Soviet cement-block aspect. Most of the old town had been destroyed by an earthquake in the 1960s. We passed by the old radio station where the clock tower, still standing, read perpetually 6:42, the precise moment the quake began.

I awoke again to find myself standing in front of an exhausted-looking English woman, the only doctor at Blace Camp. I was yawning. "I'm sorry," I told her. "I've put in a fourteen-hour shift already today."

She yawned herself. "This is my second twenty-four hours in a row."

Relief-work rivalry.

I looked around the medical tent, and my eye caught my name on a posted piece of paper. The title was "Coverage for Blace Border Crossing During Urgent Situations" and then opposite Thursday was my name. I had never seen this schedule before.

"How many refugees?" I asked her.

"They say almost ten thousand in no-man's-land. The Serbs let them in past the Serb border crossing at—let's see—about nine tonight. And another twenty thousand still in Kosovo. But of course, it doesn't make any difference what the Serbs do if the Macedonians keep their side closed."

"Is there any word?"

She shrugged. "No, of course not. That would make it easy."

The medical tent was actually essentially empty except for a woman with a squalling child who had managed to make it alone across the Kosovar border through mine-ridden no-man's-land. One of the aid workers found her shivering by the side of the road and brought her here. The baby was about six months old. He had lost all his baby fat but wasn't frankly starving yet. He had obviously been wrapped in wet clothing for a long time, though. His entire body was one giant, macerated, lobster-red open

sore, the sore extending even up into his face—a whole-body diaper rash. Otherwise he was one angry baby. He squalled vehe-
mently while the nurse peeled off the plastic triangle that had
served as his diaper for God knows how long. His mother had
kept him wrapped in a piece of plastic shower curtain.

I looked around . . . missing something. Then I realized it was
Dini.

"Where is he?" I demanded of Bafti, who was sleeping in the
corner. Without opening his eyes, he lifted his hand to point outside.

"Well, wake up. We've got to get moving."

Dini was dozing in the Jeep outside. Poor Dini. Dini got roped
into everything. He drove, he translated, he held people's hands,
he carried the wounded, he counseled the stricken. There is no
part of my stay in Macedonia that does not have Dini's infinitely
weary, infinitely patient face imprinted on every memory. He was
always there, always ready to shrug, "Yes, why not," to every re-
quest, always with a lit cigarette, no matter where. I had worked
with him for a month before I found out that he had finished
medical school in Bulgaria and had come back to Pristina to continue his studies. "Why don't you work with us as a doctor?" I
asked him. He shrugged and shook his head. "He's given up," Bafti
told me and refused to say any more. "Ask Dini," he told me
when I pressed him.

Night. Open sky. A sleeping refugee camp. I pounded on a
window to wake Dini up and motioned for him to come along.
The border crossing was right next to the camp. We climbed some
rickety stairs and there it was, the border, or rather, a set of abandoned tollbooths and an old customs building off to the left. An
old sign on the building's rooftop advertised Skopsko beer. On
this side of the tollbooths, Macedonian soldiers stalked along an
imaginary line, shooing back a few sorry-looking reporters who
loitered on the road apparently waiting for something dramatic
and cameraworthy. The reporters could wait here as long as they

liked, but no one got past the abandoned tollbooths except the police and, under certain circumstances, medical personnel such as myself.

I was wearing my safari vest that had MEDICAL DOCTOR printed on the back. I sorted through the pockets, looking for my ID, but I found only a few tongue depressors. Bafti, Dini and I passed the reporters and came up to a border guard, a fatigued-looking man who glanced at Bafti's and Dini's IDs hung on chains around their necks and didn't even seem to notice me. He waved us past and just as I realized I had no ID other than the safari vest I was wearing, we were passing the tollbooths and entering no-man's-land.

It was a broad road that took off north, past the customs building. On the near side to our left were parked a crippled backhoe and few senile-looking Ladas and Yugos. From then on the scene was lit by widely spaced street lamps. Under these lights we entered a world of black and white, all the color bleached out by the night. The road was several hundred meters wide and hedged on either side by the Balkan idea of a security fence: some chicken wire supplemented with a few strands of barbed wire. Between these fences stood a wall of people, stopped to form a human embankment by a few twitchy and exhausted-looking Macedonian border guards. Behind them were more people packed in tightly and stretching out as far into the darkness as I could see. Thousands and thousands of people hemmed in on either side by a little chicken wire and kilometer after kilometer of land mines.

The guards were screaming orders at people, waving some on into a line that formed off to our left. There a column of refugees stood, everything they now possessed lying in a few bundles at their feet. All of them—even the children—looked like zombies, depleted, immobile, stricken. Everyone stood in that line, young mothers, teenagers wearing Nike caps, small children, babies, old women bent nearly double, young men wearing Budweiser beer

T-shirts and Chicago Bulls baseball caps, old men clutching their canes.

Except for the shouting by the Macedonian border guards, everyone was entirely silent. The guards moved eerily about, half trigger-happy soldiers, half harried bureaucrats. It was easy to see that they had a near lethal crowd control problem. Moving forward for each refugee could make a difference between life and death—it was easy to imagine a stampede—but these people were clearly too wiped out to do more than stand limply in the harsh glow of the border light. They huddled miserably together and walked when they were told to walk and stopped when they were told to.

It was a scene I knew even though I had never seen it before in real life. Refugees, the stateless people, the great tragedy of the twentieth century. What were the precedents? The White Russians, the Jews, the Armenians, the Romanians. Most of the people here had no identification papers, no passports—and even if they did, the passports were worthless, the papers of a stateless person.

Sometimes the patients brought their Kosovar passports into the clinic, especially when they were demanding a passage abroad. The passports had a blue-black flimsy cover over a piece of paper with the name, address and occupation clumsily typed in (mistakes typed over with X's.) The ID picture, always something from some better time, would be riveted into place, but the rivets had held so poorly that most people had to tape the pictures back into place.

This night I found myself standing next to a doctor from another relief agency who was shouldering an oversized knapsack. We both surveyed the crowd.

"How many?" I asked him.

"The problem is," he said, following his own train of thought, "the problem is, if the Macedonians don't open the border . . ."

"They've got to," I said. I surveyed the crowd before us and tried to imagine turning the people back. No wonder the border guards looked even more frantic and edgy.

He shrugged. "The same thing happened last week and nobody got through," he said. "Macedonia said they've got their fill of refugees. The U.S. has said they're going to evacuate some to the States, but that's just a promise now. And even if these guys do get across, there are twenty thousand more where they came from. Twenty thousand just that side of the border. That's what we've heard."

"Is there a plan here?" I asked him.

"No," he said. He looked out at the crowd and sighed. "Well, triage I guess. We're going to try to set up a station maybe two-three hundred yards over there." He pointed into the packed crowd. "If you can, just go through the crowd and pick out anyone who looks sick and we'll look after them."

We both walked forward the few hundred empty feet that stood between us and the crowd. Bafti and Dini followed along behind us. Then, suddenly, we were engulfed by the crowd. The ghostly faces now assumed personalized, demonic forms as people pressed in around me. Here were men with rotting teeth, stubbled faces, stinking with a two-month accumulation of road dirt, sweat and fear. Middle-aged Muslim women in their head scarves and long robe-styled coats gazed distractedly beyond me. Children's faces loomed up from below, expressionless. People tried to move aside for me but the press of bodies beyond them pushed them back against me. Bafti and Dini trailed behind, trying to keep up, Bafti shouting in Albanian, "Is anyone sick? There is a doctor here."

Then by some whim of the crowd, Bafti and Dini were ahead of me, Bafti frantically waving me down. I struggled over. Dini gestured down into a small well of empty space in the packed crowd. There I found a woman inert on the ground. She looked as though she had decided, just shy of freedom, to lie down on the road and die.

Bafti and the family members were conferring while Dini stood just beyond them, the scene reflected in his sad eyes. "What is it?" I asked him.

"The family says she's had a seizure. She's not breathing anymore."

I knelt beside her and, because it was much too dark to see, tugged her coat open so that I could get a hand on her chest. She was breathing, thank God, and—I mashed on her neck—she had a good pulse. As I did this, she opened her eyes and swiveled them, fish-like, toward me. Then she turned to look up in my direction. I recognized the expression on her face. I had seen it a hundred times over the past few weeks in the camps. It was a look that was one part exhaustion, one part terror, the look of a woman spiritually, as well as physically, at the end of her rope.

I glanced up, sighing, trying to gauge the distance to the tollbooths, the borderline, safety. On one hand she had only a few hundred meters to go, but between here and the tollbooth were those stony-faced Macedonian customs officials. And even if she made it across the border, I knew, after seeing so many like her, that you just can't turn fear on and off. Terror has a life of its own, regardless of circumstances. Even when safety comes, it doesn't just disappear. Terror is stubborn, resourceful, and lingers on in some long after it has served any constructive purpose.

I looked up at the family, who were peering down at me, awaiting my verdict. "She's okay," I said. "Let her lie here for a bit and she'll be okay."

I stood up, looking around for Dini. He was not far from me but was mired in a crowd even thicker than the one I was in, if that was possible. It took me a moment to see why. Dini was handing out cigarettes to everyone within reach. The crowd was passing around his lighter. I could see the flame flair up every few seconds, illuminating the face of the smoker, and then flick off, only to reappear a moment later, somewhere nearby.

Someone else shouted from within the crowd; I wasn't sure from where. Bafti and I struggled to our left, toward the voice that had called out. Finally Bafti was close enough to shout out, "What's the matter?" He passed on the reply to me.

"That woman there says she's pregnant."

"How pregnant?"

"She says nine months."

Oh, boy, I thought. "Is she having contractions?"

"She's not sure."

I struggled over to the woman—actually a haggard-looking nineteen-year-old-girl dressed in a Muslim scarf and overcoat. She was leaning up against a man who looked to be her father. Bafti and she muttered to each other while I palpated her belly, as if that would tell me much of anything.

"We've got to get her over to the medic area," I told Bafti as he struggled over to me.

"But she's with her family," Bafti said.

I winced. "How many in her family?"

They counted. At least ten. No way we could move them all. "She won't go without her family," Bafti told me. I knew her logic. Better deliver at a border crossing than risk never seeing your family again. I looked around for a moment, blinking mole-like in the bright light, trying to imagine myself delivering a baby onto pavement in a sea of thousands of refugees. It had been done before. A nurse-midwife we had hired delivered three babies in a railway station in Pristina during the first wave of deportation.

There was a lot of shouting from the Macedonian side of the crowd, where the border guards were trying to get people to stand in a line. I peered over the crowd and saw a frazzled-looking guard standing in front of the wall of emigrants, screaming orders in Macedonian at the crowd of faces in front of him. It was clear he wanted people to move, but nobody moved, nobody budged.

"A bloody idiot," Bafti said, while Dini just looked on sorrowfully.

"What's this now?"

"You don't need to do this," he shouted out angrily to the guard, but in English. The guard had no idea what he was saying. "You just bloody well don't need to do this." He waved his hands. "He wants the women on one side and the men on the other. He's putting the families apart."

Separating the families. The ultimate refugee nightmare. It seemed like such a small thing, but it was really one of the most powerful weapons to instill fear. I had cared for men released from Serbian prisons, who had been through taunts, beatings, starvation and deadly threats without turning a hair, but when it came to their families—God only knew where the family members were—they broke down helplessly, sobbing, inconsolable.

The pregnant woman still stood in front of me, face utterly without expression.

"Well, if she's not going to the medical unit, tell her she needs to get down to Blace Camp as soon as she's through the border."

"If she gets through the border," Bafti said grimly.

It was impossible to move farther along the road because of the packed crowd. We struggled back to the right, to the embankment that ran along the righthand side of the road, and fell behind a couple of English paramedics I knew from Senakos Camp who were lugging giant backpacks filled with medication. We clambered up the embankment until we were beyond the reach of the crowds and then we teetered along, working for each footstep, sending bursts of skree rolling down beneath us, until we finally arrived at an area, about fifty yards farther on, where the crowd started to thin out. I clambered down, reaching out for support. I was assisted by a man of about fifty dressed in an impeccable suit with an elegant tie neatly in place, reading glasses dangling from around his neck by a silk cord. He could have been the devil himself for all I knew. Beyond him, the paramedics laid down their backpacks and opened them up. With them opened now, I could see they contained everything, angiocaths, syringes, fluids—enough to stock a portable ICU should anyone be insane enough to want one here.

I moved on beyond them. Now there was enough space for people to collapse into. Whole families huddled on the ground, frozen in sleep. Children dozed in their mothers' arms, people sprawled out on their coats. Muslim women, scarves still wrapped in place, snored loudly. They lay stretched out, oblivious, while around them others stood in small groups, the tips of lit cigarettes about all that you could see of them.

In one group a man lay sleeping, face up, his hands on his belly. Something about him seemed familiar—not familiar in an everyday way—familiar on a visceral level. In his hands were some papers, and I could see there the little purple-covered Kosovar passport. Even though he was dead asleep, he was still clutching his (useless, worthless) identification papers, papers which signified that he was a citizen of a country that had seized his home, maybe killed some of his family and summarily expelled him. I remembered now where I had seen this man before, or rather someone who looked like him. It was on Macedonian TV. There was some footage of a tractor convoy, one of hundreds that had sprung up on the country roads and mountain tracts inside Kosovo during the flight of the refugees. This particular convoy had been ambushed by the Serbs, and now the dead lay scattered in the mud amid the abandoned carts and overturned tractors. The camera zoomed in on a man—a corpse, rather—who lay in the mud still clutching his passport and his identity papers. His last act must have been to try to prove his citizenship. What happened next? Did a soldier taunt him, telling him how worthless those papers actually were? Did he shoot him as casually as one child would shoot another with a toy gun? Did the soldier really think, "It's either him or me"?

I walked on, the crowd thinning as I went. As I walked along I kept calling, "Doctor, doctor," in Albanian, until I realized I was just whispering, so I gave up. I must have looked spectral myself. People looked at me and veered away, turning their faces into the darkness. At one point there was the stench of urine off to the left. A man I thought was praying in the darkness turned out to be relieving himself. I walked past families, children limply asleep on the ground underneath. Off to the right, sitting cross-legged on a pile of logs, a woman sat, head bowed, weeping deeply. It struck me that I had seen no crying here; even children didn't cry, as if there was no grief fresh enough to need relief. Then I came up close to her and realized this was one of the aid work- ers, someone in a medical safari vest, sobbing helplessly. I knelt down in front of her. "Are you all right?" I asked in clumsy Al- banian.

"No," she said in English. "No, no, no." She tried to blot up her tears with the back of her hand, got nowhere and buried her face deep into her upturned palms. "These are my people," she sobbed. "My people. I can't go any farther." She looked back up at me accusingly. *"I can't go any farther."*

I looked up and saw why. Beyond us loomed the Serbian bor- der, the dead end of no-man's-land. It was as sudden as that. The gathering of the refugees stopped there. No gate, just another imaginary line. Off to the side a sign in Cyrillic, used only by the Serbs, not by the Albanians, announced the Kosovo customs of- fice. It was completely dark beyond that, the road entirely open.

I stood up, hand to my chest. I was tempted to keep walking, something that seemed as easy to do as falling down. There were twenty thousand more refugees there in the darkness, twenty thou- sand more waiting to cross the border. How many pregnant women? old men? starving, terrified children? Then I looked down in front of me. What good was I going to do for *them* if I couldn't even help her? What was I going to do without medicine and equip- ment or—most important—some political power, while dealing with a people who would just as soon put a bullet through my head?

I turned back, stomach churning, telling myself, No, no, it's beyond that border that people really need help. But I turned back, back to the light, such as it was, back to the refugees. And what could I do? I was afraid even to try to comfort the aid worker sitting on the roadside.

Bafti sat down beside her and looked over at her with his in- nocent face. He, too, said nothing; he sat there, silently, watching her cry. I started calling out again, my voice sounding plaintive.

Someone waved at me, a small gesture. I almost didn't see it. There was an older man sitting next to what looked to be his wife and a middle-aged daughter.

"Doctor?" I asked them.

The man motioned me closer. As he did so his wife began to undress. She pulled off her coat, then a wool vest and a flowered rayon blouse. I looked around nervously, hoping no one would notice the striptease. Then the woman turned her back to me, a back plastered over with toilet paper. Her husband began peeling the toilet paper away and I saw what she had been trying to cover. It was a burn, a large burn that covered her entire back. God knows how it had happened or when, but by now it was badly infected. The toilet paper came away with a layer of formless gray goo plastered against it. There was the sickening smell that bespoke intensive care units, terminal illness. It was the smell of pseudomonas.

"Jesus," I told no one in particular. I thought now of clean gauze four-by-fours, Neosporin and Silvadine cream, sterile gloves and brisk nurses. I thought of going home.

I motioned for her husband to get her dressed and follow me. I walked this woman and her family back through the crowds of no-man's-land, past all those sleeping bodies and beyond to the crowds near the triage area. When I arrived, the pregnant woman and her husband were there as well. She was lying on her side moaning. Dini sat next to her, holding her hand. "Contractions are still ten minutes apart," he told me. "Should we try to get her across without her family?"

"You walk her to the border," I told him and sat down abruptly. My hands were shaking.

I had only sat there for a moment when suddenly there was a murmur from the crowd and a sense of movement. Everyone was shifting restlessly, and somewhere at the near side of the Macedonian side of the border there was a shout. Soon the shout was taken up by the crowd immediately behind it and then deeper and deeper into no-man's-land until it swept by us and passed on into the darkness behind us.

"Get up, get up!" Bafti called over to me. "The Macedonians are opening the border."

"Do you know who they'll let through?"

"Everyone in no-man's-land. That's what the shout says."

I dropped my face down into my hands. "Thank God. Thank God."

We walked on but stopped when someone shouted Bafti's name. "I know him," Bafti said. "He's from my town." He ran over to a shabby-looking man who was painfully thin. By the time I caught up, they were deep in animated conversation. Now that I was closer, I could see that the man was not just thin, he was emaciated—he must have been hungry for months. He looked like some of the "prisoners" we had gotten recently in the refugee camps from Kosovo. These were men who had been pulled off convoys or found hiding and taken into "custody" by the Serbs. Thousands of them had been held under concentration-camp conditions in makeshift prisons throughout Kosovo. Most had been there at least a couple of months and then were released as some kind of goodwill gesture by the Serbs. They were shattered men. They had been two months starved at least and beaten daily. Each one was nursing spectacular bruises and at least a couple of broken bones. Some had to be carried to the tents. They all told their stories in the hospital tent at night while they waited for food and first aid. The practice for the prison guards was to pick out some feature—some incidental—that would mark someone out as an individual and then beat him for it. One man was captured in a jogging suit. The Serb soldier would say, "Oh, so you're athletic, huh? We'll see how athletic you are." And then would beat him. And someone else—"Oh, so you like baseball," because he had on a baseball T-shirt, and they would beat him. One man had a harsh, throaty pitch to his voice from surgery on his larynx. The solider would taunt him. "Can't you talk? What's the matter? Can't talk?" And when he would finally be provoked to say something, they beat his face in. By the time I saw him, he had all of his teeth knocked out, a mandible and an orbital fracture.

I had been dealing with pain and suffering as a doctor for a decade, and in that time I had unconsciously developed psychological tricks to get me through the day; little emotional shock absorbers that involved the gamut of simple human defense mechanisms—humor, denial, boundary setting. None of these worked here. Each man I saw unloaded from the bus, as we tried to triage the sickest ones to the medical tent and get the walking wounded some food, each one, no matter what I said to try to comfort him, would shake his head and say, "You don't know how it was." Simply that. I would try to connect with each one, talk with him, joke with him, and each one would look at me and say, "You don't know . . . you can never know. Thanks be to God you will never know how this was."

None of this, none of these walking casualties were about war. Killing was not the point here; winning a battle was not the point. This was not just about war—this was about degradation, desecration, annihilation—annihilation not of the body, but of the soul. And there is a psychology to this, a list of ways to kill without killing; to leave your mark forever on a human soul. Rape, torture, wanton destruction.

Dini finally told me, one night, after many shots of local brandy, the story of his family's attempt to escape to Albania during the war. They lived in Dakovica. Statistics would later chillingly confirm that ethnic Albanians had the highest mortality rate in Dakovica of any city in Kosovo. After the bombing started, Dini, his mother and his father gathered a few belongings into their little Lada and headed for Albania. They were stopped by Serb military about two kilometers shy of the border. The soldiers made Dini and his parents get out of the car and told Dini's mother they wanted ten thousand deutsche marks. "Ten thousand deutsche marks or we kill your son." Dini's mother had 3,000

DM—this was all the money the family had in the world. She gave it to one of the soldiers and he threw it on the ground, saying, "Three thousand is not enough. I want ten thousand!" Dini's father then got down on his knees. "Please," he said, "kill me, kill me, just do not kill my son. Don't hurt my son." Dini flicked his cigarette in the ashtray in front of him as he told this story. He told it deadpan, with not a whiff of emotion except for a slight smile that twitched, tic-like, as he toyed with his cigarette. He was alive, he said, shrugging. He was there with us. Whatever that was worth.

That night, after hearing Dini's story, I kept dreaming—that kind of dream you have when you are half asleep, half awake— of the Skopje clock tower, the time eternally 6:42, the time of the earthquake of 1964, and of Dini's father down on his knees, and of Dini now, an empty carcass of a man.

We left at four A.M. We were all scheduled back at work in the camp clinic at eight. It was a boiling hot day. We saw the usual: earaches, sore throats, colds, "weak and dizzy" (read: depressed and sick of the camp). At three P.M., though, something a little different. A young Muslim woman in a neat head scarf and a long coat (in that heat!) came in initially complaining of belly pain. I asked her if she might be pregnant and she shrugged, head dipping shyly, and then said, "Maybe—yes."

"Let's find out."

We sent her out to get us a urine specimen while I rooted around the stock drawer looking for my stash of urine pregnancy tests. I loved doing these—there was a voodoo-like appeal to putting a few drops of urine into a little square of plastic and having the paper marker light up with a "minus" sign (negative) or a "plus" sign (bingo).

"Do you want to be pregnant?" I asked her when she returned with her urine cup. If she said no, as some women I had seen before had said, I would know why. Life in a refugee camp, with a miserably bleak future—who could ever want to raise a child here?

But this woman blushed and nodded her head. "*Po*," she said, meekly. "Yes."

Three drops of urine. Everyone, the nurses, the translators, the logistician, all gathered around the table to stare down and watch the urine diffuse across the white blotter paper. Slowly the results faded into view, a bright pink positive sign.

"Congratulations," I told her as she beamed. Beside me Bafti whispered under his breath, "She's crazy."

It was a terrible day—torturously hot and still—not a breath of wind. Once again we saw over a hundred patients in twelve hours and ahead of us was an hour-and-a-half bus ride back to Skopje. We did this only to get up to do it again tomorrow.

At nine P.M. Dini arrived at the wheel of the battered van. I crawled into the back to go to sleep, and as I closed my eyes I remembered the ride of the morning. On the way we were detoured from the main highway (the only true highway in Macedonia) back into the unalloyed nineteenth century. The road was single-lane and filled with mule carts and horse-drawn wagons. It ran past Muslim townlet after townlet until finally it returned to run adjacent to the main highway. There we saw the cause of the detour, a massive wreck. A mulberry-colored sedan had run head on into a giant semi, one of the huge, underpowered trucks that haul everything from chicken feed to schoolchildren in Macedonia. The accident was a head-on collision. The semi had jackknifed, the cab now canted sideways. What was left of the sedan was up on the embankment. A body still lay on the ground beyond it. To me, the wreck served as a firm reminder that one of the most dangerous things about the Balkans was the maniac drivers. Sacking out in the back of the van did not buy me much protection, but I figured at least it would allow me to die in my sleep.

I awoke when the engine started. Someone got in and slammed the door. I heard Bafti's voice saying, "Fourteen more buses. *Fourteen*." This meant more refugees. I opened my eyes and turned my

head to see one of the buses parked next to us, two small children and an exhausted mother staring down at me from behind
the bus window. Then the van started moving forward and there
were more faces staring down through that window, then the next,
then another bus with window after window, each like a film
frame, jerking forward slowly, a little rectangle of distraught faces
and hands pressed up against glass, each frame passing more quickly
than the last until the last bus was passed, the film broke and
there was nothing but darkness beyond.

14

WHY I DO WHAT I DO

MIDNIGHT SHIFT, Saturday night, shortly before bar rush. Tonight, by some megrim of the scheduler, I have the honor of working with the departmental chairman, Dr. B. Fortunately this is rare—not that we interact all that much even then. As I write this on hospital progress note paper, he is standing way over by the telemetry radio talking into his personal Dictaphone, as far away from the action as you can possibly be and still be in the ER. I contemplate him as he stands there, his white lab coat gleaming in the pale light. Under that white coat he is wearing a golf sweater and a blue shirt with French cuffs and cuff links that also catch the light. Right down to the inevitable penny loafers and crossed-golf-clubs tie tack, he looks like what he is, a country club kind of guy, pretentiously Ivy League and very twee. He really does belong on some golf course somewhere. How ever did he end up here?

But then B. is not really happy as an ER doctor. He doesn't like drunks, he doesn't like the psychiatric patients, he doesn't like street people and he doesn't like doctors like me. I may be a good clinician but I am bad with *charts*. I don't document well. (Doctors never *write*; they *document*). This makes me, according to him, a medical legal risk. "Look here," he said to me the other day, "you didn't document the patient's condition on discharge." "That patient was dead," I told him in return. "Well, you need to document that." Fortunately, as he said this he was standing in front of me, not looking at me. He didn't see me roll my eyes at him. But I am always rolling my eyes. Every time we talk I am reminded of the awful destructive power of mediocrity. I look at him sometimes and think: Born to Do Hospital Administration.

So B. and I are together tonight. As I sit here tonight, still gazing at him, I idly consider the differences between his lab coat and my own. His is pristine white—there is an ironed crease running down each arm. I, on the other hand, can trace a complete history of this previous week's shifts based on my lab coat stains. There was the patient from two days ago, victim of a motor vehicle accident, drunk and out of control, who bled all over me. Here the little kid from Wednesday who vomited pink Kool-Aid on my sleeve. The black blotches on the front were spray painted by a suicidal sixteen-year-old girl who kept spitting up charcoal as fast as we poured it in. All this, of course, is overlaid with the trail of coffee stains I have spilled on myself over the course of the week. I contemplate these stains, thinking: I was born to wallow in this sea of bodily fluids. B. definitely was not.

Born to this or no, tonight I'm in survival mode, sitting in the nurses' station in my favorite chair, head down, feet up on the desk, an unread *New England Journal of Medicine* in my lap, coffee cup half filled with stale coffee in my hand. Next to me, facedown on the counter, is the medical thriller B. is reading. There's a picture of the handsome doctor-author on the back, stethoscope draped casually over his neck (but he's an ophthalmologist).

B. is writing his own medical thriller so he can be a doctor-author too. In other words, he is desperate to leave medicine, as is almost everyone else who works down here. This is it, the most "exciting" medical specialty there is, and we all would do anything to get out, quit the constant headaches, the pressure, the nights, the weekends, the drunks, the strung-out, end-stage addicts. We don't have many plausible options available though; almost all of us have invested a lifetime in education to get to this place. The only ways out seem to be either to hit the jackpot (same chance as everyone else standing in line waiting to buy a couple of lottery tickets and a carton of cigarettes at the quick-stop store) or write a bestselling medical thriller. Both are about as likely. B. is serious about his book, though. He has produced a 420-page manuscript that he is pretty sure could be a major best-seller. I've read a couple of chapters. The story involves your typical multinational terrorist organization that hijacks the last living sample of the smallpox virus and threatens to cause a worldwide pandemic. I note the genre differences. If the forces of truth, justice and public health prevail it's a thriller; if the virus is set loose and ravages the world, it's science fiction. B. apparently plans to stick to the thriller side of things. There is the beautiful young emergency room doctor as the heroine. The hero is a brilliant young scientist from the Centers for Disease Control. I point out to B. that CDC employees are actually federal agents who have the power to arrest private citizens. To me that seems more comical than anything, but B. loves it. "Great," he says. "I can use that." Meanwhile the real world of medicine stumbles on around us.

What is the real world of medicine? What is the everyday stuff that never makes it into mystery thrillers? Well—I'm looking around at the detritus in front of me—a great deal of it is simple advertising. A fact of modern medicine; it's everywhere you look. The magazine on my lap features an advertisement where a young woman windsurfs through a field of flowering alfalfa to advertise an allergy medication. On another page an exuberant woman romps with a beaming young child to celebrate some antidepressants. Scattered on the desk is the usual: a pad of Post-It notes featuring an ad for Zapnia, an antibiotic ("Go for Freedom!!"). A coffee cup features a sunrise over mountains and the words: "It's Going to be a Noxenal Day!" (an antidepressant). My pens: the one I am writing with advertises an antihypertensive on the clip ("Defuse the High Pressure Time Bomb!"). The one in my pocket features a drug for reducing cholesterol—no slogan, just the name.

All these courtesy of the various drug representatives, the "drug reps."

The poor drug reps. We get a visitation every day. Once upon a time they were unsmiling men dressed in cut-rate brown suits, carrying stodgy sample satchels. Now they are attractive young women, well dressed and elaborately coiffured, the clip, clip, clip of their high heels a marked contrast to the soft padding sound of the usual ward sneakers. They come bearing gifts: drugs—often hundreds of dollars' worth of samples—for the doctors to pass on to their patients, friends and family. Then the added inducements: notepads, calendars, expensive pens, refrigerator magnets, ice cream scoops, flashlights, clinical guides, business card holders, boxes of tissues, timers, T-shirts, canvas bags, key rings, decks of cards.

The problem is, of course, that in order to dispense these gifts, those well-dressed, well-heeled young women have to actually come *into* the ER and see this life firsthand. Yesterday, for example, the pleasant, terminally blond Abbott drug rep stood giving her usual speech ("This drug extends the spectrum of coverage to include Varicella and *Yersinia pestis*") while opposite her in room 10 a pathetically manic woman, who an hour before had set fire to her hair, sat up on the gurney screaming at her: "Fuck me, fuck me, fuck me, you Teutonic goddess."

This is the real world of the ER. And tonight it's all around, evanescent yet eternal, lit only by cold fluorescent light, the sole illumination for this nightless place.

I glance at my watch. Ten after two; the trauma phone should be going off shortly for our first drunk-driving accident of the evening. Meanwhile there are a stack of charts in front of me that need to be dictated, another stack that needs to be signed, yet I just sit here, not reading the magazine in my lap. I should really be thinking about my future, my life post–emergency medicine. After all, I've done this now for over ten years. Isn't it time to stop spending my life hunkered down over screaming, manic burn patients and start thinking about a career? But try as I might,

I can't imagine life without this place—the crazy hours, the scream-ing babies, angry mothers, the bizarre drunk William Burroughs look-alikes, the respectable businessmen wearing nylon stockings and panties under their suits, the psychotic rap poetry issuing from an out-of-control schizophrenic tied down in the psych cubicle. I could leave them all behind and return to the world of the liv-ing, a world where no one could ever imagine that this other world, almost an anti-world, existed.

Over the years I have tried to tell people about what life is like in these little rooms. The best I have done is to come up with this analogy. Imagine you are standing in a field somewhere, a brightly sunlit field with flowers, trees and birds. There is also a rock at your feet. You bend down and pick the rock up to look at the ground underneath it. There you see worms and bugs and slimy slugs and things that scurry to get out of the light.

That's what life is like in the ER. Every day at work is like picking up a rock just to see what's underneath. And whatever it is, it's pretty much guaranteed not to be a pretty sight.

Two weeks ago I was asked to appear on a panel, a presenta-tion about emergency medicine for a medical student "Career Day." There were five of us official emergency medicine physi-cians sitting in a row at a table in the front of a lecture hall. Three dozen students gazed down at us as we each gave a little rundown on our lives and our "lifestyles." Most of it was party-line stuff. During the question-and-answer period, though, one of the students startled a panelist into an honest answer. "Why did you," he said, looking at the doctor sitting next to me, "go into ER?"

My colleague thoughtfully searched the ceiling. Everyone sat very still; even we panelists wondered what he would say. Wasn't this the most important question?

"Because I have a very short attention span," he said, scratch-ing the back of his head and smiling.

There was silence and then a number of students started coughing. Nobody laughed. Remember—this was a group obsessed about their future. Then the question was passed down the line of panelists. The woman to the left, a director of a large suburban emergency room, said she got into ER in order to get out of an impossible surgery residency. An academic physician next to her said he liked the trauma and liked the research questions that could be asked about trauma.

After the last of the others on the panel trotted out his or her answer, they passed the microphone to me. I held on to it for a moment, trying to compose my thoughts, what thoughts there were. As I did so, I stared across at the sea of faces in front of us, all so young, so splendidly well educated, so wealthy, privileged and impossibly naive.

"Well," I said, trying to smile, "my mother was an alcoholic."

All sound evaporated. The room became perfectly still, not another cough.

"And my grandfather, my dad's dad, was an alcoholic."

No one moved.

"I know this doesn't answer your question in any way that applies directly to you—everyone has to find his own way. But in some ways, for me ER is all about family baggage, the stuff I dragged into adulthood with me." I could feel myself groping for a moment. "Like my granddad." I made a gesture meant to evoke a distant prairie. "It's funny, because I never met him. He was my dad's father. Dad was raised on a farm on the plains in eastern Montana which is the poorest, most godforsaken piece of tundra you ever want to see. In the thirties it was the northernmost reach of the Dust Bowl of the Great Depression. You can't—none of you sitting here can really quite imagine it. That land was bitter cold in the winter, and it was winter up there pretty much all the time. Martin—my grandfather—tried to farm it all the way through the Depression years, but he was a man who never had a bit of luck. There was no water—no rain—nobody to sell anything to, no nothing, for over ten years.

"You know those courageous settlers who came here from the

old country with just a dream and ended up in a new world rich beyond their imagination? Well, Granddad wasn't one of them. At the tail end of the Depression he gave the farm up. In 1940, or thereabouts, his youngest daughter died and my grandmother left him. A year later his three boys went off to fight in World War Two. Granddad was left alone up there in the badlands with nothing but drink to keep him company.

"The last time my dad saw him was after the war. It was the middle of another bitter-cold winter. Granddad was working on a dam project down south of Bozeman. He was in his fifties by then, living out of a little wooden shell he had built himself on the back of his pickup truck. He was pouring cement all day and drinking two pints of whiskey a night. By then he was coughing so bad he could scarcely smoke a cigarette. So Dad took him up to Missoula to a tuberculosis sanatorium. And Granddad died there of advanced TB: a drunkard's death. Nobody knows where he's buried."

I paused.

"That was my granddad." I shrugged. "And my mother . . ."

I stopped again. The room remained ghostly quiet. I could hear myself breathing. I was afraid of what I was going to say next.

"Every day," I said, "every day I go to work and I see my grand-dad. I see the drunks and the addicts, the people who have fallen right off the edge of the earth. I see people who have made every bad move anyone could make, made every major mistake there was to be made, and by the time I see them, they are paying for it, sometimes with their lives. That's why they came to the ER.

"When you work in emergency medicine, you are seeing pa-tients who are the least common denominator as far as human beings go; people who are heartbreakingly stupid and dirty and drunk and high and obnoxious—unbelievably obnoxious. These people have all flowed out of the darkest side of life. And when you are finished with them, that's mostly where they'll return. So each of you who is thinking you want to go into emergency medicine will have to ask yourself, 'Do I really want to do this?'" I tapped my chest. "I know the answer for myself—every day I work I'm taking care of someone who is just like my grandfather, someone just like my mother. But everyone in this room needs to ask himself or herself, 'Do I want to spend the rest of my life with addicts and idiots and drunks and psychotics? Is this what will make me happy?'"

I peered at all of them over the top of the microphone. "Very few sane people answer yes."

I passed the microphone on. I had said my piece and made a complete fool of myself to boot. I scanned the faces in front of me. Everyone was staring toward me, but not actually at me, each face with mouth slightly ajar. I had a feeling deep in my bones, a not unpleasant and faintly snobbish feeling, that of all the young students sitting in that room that day, not one would go into emergency medicine.

B. now sits down next to me, steeples his bloodless hands and picks up his paperback. Next to him on the desk is a thermosstyle coffee cup with a drug company logo on its side. There's the reality issue again. I lean forward. "You should put that in your book," I tell him, pointing. He looks at the cup and then back at me. "You mean . . . the coffee cup?" I look at him and realize that he isn't my problem. I am my problem. Just as I think this, the trauma bell goes off.

"I'll take it," I say, patting him on the back as I stand. Better to keep busy. B. nods, absentmindedly tapping the Dictaphone in his breast pocket. A man without demons.

I head out toward triage looking for Donna. From the hallway, I can see her sitting at the triage desk, musing over the electronic blood pressure monitor. Digital readout is 123/99.

"What's coming in?" I ask her as I reach the door.

"Trauma-wise?" She shrugs. "No idea."

"Who took the call?"

She shrugs again. I lean a little further into the triage room and can now see the patient whose blood pressure she is taking. He is a middle-aged man in a business suit, the suit coat folded carefully on his lap, and he's wearing aluminum foil. He has an aluminum foil hat perched on his immaculately bald head, aluminum foil tents on each shoulder and rings fashioned from aluminum foil on each finger of his right hand.

"Well, the thing is," Donna is telling him, "when they talk about safe sex, what they really mean is *condoms*..."

I walk on. I don't want to know any more. Another inexplicable patient. *Inexplicable*. This was the second one tonight. Donna had triaged one just hours before. She told us the story. A man brought in a very pregnant woman, clearly far into active labor. He ran up to the triage window and screamed—panic stricken— *"She's gonna have a baby right now."*

Donna barely looked up.

"You the father?" she asked him.

"Of course I'm the father."

She pulled out a triage form. "What's the patient's name?"

He turned to lean over the mother of his child and asked, "Honey, what's your name?"

Donna gave me the look she gave him: deadpan incredulity. "He didn't know her name," she said, shaking her head. "Didn't know her name..."

There was another inexplicable case yesterday, a trauma that did not go well. It was the worst kind of case, tragic and, well, weird. A man of thirty-five came in via EMS—gunshot wound to the abdomen. He had an innocent-appearing injury, a single, small jagged hole in the right lower abdomen from which a small tongue-like piece of fat extruded. The patient was alert and awake, but his blood pressure wasn't so great. As I checked him over, I started my usual trauma history routine.

"What's your name?"

... Jamie Something ...

"How old are you, Jamie?"

"Fifty-two."

"You have any medical problems?"

"No."

"Take any medicines?"

He looked at me. "Yeah."

"Yeah, what?"

"I took a lot of pills."

"You *took?*"

"Yeah, I took."

"Today?"

"Yeah, today."

"What did you take?"

"Aspirin, man, I took a bottle full of aspirin. Then I drank bleach, you know, bleach for clothes."

"Were you trying to hurt yourself?"

He looked at me, scowling. "I was trying to *kill* myself."

"And then you got shot?"

"Yeah."

I gazed at him, confused. "Did you shoot yourself?"

He gave me another look. "Are you crazy?" he said. "Why would I shoot myself?"

I opened my mouth, closed it and opened it again. I was trying to figure out what to ask him when Donna said, "Oh boy, guys. We're losing his pressure here."

There it was: 62/40. While we were chitchatting, the patient was drifting away.

"I got a bad feeling," Donna said as she prepared a second line.

The patient's words echoed in my head. ". . . aspirin, man, I took a bottle full of aspirin." I had that same bad feeling. This guy was going to die

I put a central line in, put down an NG tube to wash out the aspirin, started blood, clotting factors, everything. The surgical team arrived, took one look at the patient and whisked him immediately (stat!) to surgery. There they found that the bullet had transected the right iliac artery, one of the twinned vessels that reaches down to supply the legs. Also there were by now several liters of blood in his gut. All this was fixable; what he needed was blood transfusions and a vascular repair. But even with transfusions at maximum volume, he remained severely hypotensive—and even after an uneventful vascular reanastomosis and a quick closure, he was just barely hanging in there. And then he, quite undramatically, faded away—died—the next day, at noon, twenty-three hours after he arrived. Everyone knew what he died of: diseases with lots of initials (ARDS, DIC, ASA OD) but no one I talked to had any idea how a man who wanted to kill himself with an overdose of aspirin somehow came to be shot by somebody else.

And so it always goes, the life of a doctor—stories, stories, stories. Some that end in a great denouement and a life saved. Others that fade to nothing or fade to death. And each story takes place in a setting of complex banality—the ER with the triage desk littered with coffee cups and streaks of dried blood, the dingy linoleum floors, the posters: YOU HAVE THE RIGHT TO A SCREENING EXAM and SEATBELTS SAVE LIVES. The zombie paramedics, surly nurses smoking out in the well light of the ambulance bay, breath smoky from the cold alone.

While I was thinking this, I had walked out through the wheezing automatic doors, and now I stood in the well of the ambulance bay, looking out into the night. In the distance a siren began to wail. Was this the trauma victim coming to us this soon? I should be inside, I tell myself, starting to get the intubation equipment set up. But still I linger here, staring up at the night sky, listening to the siren. I hear it now as I heard it when I was young, before I became a doctor, back when that sound always stood for the lonely city, empty streets at three A.M., rain, lost luck and the end of the line. Plus an echo of something more haunting; an echo of the long-ago sound of a freight train, a sound that spoke of other places, lives better spent and long, inexorable travels into darkness and night.

The siren passes. It's not for us.

One of the security guards now comes ambling down the driveway. He sees me, holds his arms up and out, leaning back to address the sky. "What are we doing inside on a beautiful night like this?" he shouts.

"Oh, you know," I shout up at him in return. "The usual. Saving lives. All that."

The doors wheeze open and Tony, the other security guard on tonight, leans out. "Trauma coming in," he tells us.

"Yeah, okay," I say. "I'm aware."

"Well, they're waiting for you in trauma. Nudge, nudge, wink, wink."

I sigh and trudge back through the electronic doors, away from the night and into the blue fluorescent light.

Donna and Mary Ellen are already in the trauma room. Donna is opening up the medication cart. Mary Ellen is laying out the form for record keeping. Bill, the tech, is doing pushups.

"Fifty-six," he says, "fifty-seven, fifty-eight . . "

"Anybody hear anything more?" I ask.

"EMS called again—they're transporting now," Donna tells me. "A car hit a pedestrian and then ran into a bridge. They already pronounced the two in the car DOA. They're bringing in the pedestrian."

"EMS pronounced people dead in the field?" I ask, puzzled. Usually our EMS transported anything that looked to be alive in the last thirty days.

"I don't know," Donna says, leaning casually up against one of the cabinets. "I think they were *very clearly dead*."

We both stand there thinking the same thing, I'm sure: decapitation.

"Beauty," Bill says, rising up from the floor and dusting off his hands.

"So what about the pedestrian?" I ask. I start stripping off my dirty white coat and strapping on a blue plastic gown.

"Chest trauma is all they said."

I hit the intercom with my elbow. "Call upstairs," I tell Mary at the desk. "See if you can track down Surgery." Her response is an electronic squawk.

I move to the head of the bed and run through the intubation equipment. I know these things as if they were a lover's face. The arched endotracheal tube with its deflated balloon cuff. The laryngoscope handle and, as I fit it into place, the laryngoscope blade. I open the blade up to ignite the light at the tip, the intubation "beacon of hope" or "sentinel of disaster." As I do, I try to ignore the image that always sits in my heart, a well-worn image: that of a box, a plain cardboard box. While I organize the equipment I also mentally do what I am powerless not to do. I open the box and look inside. There they all are, all my failed intubations, every one of those times that, for whatever reason, I couldn't get the big tube down that little hole. Included are the times I couldn't get the tongue out of the way, or the vocal cords were so far anterior I couldn't get to them, or the patient vomited and I couldn't see, or any one of a thousand catastrophes.

There's a special section of the box devoted to blunt trauma, like what is coming in tonight. Blunt trauma victims are usually the worst kind of patients to intubate. The face can be mangled beyond recognition. Sometimes you're not sure at all where the airway is; you have to follow the bubbles down to their place of origin. What's more, you have to intubate without moving the neck at all, because if the patient has a fracture of the cervical spine and you move the neck, you'll pith him like a frog in some biology experiment. And there it is: lifelong paralysis—that knowledge sits in the box as well.

There's more stuff in the box. Can't get an airway through the mouth? That's when you need to do a "crike," a crichothyroidotomy. To do this, you take a knife and plunge it directly through the soft tissues of the neck and then into the trachea. Follow it with a small plastic tube you use to breathe for the patient. Connect the Ambu bag and there you go. It sounds easy.

It is not easy.

I pull on a pair of latex gloves and then slide another pair over them. HIV and AIDS have raised the ante for physicians who do invasive procedures. As everyone knows, any patients we care for could be infected. Years ago in Baltimore, researchers demonstrated that 15 percent of all trauma patients were positive for HIV. It's probably higher now. Ergo: any errant needle stick or mishap with a scalpel could change my life.

I thought about being with Doctors without Borders in Nigeria, smiling to myself. Perhaps no one put an actual gun to anyone's head, but each person had risked his or her own life in their own way—all that cigarette smoke and not a glove to be had. But then, they saved lives . . . so many lives.

Well, I think, as I set up the suction, I could leave all this—the failed intubations and the crikes, the nights, the drunks, the two A.M. train wrecks, the heroin ODs, the long-time shooters who will risk my life as much as they have risked their own. There I could be, harvesting hair sproutlets, Kenny G in the background, assisted by a nurse who would not say, as Donna is saying right now, apropos of something I did not catch, ". . . and I'm tellin' ya, fuck all of 'em. What the fuck do they know about this?"

I close my eyes for a moment, and as I do so, I see a hair transplant patient lying in a darkened room—something like a tomb—and me with my blue plastic gown on sitting over him, acting somehow like a Nazi doctor experimenting on bald heads. And the darkness of that room hurts my eyes like bright light.

I open my eyes again suddenly. Now I remember a woman patient I had last week. She was in a bad auto accident—luckily her only injury was a broken ankle—but that ankle had been smashed to smithereens. She would have to go to the OR to have it repaired. She was also an old shooter; she shot heroin IV. I found telltale needle marks, including fresh ones, all up and down her arms and legs. The skin rarely lies.

And she was pregnant.

As part of her workup I was going to order an HIV test. The hospital requires that the patient sign a form giving permission for the test. I gave her our form along with a pen advertising some antidepressant to sign it with.

"I don't want no HIV test," she said, handing the pen back to me.

I was taken aback. "Why not?"

"I don't want to know what it shows."

"Honey, we need to know. You're going to surgery."

"I don't want to know."

"But if you have HIV, there are drugs you need to take. Drugs that can make you live a lot longer."

"I told you, I don't want to know."

"And there are drugs you can take so your baby won't catch the virus from you."

She fixed me with a baleful gaze. "*I don't want to know.*"

There it was again, the inexplicable. Just think, I tell myself, I could walk away from her and, in time, even get rid of her memory. That was the most important thing, the memory . . .

Other things, too, other memories. An eight-month-old boy had fallen out of bed and suffered a skull fracture. The mother was crying, Dad was stoical, but I couldn't look at either one, couldn't even stand near them. I had to walk away, shaking my head in disgust. That's because when we first got the baby, as we were cutting her little yellow jumpsuit away, we found the child also had a broken arm and large bruises on the legs. No kid gets that from rolling out of bed. It was child abuse and nothing but child abuse.

We lost the baby's pulse almost immediately on arrival, and after that it was all downhill. She died—officially—about forty minutes later; there was nothing we could do. It was the only time I ever saw Donna cry. I found her sitting out in the ambulance bay, smoking a cigarette, sobbing. "I just can't take this stuff," she told me as I patted at her shoulder in an inadequate way. "I just never could take stuff like this."

But no more. It is time to come back to the present. Donna, now, is turning on the heart monitor and disentangling the spidery, pentapod set of monitor leads. The respiratory therapist has shown up, looking dazed by the light. Tim, the x-ray tech, has wheeled in the portable x-ray machine. He now leans against it, eyes closed.

I check my watch, wondering where the surgeon is. We all stand now in various slack postures, waiting. For what, nobody knows; we never know. Anything could roll through those doors. As I stand here, another trauma comes to mind. A year ago we had a kid come in via EMS, twenty years old—front seat, non-belted driver, airbag deployed—who seemed to have nothing wrong with him except his feet were slightly blue. Nothing, maybe, except he kept telling me he "felt funny." Just as we were getting his chest x-ray, he crashed and burned, no blood pressure, no pulse, nothing, nothing. He died, right there in front of us. We never got anything back. His autopsy showed he had a ruptured aorta—a common injury in those accidents that involve an airbag and someone with no seatbelt. I was the one who went out and told his wife. They had been driving to Florida for their honeymoon. They had been married for six hours.

"But he was fine afterward," she kept saying. "He said he was just fine."

Inexplicable, another in a long line of inexplicable patients. What was God thinking?

As I ponder this, I can hear the warning buzz of the ambulance as it backs up into the ambulance bay. Here we go.

I think suddenly of B., in his white coat, demonless, sitting out in the ER proper. Aren't I still missing the point? I ask myself. Doesn't the ultimate case of the inexplicable boil down to me, my story? Who really cares about B.? What am I doing here? Was it really my grandfather? Is that how I came to be standing here in a trauma room in a smoldering ghetto in some rustbelt of a town in the heart of the Midwest at 2:47 in the morning, without enough sleep and with too much coffee, waiting for whatever might roll through the door? And in this case, whatever comes through the door could be thought of as, truly, anything.

The doors open. Mary shuffles in.

"Where's Surgery?" I ask her irritably.

She raises her hands. "Surgery's coming," she says. "Don't get your knickers in a twist."

Donna, fiddling with the monitor in the corner, says, "Sweet Jesus," about something we cannot see.

The doors bang open again. This time it's the paramedics wheeling in a cart followed by some EMTs, some firefighters and a police officer. "Walking down the fucking street," the firefighter is shouting as she comes through the door, while the lead paramedic shouts over her, "We've lost the pulse."

The room fills quickly. Another typical disaster, routine chaos until I realize what's on the cart—a child, no more than three or four. A little boy. And the paramedics aren't in their usual sweating, paramedic mode. They look terrified.

"Talking at the scene," the rear paramedic continues. He is holding a bag of normal saline aloft while trying to negotiate the turn with the gurney. "Family just got home from Alabama. Grandma was walking the kid to the house when the other car lost control. It hit him and then he hit a tree, we think."

"How old?" I say but don't listen for an answer.

Donna is shouting, "Move it, move it, move it," as the respiratory therapist stumbles past her trying to get at the Ambu bag. I push Mary Ellen out of the way to try to feel for a pulse at the kid's neck. As I do, everyone else crowds up, trying to pull the kid off the gurney onto the cart.

I grope for the pulse. There's nothing. The kid is blue, not breathing.

"Let's start CPR here, come on, come on. I've got to intubate." I fight my way to the head of the bed, past Bill, who has climbed up on the stool to start CPR. There it is, all my equipment. But the endotracheal tube I have laid out is adult size, no way it will fit a four-year-old.

"I need a five, I need a size-five ET tube," I shout as I paw helplessly through what's before me.

Meanwhile Donna is shouting, "Damn, damn, damn, damn, damn. We have a rhythm on the monitor here, folks. If that means anything."

"Weird," Bill tells me after a moment, "very, very . . ."

"Hold CPR. Check for a pulse again," I say. I've found the size 5 tube and pull out a 4 just in case. I turn back to the patient. The respiratory therapist now lifts the mask away for me, and I get my first view of his face. It's bloodless, gray-white, blue at the lips. This is a very dead child.

"Heart rate of forty. Still no pulse."

So here it is. How often have I seen it, that nightmare confluence of velocity and deceleration, cell disruption and denatured proteins, rarefaction and sudden impact, all that blind science of night and darkness that I know as surely as I am blind to the workings of all those other great mysteries, including the workings of my own heart? I stand there helplessly for a moment and then think, Intubate, intubate.

"Restart CPR. Epi, atropine. We need another IV."

Who's saying this? Me? Donna? Mary Ellen?

I slip the blade into the mouth and peer down. This time it is going to be easy. There are the cords and I can see the beveled edge of the tube slip right through. No struggles here. It's textbook.

I straighten up, pulling the stylet out. "We're in," I say. "Hold CPR."

"I'm tellin' you," Bill says, halting, "something feels very weird here."

The respiratory therapist starts bagging and I watch the chest rise and fall as I fumble for my stethoscope—but this doesn't look right. Only the left side seems to expand. I listen: once, twice. Something, some kind of breath sound on the left, but not much. And on the right there is this weird hollow resonance, but not even a whisper of real breath sounds. I listen over the stomach— nothing there. The tube is in the right place, I'm sure. What is going on?

"You're not in," the respiratory therapist says.

"No, no," I tell her. By now I have my hands down on the patient's chest and feel for the first time the right chest wall. It gives way a little as I press, collapsing inward. Rib fractures. Several. I can feel them and I can feel as well fine crepitance, bubbles of air in the chest wall that collapse under my touch.

"That's all we need tonight," Donna says. "A fucking dead kid."

"No!" I say.

I know now what is going on. I press on the chest wall, which gives again, just like before. "Tension pneumo," I say. "We've got to needle the chest."

"Heart rate thirty-five," Mary Ellen says.

Tension pneumothorax. The kid's rib fracture has torn a hole in the lining of the lung and as the lung collapses, a pocket of air forms next to it. With each breath the air pocket has gotten larger and larger, and now the lung has completely collapsed up against the heart, squeezing it so that the heart can no longer pump. Deadly, deadly, unless you fix it, and it is actually easy enough to fix. Just put a hole in the chest wall and let the air escape. The lung collapses back into place and the heart can start pumping again. You can save a life that way—once in a while.

I glance at the clock. The boy has been here for a little over three minutes, three precious minutes.

"Give me a fourteen."

A 14-gauge angiocath, a whopper-sized needle to any doctor or nurse or paramedic who tries to fit it in a thread-sized vein, but still, so slender, really, no bigger than a very small piece of straw.

I take the package from Mary Ellen, strip off the paper cover and fold the plastic back. The needle, the plastic catheter sheath, the flange, the hub. I don't even look; I know what's there. I gently nudge Bill to move him out of the way. Now for the easy part. Go to the middle of the collarbone and then drop down about an inch or two until you are just above the third rib. Steady your wrist against the chest wall and then don't think, just act. Push the needle through the chest wall and keep going. Especially don't think about the fact that if you are wrong, you are making things much worse, tearing a hole in the lining of the lung—*causing* a pneumothorax, if one wasn't there before.

Push *now*. Now listen.

What you are listening for is a rush of air, the sound of a deflating balloon only just barely audible.

"I swear I hear something," I say. "Check for a pulse."

"Nada," Donna says. She has her hand on the child's carotid.

Mary Ellen is looking up at the monitor. "Heart rate is coming up, though."

We all look up. There it is: 52 . . . 54 . . . 55.

"Whoopee," Bill says without enthusiasm.

"More epi?" Donna asks and then, "Wait a minute. I swear I feel something."

My heart is everywhere at once. I put my hand on the child's right groin, searching for a femoral pulse. "I think . . . I think . . . Recycle the blood pressure cuff. Get the Doppler . . . Have we got that second IV? We need a blood gas for Christ's sake." I keep barking orders, but as I do so I remain just standing there, not thinking, not moving, just feeling with my fingertips. Yes, no, yes, no.

"Seventy-five," the respiratory therapist says. I look up at the monitor. Heart rate: 75 . . . 76 . . . 77.

"There is a pulse here," Donna says. "Now I really can feel it."

The blood pressure reading comes up: 45/30. Terrible. But there. The kid has a blood pressure.

"Would you look at that," one of the paramedics says. I didn't realize they were all still in the room but they've stayed on. But then, this is why they are paramedics—because of patients like this.

"I don't believe it," Mary Ellen is saying, a voice filled with wonder.

"Well, let's keep going, guys," I prod. "We need a blood gas, chest x-ray. And where *is* Surgery by the way?"

But I don't want to go on. I've done this for so long that I know how deceptive things can be—maybe this is a tension pneumo, a save maybe, but saves tend to go sour again. Fix one thing and then discover something else just as lethal that you can do nothing about What I really want to do is just stay here in this moment. But I know what I need to do, go back to check out the lungs again, the heart, those pulses. Cut off the rest of the clothes, do a limited neurological exam . . .

Even here, in my mind's eye, I balk. It is one thing to save the rest of the body but what about the brain? How long had the kid been out without a blood pressure or a pulse?

"Repeat blood pressure seventy-four over fifty-two."

"Miracle," I breathe, despite myself.

Donna must have been thinking along the same lines as I because she sighs. "Let's hope it's not one of those *bad* miracles."

"His hand is twitching," Bill says.

We all look down. His right hand is motionless.

"No way," Donna says.

Then it does twitch; we can see it. It jerks and the fingers start wiggling.

"The kid needs a chest tube," I say. I finally unstick myself and go to the head of the bed, back in ER mode now, back to myself again, brusque, emotionless, and thinking, What next? what must I do next? because that's all that matters. Look after the kid's heart, stop thinking about my own.

The kid's other hand is moving now, fingers wiggling as well. I look down at the child's face. A small bruise runs along his right cheek. I think of his parents . . . his grandmother walking him to the house . . . all those parents . . . grandmothers. . . . I think of Nigeria . . . the little boy whose life we saved with that tiny IV cannula. I think of the tools in front of me, the laryngoscope, the blade, an ET tube, a monitor, a defibrillator, the chest tube, my hands . . .

"Leave this world," I think suddenly, and despite myself, despite where I am and what's going on, I laugh. As if anyone, anyone here, could ever truly leave.

I can see now as I strip open the chest tube tray that there are no certain answers for me, no absolute solutions, no wise moves that will ensure my happiness. There is only the late night and Donna and Mary Ellen, Bill and me, the paramedics, Mary and the rest, all of us bent over this tiny figure, naked, hopelessly fragile, yet resiliently young and, I hadn't noticed before, now suddenly radiant—radiant with a kind of roseate flesh that seems lit up from within. I stop for a moment to look up at the monitor. Oxygen saturation: 100 percent; blood pressure: 129/68. Well, perhaps there is no clear future for me, but for this little one, I believe with all my heart, the future is an open book.

The paramedics start drifting out, satisfied, while we bustle around like mad, mumbling orders, repeating them, bumping into each other, swearing. It looks like chaos and it is chaos, but if you have specially trained eyes, you can see what all of us are thinking, and you can hear, as we stumble through our paces, what all of us are mumbling.

It is that this little one is going to wake up and live.

FOLLOW UP

BAFTI, HIS BROTHER IRFAN, AND DINI are currently studying in the United States.

Doctors without Borders won the Nobel Peace Prize despite my contribution to their overall efforts.

Dr. Daiquiri voluntarily surrendered his medical license after pleading guilty to thirty-one felony counts of trafficking in drugs. He was sentenced to five years in prison.

REASON FOR HOPE
A Spiritual Journey
by Jane Goodall with Phillip Berman

The *New York Times* Bestseller

Jane Goodall's revolutionary studies of Tanzania's chimpanzees forever altered our definition of "humanity." Now, intriguing as always, she explores her deepest convictions in a heartfelt memoir that takes her from the London Blitz to Louis Leakey's famous excavations in Africa and then into the forest of Gombe. Thoughtfully exploring the challenges of both science and the soul, Goodall offers an inspiring, optimistic message that gives us all Reason for Hope.

"A remarkable story...passionate and convincing."
—*Washington Post Book World*